1975   Years)

CU01461200

72490

$\dfrac{30-}{TH}$
K_R

Florence Farr:
Bernard Shaw's 'New Woman'

Florence Farr in New York, 1907.

Florence Farr

Bernard Shaw's 'New Woman'

Josephine Johnson

COLIN SMYTHE
Gerrards Cross 1975

U.S. DISTRIBUTOR
DUFOUR EDITIONS
CHESTER SPRINGS,
PA 19425-0449
(215) 458-5005

iv

For my parents

Preface

When Florence Farr had preceded most of her friends in death, the poet William Butler Yeats wrote to her niece for some photographs. He planned, he said, to write a book about her, since 'not enough has been said'. Dorothy Rhodes persuaded her mother Henrietta Paget to let her send 'among other things a photo she prized very much, asking for its ultimate return'. Months later, Mrs. Rhodes reminded Yeats about the photograph. 'He replied that his wife, who was at the moment on a walking holiday, saw to these matters and he would get her to attend to it on her return. I never heard another word.'

A half century after Yeats had expressed his wish to write about Florence Farr, I informed Geoffrey Walter Paget, Dorothy Rhodes's brother, of my intention to write about his aunt. Slightly incredulous, Mr. Paget wondered who on earth would be interested in reading about her. To him, she was simply a good-natured soul, terribly untidy and restless, who probably ate her meals out of a brown paper bag. Moreover, as his wife added, Florence made a dreadful noise twanging on that silly instrument. It was a relief, in fact, when a string would break. Besides, Yeats was dead, and really, Willie was such an ordinary young man in the Bedford Park days that Florence could not possibly have been interested in him. And more, all the Bedford Park people were quite forgotten.

Nevertheless, it is in part through her family's memories, and hitherto unpublished correspondence that I document the life of a 'New Woman' whose name must always crop up in the context of Yeats, Bernard Shaw, John Quinn, Jacob Grein, Ezra Pound, and a host of lesser and great notables of the late eighteen hundreds and early twentieth century. A woman emerges of artistic sensibility smothered by weak execution; a woman of immense personal dignity who wrote about passion but perhaps never experienced it; one who was to Yeats an everlasting companion of the spirit, and to Shaw, an enormously significant part of his manhood. Though she stirred the souls of others, contrary to all myths, her 'Leperello list', as Shaw named it, shows no additions, according to his calculations, after he was placed on it. Florence Farr no doubt cared too much for her independence to successfully submit to a permanent male relationship. But time has it that in her liaisons with 'great minds', as Pound wrote, she was 'second always'.

Because Florence's father William Farr was in a sense a 'New Man' and no less stamped on his age than his daughter, I include first a brief sketch of his life. It is by way of introducing the family which, to a certain extent, shaped the life of a very interesting human being.

Acknowledgements

I extend my deepest gratitude to Ellic Howe, Dan H. Laurence, and William Murphy for their generous gifts of time, MSS, and other valuable information during the search for this book. A Norman Jeffares's encouragement from the outset was constantly available, and to him I offer thanks as well as apologies for any unperceived editorial imperfections.

The following individuals, societies, institutions, and publishers have rendered me information, MSS, and where applicable, permission to quote for publication: Mrs. Dorothy Rhodes, Mr. Geoffrey Paget, Senator Michael B. Yeats, Miss Anne Yeats, Mr. Geoffrey Watkins, Mr. Anthony S. Latham, Mr. Roy Schutz, Mrs. Marjorie Todhunter, Dr. Thomas F. Conroy, Mr. Gerald Yorke, Mrs. Christina P. Cox, Mr. Robert K. Brady, Miss Ceridwen Oliver, Miss Rietta and Mr. D. C. Sturge Moore, Mr. G. W. Smith, Mr. Herbert Van Thal, Monsieur Michael Gambazini, Professors John Kelly, Richard Londraville, the late Dr. Lucien de Zilwa, Mr. Carl Dolmetsch, Professor Jayanta Padmanabha, Mr. G. Goossens, Mr. Raymond Mander, Mr. Joe Mitchenson, the William M. Murphy-Jeanne R. Foster Collection, the Society of Antiquaries of London, The Library, University of Manchester, The Enthoven Theatre Collection, The University of Toronto Library, The Beinecke Rare Book and Manuscript Library at Yale University, The British Museum, The National Library of Ireland, The Governors and Guardians of The National Gallery of Ireland, and Royal Academy of Dramatic Art, The Society of Authors, A.P. Watt & Son, The Library, University of Reading, The John Quinn Memorial Collection at The New York Public Library, Astor Lenox and Tilden Foundations, Westminister Public Library, Bryn Mawr College Library, Central Library, Bromley, Department of Western Manuscripts, Bodleian Library, Oxford, Chiswick District

Library, Department of Rare Books, Cornell University Library, the Burgander Collection at Cornell University, Dr. Percy M. Young and the Executors of the late Miss Harriet Cohen, Wing Commander S. M. MacIldowie at The Cheltenham Ladies' College, Florence G. Healy at the New York Medical College, Isabella Stewart Gardner Museum, Mary Lynn McCree at Jane Addams' Hull House, The London School of Economics and Political Science, Miss J. Gibbs and the University of London Library, Faber and Faber Limited for 'Portrait d'Une Femme' from the Collected Shorter Poems and verses from The Cantos of Ezra Pound, R. J. Hill, Secretary Lord Chamberlain's Office, C. J. P. Beathy, the Pennsylvania State University, Fales Library at New York University.

I thank all of the above for their extraordinary assistance, and those whose names I have erroneously omitted. And, my acknowledgement to Gene who walked many of the miles.

JJ
August, 1974

CONTENTS

ILLUSTRATIONS

1

William Farr,

M.D., F.R.S., D.C.L., L.S.A.
1807-1883

More than a century before the word 'new' became redundant in the English vocabulary in relation to New Woman, New Drama, New Art, William Farr[1] was born in the small village of Kenley, Shropshire. William's paternal grandfather was a small farmer in the parish and William's father John followed a similar pursuit, but as a farm labourer. Shortly after his son's birth, he found employment on the estate of a retired cab proprietor from Bath, Joseph Pryce. John worked for Pryce as bailiff and gardener while William's mother Catherine earned her keep as general houseworker.[2]

When William was two the young Farrs left their employer to settle elsewhere, and, as the story goes, the child remained in the care of the elderly Pryce. He grew to enjoy a social climate not available to his younger brothers, James, Thomas, Henry, or a sister, Anne-James. The squire doted on William who, 'when the wind blew high' could always find refuge between the old man's knees. And there is a Dickensian touch supplied to the scene by Pryce's recollections of how, in those early years, William would 'salve and plaster the servants from any temporary ailment', a tale told when the boy first displayed an aptitude for medicine.

At sixteen William had completed a mediocre education and at nineteen he was ready to strike out on his own. Pryce's attachment to his ward did prevent the local apothecaries from taking William for a pupil but an incident in 1826 directed the course of his future. A friend of Pryce's, Dr. Webster, called one evening for a sociable chat. When the conversation turned to medicine, the guest discussed with his hosts a recent article on the subject of contagion. So impressed was William by the Doctor's learned discussion that when he next visited Shrewsbury he called upon Dr. Webster at his home there. The two devised a plan: William would study with the Surgeon, and, under his guidance, become a dresser in the local infirmary. The agreement arranged, William walked the fourteen miles to Shrewsbury and back every day that summer to fulfil the contract until Pryce, approving of Farr's determination, bought him a good bay mare on which to make the journey.

Late in 1828, William became ill with acute bronchitis, an ailment that recurred until his death. Pryce oversaw his recovery with 'indefatigable' care, as his ward put it, perhaps with more than his strength allowed, for shortly after, the old man developed pneumonia and died within a few days of its onset. He was ninety and he left a legacy of five hundred pounds to William who was then twenty-one.

The sum enabled young Farr to travel to London and from there to Paris to study medicine at the University. After a period of intense study and exploration on the continent, his sojourn in Paris ended abruptly. Walking in the gardens of the Palais Royal one day, not long after the July Revolution of 1830, he came close to being shot. He managed to escape capture, fled to Calais, and so crossed the Channel to England.

Back on English soil, William established himself in London in order to attend the University Hospital in Gower Street. These studies were interrupted by a call from his mentor Dr. Webster to return to Shrewsbury. The surgeon had brought about a temporary appointment as House Surgeon to the City Infirmary. It was William's wish to stay on at the institution of his apprenticeship on a more permanent basis but without medical qualifications he was obliged to return to London. Before his departure, eight pupils of the Salop Infirmary presented him with a snuff box, 'desirous of expressing our gratitude to you, for the very marked attention you paid us . . . as well as for the readiness and ability with which you promoted our professional studies'.[3]

In London, William reapplied himself to his study at University College and on 29 March 1832, he passed his examinations at Apothecaries' Hall. The L.S.A. was the only qualification he earned by examination, his later accomplishments being acknowledged by various honorary awards.

By 1833, just able to support a household in modest fashion, William married a Miss Langford, the daughter of a miller from Pool Quay on the Severn, near Shrewsbury. For several years number 8 Grafton Street, between Huntley Street and the Tottenham Court

Road, became the Farrs' domicile and William taught and practiced medicine in this rented house on the small street now called Grafton Way. (8 Grafton Street was not far from Fitzroy Square where, fifty-four years later, George Bernard Shaw became intimately attached to William's daughter Florence. Shaw knew the resident who had lived at number 8 only as a man who 'survived his wits and lost most of his means by senile speculation.')[4]

The smallness of William's medical practice soon prompted the young couple to rent out rooms. Their penurious circumstances also challenged the young practitioner to attempt a course of lectures on the subject of Hygiology. (The word 'Hygiene' struck him as a 'naturalised French word, not agreeable to the ear.') Unable to find a ready audience, William submitted the contents of the lectures in a series of papers to the *Lancet*. It was not long before he received recognition for his marked propensity for statistics and soon he was called upon to edit the *British Annals of Medicine*. Of enormous consequence to his career at this time was his article 'Vital Statistics' for McCulloch's *Account of the British Empire*. This work demanded an investigation of deplorable standards of public health existing in Victorian England.

1837 was a difficult year for William. Dr. Webster died but leaving William his personal library and the sum of five hundred pounds. That year too, William's young wife died of consumption. Nevertheless, the young doctor's career was in the ascendancy. In 1837 England was preparing to require the civil registration of all births, deaths, and marriages. Vital to the plan was the need for scientific minds to assemble and record these facts. William Farr was urged for an appointment and by 10 July 1839, he had become Compiler of Abstracts for the new scheme, a position that marked the beginning of a forty year long career in the General Register Office at Somerset House. His appointment was accompanied by the announcement that Farr was 'a gentleman of the medical profession, whose scientific knowledge and intimate acquaintance with statistical inquiries are ample pledges of his peculiar fitness for the post.[5] Supporting the title were three hundred and fifty pounds a year, a sum which represented to William the security of an annual income that had not come his way before in a medical practice.

Sometime in 1841 William Farr left Grafton Street for Stoke Newington (an area where Dr. Woodman, an occultist friend of Florence Farr also resided, but in the 1860s) and on the first of January in the following year he married Mary Elizabeth Whittall.

William's second wife was the daughter of Joseph Whittall of Deal and formerly of Shropshire.

There were no children from William's first marriage[6] but Mary Elizabeth gave birth to eight children. Only the six who survived are remembered by their niece Dorothy Rhodes who, in 1894, played the faery child in W. B. Yeats's *Land of Heart's Desire*. Five of these children lived to survive their father. Of the four girls there was Mary Catherine born in 1843, Emily Alice in 1851, Henrietta, or Etta as her family called her, in 1853, and Florence Beatrice in 1860. There were two boys, Fred and William. Fred, under the assumed surname of Clarke, ran away to the United States in 1861 to enlist in the Northern Army during the Civil War. His misadventure ended when he was taken prisoner by the Rebels who removed him to Mayo Hospital, Richmond. On 23 March, 1864, he died of fever, his death occurring while his parents negotiated for his return as a minor and a British subject.

The Farrs' remaining son William rose to the rank of Lieutenant on Her Majesty's ship *Hector* to that of Commander. He married but had no children and returning from his last sea duty took on the work of shore patrolling with the Coast Guard. Later he settled at Whitby in Yorkshire where he died and was buried in the late 1880s.

Except for William, only two more of the Farr children were to marry, Henrietta and Florence. Henrietta became the wife of the artist Henry Marriott Paget in 1881. Mary was a spinster who preferred to live alone. When she was too aged to live unattended any longer, Henrietta found her a pleasant room in a house in Heath Drive, Hampstead run by two retired nurses. 'She received every care and comfort' and died one night in her sleep in 1928.

Emily Alice, semi-invalided with a hip disease, was tall and 'resembled Florence in face and voice.' She lived with Henrietta and her husband for some years in Bedford Park and then 'in various furnished rooms all her life.' In 1927 she was renting from a 'charming landlady' in Denham Drive, Golders Green when she died on 12 January at seventy-six. Mary and Emily were cremated within a year of each other in the Golders Green Crematorium in Hoop Lane.

In 1845 the Farrs decided to leave their home in Percy Villas, Lordship Road and move to a new dwelling in Melina Place, St. John's Wood. The little cottages in the *cul de sac* off Grove End Road (the scene of an adventure in A. Montgomery Eyre's *History of St. John's Wood*) were built in 1820 for the gardeners of the surrounding houses. Constructed with interior walls more than a foot thick to keep out the cold, the Farrs' cottage at number 1 was set amongst lilac trees which now crowd the high walls along the garden pathways. Except for a block of flats at the corner of Grove End Road, the delightful street remains today much as the Farrs knew it, a country haven in the midst of London.

It was during his stay at Melina Place that William Farr began writing the formidable body of articles that are represented in the memorial volume, *Vital Statistics*. His research shows a dedication to the specific area of statistical nosology which represented to the self-taught statistician a breakthrough for preventive medicine. A new approach to medical science could be accomplished, he believed, by the discovery of the causes of diseases and the exactness of diagnosis with its precision of nomenclature. An investigation, submitted in the First Annual Report of the Registrar-General, carried William Farr's statement

> Each disease has, in many instances, been denoted by three or four terms, and each term has been applied to as many diseases; vague inconvenient terms have been employed or complications have been registered instead of primary diseases. [7]

(Before he met Florence Farr, Shaw touched upon this subject in his *Unsocial Socialist* after a fictitious young woman's death in St. John's Wood.)

By mid-century, William Farr's recorded facts were co-existing with 'great eloquence and pure philosophy.' He was certainly recognised as a man of scientific letters. Seldom was there an area of public concern that was untouched by his inquisitive mind, and indeed, his enlightened activity had been recognised in 1847 with an honorary medical degree from New York which he attached to his name thereafter. Yet much of Farr's work was accompanied by exasperation for when in 1852 he published his findings of the causes of the Cholera epidemic of 1848-49, he was impotent without the support of the government to prevent the recurrence of the disease.

Shortly after William's frustration during the 1853 Cholera epidemic, he began an enduring friendship with another proponent in the fight against ignorance and disease, Florence Nightingale. (The nature of this relationship was echoed in many of Florence Farr's later friendships.) By 1855, after her return from the Crimean War, Florence Nightingale was a household word throughout England and countless children were named for her including, quite likely, Florence Farr. Through an almost daily correspondence between the nurse and William Farr a glimpse is caught of two very warm but often cantankerous personalities. In February 1857 there is an example of the pleasure Farr expected to receive from their mutual objectives.

> It will always give me the greatest pleasure to rend you any assistance I can in promoting the health of the army. We shall ask your assistance in return in the attempts that are now being made to improve the health of the civil population. It is in the *House*—the *Home* that sound principles will work most salutarily, and the effective agents must be the women of the country.[8]

William Farr anticipated Women's Rights before his daughter Florence was born. His peculiar vision may not have included the vote for women or unlicensed connubiality but it did embody the concepts of equal education and professional opportunity. Taking precedence were good nurses. They can, he was assured, 'be created by you [Florence Nightingale] out of English women; and if only two or three are completely formed—they will multiply in a geometrical progression 1 2 4 8'.[9]

Florence Nightingale was not so sure; her experiences led her to believe that women were unmalleable. Not only did they possess noticeable incapacities for sympathy but they were crying about 'Women's Rights' and the 'want of a field,' and not one of them could measure up to the qualifications of a good secretary.[10] Nearly a decade later she was still frustrated by her efforts to produce good nurses. From her home at 35 South Street, Park Lane she complained to her colleague

> The *Lancet* . . . says 'the nursing by *ladies* is the very best nursing England has seen' . . . Because 'ladies' have happened to produce nurses, who are better than drunken sots therefore *all* 'ladies' are good nurses![11]

There is nothing in this intimate correspondence to imply that Florence Nightingale was not welcomed by Mary Elizabeth Farr at Melina Place. On the contrary, it is a disappointed household that misses her company when she is away, or thanks her for the 'fine brace of pheasants', and wishes to offer her 'some of the nectar' which they know she does not 'disdain'. And when William was unable to meet Miss Nightingale during their working hours, he often sent her a note to herald an evening visit. 'I may be able to look in . . . 6-7 o'clock.' He was anxious to discuss the mortality of the British army in India. 'In half', he said, 'it is a thing beyond all doubt to be done at any expense or sacrifice.'[12] The wastefulness of years through illness, disease, and war were an insult to human dignity. Man could not aspire for the hope of a hundred years of athletic life for there must always be a twilight in the evening of the Natural life; the soul as it sinks away or rises? leaves some fading light in the body. What is unnatural—is the cessation—the destruction of life in the middle of its career—before its work is done.[13]

In 1858 the Government appointed a committee to report on the preparation of army medical statistics, and a year later Queen Victoria signed a warrant for 'The Royal Commission for Inquiry into the Sanitary Condition of the Army in India.' Dr. Farr was invited to join the Committee. The work was a basis for an accelerated correspondence with Florence Nightingale, often twice a day, when William Farr remembered some new point in her evidence with which he wished 'to find as much fault as I can.' And she, with unfailing admiration would avail herself of his wishes.

I am coming to town next week, when I hope to have the pleasure of crawling at your feet a little more for a few more favours. La reconnaissance n'est qu'un vif sentiment des bienfaits futurs. [Acknowledgement is but an active feeling of future kindnesses] as I have often told you.[14]

This New Woman was soon to rely almost exclusively upon the strength and optimism of William Farr. Known for her exasperation with women, she was fast losing her respect for men.

I have too painful an experience of mankind and should reverse your maxim thus—*Quand* 'la pudeur s'est refugiee sur les levres' c'est parcequ'elle s'est enfuie du coeur.' [When modesty finds refuge upon the lips it is because it has left the heart.] Such is my experience at least of the Army. When a person talks about his conscience or his sacrifices, I know he is incurably selfish—when he offers to take his oath he never touches spirits, I know he is incurably drunken, when he is particularly prudish as to what women should do or not do, I know he is incurably bad.[15]

Sometime in 1859 William Farr was told by a mutual friend that Florence Nightingale believed she was dying and wished her correspondence destroyed. Dr. Farr answered that he had always considered her communications confidential 'and I have this morning (with great regret) burnt all of them I could find.' In so doing, he had found in their contents so much wit and wisdom that he felt guilty in their destruction, of a 'sort of sacrilege for which we must ask the Gods to forgive me.'[16] (The correspondence overlooked by Dr. Farr and the diminishing letters of the future years were carefully preserved by Mary Catherine.)

In 1860 William Farr's daughter Mary and his sons were in their teens; Emily and Henrietta Farr were nine and seven respectively, and William's wife Mary Elizabeth was with child. A salary of eight hundred pounds a year and an expanding family, which included John Farr who had lived with William since Catherine Farr's death in 1844, prompted Dr. Farr to search for a house out in the country. By May, the family had moved to Bickley, ten miles from the centre of London, but not far enough for the countryside to have changed into the prettier scenes of Kent. (Disguised as 'Bromstead' the town was well described, Florence Farr later remarked, in H. G. Wells's *The New Machiavelli*.) Bromley, with Bickley incorporated into it, was on the main road from London to Hastings, and, in those years, a market town free from any industry. The Farr residence, 'Southlands House', number 3 Southlands Road, was one of a thousand houses in a community of 5,500 people. Southlands is a gently ascending street off the main road which leads from the railway station to Bromley Common. If the children cut across country they could arrive in half an hour at Holy Trinity. The Farrs were active in the church, paid pew rent, and were well known to the Vicar A. Rawson. At the back of Holy Trinity and across the way from the Rector's house, lay the property on which the Bromley Common National School was completed in 1864. In the opposite direction, what was to be called the 'Bird in Hand' operated as a beer shop and next to this establishment, the undertaker resided at the present number 60 Gravel Road.

Shortly after William Farr had established his family in Kent, Florence Beatrice was born on 7 July at 6.27 in the morning. On 11 August her parents registered her birth with Mr. Charles Bourne in the district of Bromley. Mary Elizabeth was forty-three that year and her husband ten years her senior; Shaw's future comment about the situation was that 'Florence had been born unexpectedly long after her mother had apparently ceased childbearing.'[17] Perhaps William Farr's delight with the event, combined with the distance from London, caused some estrangement from the other Florence. With September there was an impatient note from London: 'I have heard *nothing* from you about anything.'[18]

Florence Farr grew to know her father as a man of exceptional mental and physical vigour. His work at Somerset House earned him the honours of Treasurer in the Statistical Society, Vice-President, and then President. Representing England at the Statistical Congresses, he visited Berlin, Florence (Italy) and the Hague during the sixties, and the following decade, St. Petersburg and Buda-Pest. In Russia, the Emperor presented him with a diamond ring and on the visit to Buda-Pest Mary Catherine accompanied her father delighting him, no doubt, with her remarkable knack for reciting the genealogies of all the Royal families in Europe. It was at the Hague that Dr. Farr, a century before the British currency was converted, delivered a report on coinage and metric weights and measurements in which he argued for an international system of metric coinage.

Unfortunately, the self-taught statistician did not appear to be as capable in his private business affairs as in his civic responsibilities. When, in the sixties, his income permitted him the luxury of small investments, he foolishly allied himself to several precarious enterprises. Neither was it unusual for associates to use his name to further their own ends or to attach blame. During one such incident, George Scott, a past actuary for the bankrupt Consols Company, attempted to clear Dr. Farr's reputation with James Thompson, a controlling member of the East India Irrigation Company,

> My friend Dr. Farr of the Registrar General Office has just called here during my absence and from a note hastily written by him . . . I learn for the first time that the soundness of his views and the accuracy of his calculations have been impeached and that it has been asserted that the ruin of the Consols Insurance Association... is mainly traceable to the misguidance of Dr. Farr. To such a charge against such a man I unhesitatingly say that nothing could be farther from the truth . . . to attach blame or discredit him in respect of the failure of the Consols can only be regarded as a foul injustice done in a spirit of gross ignorance and malevolence. [19]

Florence's grandfather Farr died when she was four. That year, 1864, William Farr met with unequivocal success in the construction of the English Life Tables which he prepared from the return of the Censuses containing six million deaths in seventeen years. Employing the aid of Scheutz's calculating machine which he presently preferred to the earlier devices of Babbage and Shenty, Dr. Farr enabled Insurance Companies to base their assurance rates more accurately on the probabilities of English life. His charts led to the system of Post Office Insurance which went into effect that year with the Doctor acting as the consulting actuary, an advisory position he continued to occupy for several consecutive years without remuneration.

The following year, England experienced her third Cholera epidemic since 1848. Dr. Farr's analysis of the plague presented the sort of proof that immediately became a sore spot with the shareholders of the London Water Company. Moreover, John Sutherland, the Doctor's very good friend, withheld his support. Constantly battling against the attitudes of mind which permitted filth to remain rampant in England, Farr mentioned his despair to Florence Nightingale:

> I know you will pardon me for wishing you in the old fashion of England—a Happy New Year! How much the word means in your case—it is impossible to say in one word—or a thousand. While our friends fall away from us in the great struggle—we thank God that you still remain as the great leader in the good cause—and pray that he may make life half as agreeable as it is beneficient.[20]

Disappointments, brought about by the lack of implementation of Dr. Farr's suggestions, were offset by further honours. Already in receipt of the D.L.C. from Oxford in 1865, he was proposed as an Honorary Fellow of the Kings and Queens College of Physicians in Dublin. In October of that year, his election was approved on the ground of 'high scientific attainments.'[21]

When Florence was thirteen, her father applied to the Cheltenham Ladies' College in Gloucestershire for her admission. At that time, it was necessary for a controlling member of the Board to voice the recommendation so that during a meeting held on 13 September 1873 to consider nominations, a Mr. Louis W. Montagon proposed Florence. The Board approved his recommendation and she entered the College that month as a day pupil. Her family arranged for her to board with a cousin, Miss Stubbings, who latterly became Bursar at Cheltenham. Florence had 'great respect' for Cousin 'Emma' and enjoyed being in her care until her parents, Mamma and Papa, as she called them, thought she was old enough to board at the School.

Apart from some marked absentmindedness, Florence's father remained in good health until a dysentery attack which occurred in the autumn of 1876. The illness interfered with his previous stamina and then, on 18 December that year, Florence's mother died at the age of fifty-eight. Four days later, William Farr buried Mary Elizabeth next to the stone wall that separates Holy Trinity from the school house. William had ordered cut for her simple grave-stone: 'A Good Wife, A Devoted Mother—I Know That My Redeemer Liveth.'

Dr. Farr's health rapidly failed after his wife's death, but when Major Graham retired from Somerset House in 1879, the Doctor hoped to be appointed Registrar-General, a position he had long coveted. In accordance with the current custom he sent his application to the Prime-Minister Benjamin Disraeli who alone could bestow the 'gift'. Upon learning of her friend's ambition. Florence Nightingale offered her good wishes: 'May God bless your labours, may He entirely preserve your health, may you be our Registrar General, is the fervent wish'.[22]

Benjamin Disraeli in due course refused to consider Dr. Farr for the post letting it be known that the Assistant Registrar-General was suffering from incipient 'softening of the brain'. It was true that Dr. Farr was forgetful yet truer still that the favoured candidate Sir Bridges Henniker was married to the sister of Lady John Manners. The Conservative party saw this as an element that might assist them in their politics. On the other hand, Dr. Farr was thought to be unfit as a public administrator since he was 'studious and not of business tastes and habits.' It was a characteristic that later described Florence Farr.

When Sir Bridges Henniker received the appointment, Dr. Farr resigned from Somerset House, bitterly disappointed. It had never occurred to him that he might not be selected for the position; indeed, in expectation of being appointed he had moved back to London to be nearer his presumed place of work. Disraeli's choice saddened many, especially Florence Nightingale who immediately set about procuring a pension for her friend. His work, she reminded him, 'will remain and grow for all time for Europe as for England and India.'[23]

At the time of his resignation, Dr. Farr's salary was eleven hundred pounds a year, just a hundred short of the Registrar-General's. Shortly thereafter a Committee of well-wishers formed to raise a subscription to supplement William Farr's superannuation. Eleven hundred pounds were collected, a sum that was converted to Bank of England stock for the eventual provision of the Farr sisters. Later the annuities were converted back to cash and became part of an estate amounting to £1,724.17s.0d. It was to this Bernard Shaw referred when he wrote that Florence had enough 'to live modestly without having to sell herself in any fashion, or do anything that was distasteful to her.'[24]

78 Portsdown Road, Maida Vale became William Farr's last residence in London. In 1880 the tree-lined street was illuminated by gas-light, and on winter afternoons muffin men in green baize uniforms balanced trays of hot muffins on their heads. A reminder of the Paddington of those years prevails in the cries of mussel vendors who still sell their wares on Sunday afternoons. Portsdown Road has become increasingly shabby since it was renamed Randolph Avenue during the Second World War, (the change came about when the neighbourhood was notorious for its women of ill repute) but 78 still stands, a four storey dwelling with a basement and first floor balcony.

Dr. Farr ceased to earn further professional recognition while he lived at Maida Vale. He had approached the time, as he once wrote to

Florence Nightingale, when 'the soul . . . sinks away or rises?' He did enquire about publishing a four hundred and eighty page MS of the *History of the Medical Profession* but Messrs Longman and Company indicated they could perhaps only accept the manuscript on the condition that Dr. Farr would pay the publishing costs. When he had reduced his MS to a modified form the publishers then doubted after all 'whether it would prove a remunerative publication.'[25]

Shortly after this, William Farr developed 'paralysis of the brain'. Florence observed her father's decline with great bitterness:

> I do not think that any other training has such an effect on the young as that long watching of a case of senile paralysis: to see some capable strong-minded man . . . gradually change; the body just a little feebler month by month . . . the intellect evaporating and the friend one knew vanishing and needing nothing but the attentions that a one-year-old child requires of its nurse. To watch this heart rending disease saps all one's belief in the immortality of intellect and in the values of individual endeavour.[26]

Dr. Farr died during the night of 14 April 1883. The death report read 'cerebral three years; bronchitis eight days.' On 20 April, his children brought his body to Kent for burial next to his wife at Bromley Common. Fellows of the Statistical Society, neighbourhood friends of Bromley and Bickley, and 'chief male mourners' Lieutenant William Farr, Mary Elizabeth's brother Joseph Whittal, and Henry Marriott Paget attended the rights performed by Mr. Arthur Wright. William Farr's stone, now covered with moss and weeds reads, 'The good that men do is their eternal monument and its survival their highest reward.'

Excepting his diamond ring and his silver snuff box which went to William, Dr. Farr's Will provided that his children should divide between themselves his 'plate linen glass jewellery . . . books philosophical instruments pictures prints ornaments wearing apparel wines liquors'.

To Emily Alice he left the sum of two hundred pounds above and beyond her share of the estate, and to Henrietta who had married, and to William and Florence, he had previously paid two hundred pounds out-right. The remainder of his estate was to be divided equally between Mary Catherine, Emily Alice and Florence Beatrice.

Following their father's death, the three unmarried sisters were living as follows. Mary, presently forty-one, had taken comfortable rooms in the rather grim 'Oakley Street Flats', Oakley Street,

Chelsea. She was not badly off with an income of £70 a year by means of an annuity arranged through an insurance office. Joseph Whittall considered her to be 'well adapted for a companionship with refined people.'

Emily moved in with Henrietta. She was a 'fair musician' with the violin and looked forward to taking on a young pupil. An industrious woman, she had already begun to increase her income of £52 a year by accepting several small commissions for her skillful needlework.

Florence, by this time, had passed the Oxford Woman's Examination, and her uncle Joseph Whittall thought her a 'clever' girl although she had 'failed' in teaching. In deference to her father's wishes she had assumed the unaccounted for name of Mary Lester and was trying her luck on the London stage. Her share of the estate amounted to £50 a year.

The girls were not considered 'well-off' and before probate was granted, William immediately addressed himself through his father's friend Lordy Derby to Gladstone, then Prime-Minister. He hoped for a pension for his sisters. A reply from 10 Downing Street written on 25 April advised him that Mr. Gladstone was unable to comply with his wishes but that he was willing to recommend a grant of three hundred pounds. William had little choice but to accept with an appeal that Mr. Gladstone increase the sum. The Prime-Minister made a new offer of £400 which became the final settlement.[27]

Florence Nightingale consequently made several attempts to influence others in the matter of the pension for

what a great debt we owe *him*—who, with A. Quetelet we may say originated the practical application . . . of a science without which all other sciences—moral, political, or administrative, cd. not exist as sciences at all. I mean verifying & registering by statistics the results of social habits . . . with a view to determining what our course shall be in the future.[28]

Further efforts by friends of the family failed to reach the Government and, accepting their limited resources, the Farr sisters welcomed a different token of regard for their father's life-long efforts. Through Professor W. T. Gardiner in Glasgow, five hundred subscribers became responsible for the posthumous publication by William Farr, *Vital Statistics*.

It is hardly possible to think of Somerset House to-day without remembering Dr. William Farr. Yet his name is not generally well-known. His granddaughter Dorothy Rhodes is proud that it is still seen on the stone ballustrade of the School of Hygiene and Tropical Diseases in Gower Street. In further memory, the London School of

Economics and Political Sciences in Houghton Street awards a yearly 'Farr' prize to the student who performs 'meritorious work in vital statistics to perpetuate Dr. Farr's work.' The event has some little family history since it came about through the efforts of Joseph Whittall's son William who at one time was very much in love with his cousin Florence. Sometime before 1923, and after Florence Farr's death, he gave a quantity of Dr. Farr's MSS to the Library and during that year, discovering an additional box of material, offered the collection to the librarian, Mr. W. Headicar. In so doing, Mr Whittall had high hopes that a biography would be written about his uncle.[29] Before placing these last effects at the School, he corresponded with Mary Catherine Farr concerning their deposit and, in turn, Mary carried the news to Etta who was then living at 76 Parkhill Road, Hampstead. Both sisters were keenly interested that their father's papers should rest in 'such a safe place' and they decided to donate to the collection the Gold Medal presented by the British Medical Association to their father in 1880, a small portrait presented to their mother by the staff at Somerset House, three tin cases 'stuffed with diplomas' from the representatives of the 'whole civilised world, I think!' and a diploma from Italy 'over a yard wide, & very fanciful design.' [30]

In receipt of a very generous cheque from 'Will' who was much too good to his old cousin, Mary said, she invited him to collect the memorabilia from her rooms. She still lived in the Oakley Street Flats near the river but with the prospect of acquiring a new landlady, Miss Cecil Gradwill. At the moment, Mary reminded her cousin, there was no lift in Adair House but the steps to her first floor rooms were easy.

In due course William Whittall placed the collection at L.S.E. and in addition agreed to donate a prize. He was also to assume the expense of ninety guineas for the striking of a medal by Allan G. Wynn, 80 Boundary Lane, St. John's Wood. The School subsequently arranged a lecture to commemorate Dr. Farr's work and to introduce the subject of the prize. Emily, Mary, and Henrietta attended the event with their cousin Will; 'We had such an exciting hour,' he said, 'My poor old cousins were so pleased and gratified.'

A silver medal and £5 were first awarded in 1923 but Mr. Wynn's medal was not available until two years later. Hindered by the absence of a profile photograph of his subject, the medalist required the Pagets to direct the modelling on several occasions until he 'nearly' got it right. The likeness eventually turned out to be 'quite nice', Will Whittall thought, 'for anyone who did not know Dr. Farr.' In

1925 Mrs. Emily Joyce Murfitt received the first of Mr. Wynn's medals. William Whittall acknowledged the New Woman's superiority with true Farr spirit. 'I am so glad the Farr medal is awarded to a woman![32]

Florence Farr's cousin remained active in his correspondence with the London School of Economics in several matters until his death, 4 July 1932. Of special interest here are his letters concerning the musician Arnold Dolmetsch who collaborated with Florence and W. B. Yeats in 'The Music of Speech'. For several years, Mr. Whittall cultivated an exotic demesne next to the Dolmetsch residence 'Jesses' at Haslemere, Surrey. Perhaps not a little out of sentiment for Florence, he was exceedingly generous to Arnold Dolmetsch and in the late twenties he became Treasurer of the Dolmetsch Foundation at 37 Walbrook, London. Their intent was to recruit scholars and to

> assist financially in providing the requisite space for more workers, and thus increasing incidentally the output of Mr. Dolmetsch's' workshop . . . to remember the soul as well as the body of Mr. Dolmetsch's work.[33]

Apart from Dorothy Rhodes and Geoffrey Paget, there seems to be only one more member of the Farr-Whittall family tree whose life in some fashion commingles with William Farr's daughter Florence. Miss Florence Whittall, William Whittall's daughter, answers to a link in her association with Arnold Dolmetsch's surviving son Carl. An extraordinary musician, as well, the latter perpetuates the Dolmetsch factory and, most especially, the Dolmetsch artistry. A visit to Haslemere today, or to any concert hall where he plays recalls the mood of the *fin de siècle*, the period when Florence Farr and Yeats were struggling for recognition with their 'New Art'.

NOTES

1 The name 'Farr' has a gypsy derivation and is also Old English for 'fearr' a bull. P.H. Reany, *The Origin of British Surnames* (London 1958), 263

2 Early childhood biographical data is selected from F.A.C. Hare, *Tracts*, (London 1883), and Noel E. Humphreys, ed. *Vital Statistics*, (London 1885).

3 London School of Economics. This collection will be referred to as L.S.E. henceforth.

4 TS copy, 'An Explanatory Word From Shaw.' Courtesy of Senator Michael B. Yeats.

5 Humphreys, *op. cit.*, viii-ix.

6 This fact suggests a doubt that *A Medical Guide to Nice* was written by William Farr. The writer refers to his children and also attaches an M.D. to his name which was not William Farr's custom until 1847.

7 Humphreys, *op. cit.,* xii.

8 British Museum Manuscript Collection. Henceforth this collection will be referred to as BM. (February 1857).

9 BM, (March 20 1857)

10 Cecil Woodham-Smith, *Florence Nightingale,* (London 1950), 58.

11 BM.

12 BM, (June 21 1857).

13 BM, (July 23 1857).

14 BM, (February 5 1858).

15 BM, (February 26 1859).

16 BM, (June 2 1859).

17 Shaw, *op. cit.*

18 BM, (September 16 1860).

19 L.S.E.

20 BM, (January 1865).

21 F.A.C. Hare, an actuary and some-time admirer of William Farr questioned the validity of the M.D.T.C.D. degree which accompanied the recognition of Fellow. Upon investigation he discovered that although Dublin had not actually conferred the degree upon Farr, until 1867 the K.Q.C.P. maintained that the Charter of William and Mary, and the Act of Parliament by George III, conferred on their Fellows and Licentiates the title of M.D.T.C.D. Since it was not until 1868 that the claim was 'legally contested and disallowed' Hare finally admitted that Farr was entitled to the associative degree.

22 L.S.E., (August 6 1879).

23 L.S.E., (January 9 1880).

24 Shaw, *op. cit.*

25 L.S.E., (March 9 1881).

26 Florence Farr, *The New Age,* (London, October 31 1907).

27 L.S.E.

28 L.S.E., (June 25 1883).

29 An attempt was subsequently made by a student at Cornell University for 'A Search of Materials,' a thesis, 'On The Life and Writings of Dr. William Farr.' More recently, J.M. Eyler completed a dissertation 'An Intellectual Biography Of A Social Pathologist', (University of Wisconsin).

30 L.S.E., (April 18 1923).

31 L.S.E., (October 15 1923).

32 L.S.E.

33 L.S.E.

2
The Beginning of a New Woman
Queen's College and Edward Emery
1877-1888

The New Woman is just now exerting her energies in starting a football club to be called the 'British Ladies.' It will . . . consist of ladies only. The players's garb will be . . . short, fully navy-blue knickerbockers, strong football boots, legguards, blouses . . . half the number pale blue, and the other half bright red, and small peaked caps. The game is to be 'Association,' and the fair footballers intend to show the sterner sex that, even in the accomplishment of kicking, there is no such thing as masculine superiority.[1]

In 1876 Florence Farr became engaged, a 'bad year' she noted, when preparing her horoscope. The following year she entered Queen's College, London for the Second Junior Term. By then, Britain's 'New Women', as the genre were loosely termed, were pursuing their rights to equal privileges with men.

Some thirty years before, Alfred Lord Tennyson predicted their emergence from Victorianism with his bold poem 'The Princess: A Medley.' (Some called it a 'splendid failure.')

Oh I wish that I were some great princess, I would build
Far off from man a college like man's,
And I would teach them all that men are taught:
We are twice as quick!

Mindful that men 'hated learned women,' the poet nevertheless took part in the formal discussions with Charles Kingsley and theologian Frederick Denison Maurice which led to the founding of the first college for women in London, Queen's.

When Florence knew the School, she entered at 43 and 45 Harley Street. Designed as private residences, the buildings were very pleasant; there was a library on the ground floor as well as a 'waiting' room with a pastoral ceiling which was embossed with baroque cherubs. Elocution or 'reading' classes (a more advanced title) met upstairs in the recital room. Young Maud Holt studied here with Florence and returned to teach Latin in 1881 until her marriage to the actor-manager Beerbohm Tree a year later.

Not seeming to possess her father's attitude toward hard work, Florence did not prepare for the external degree of the University of London; nor did she work for an Associateship of the College. William Farr, however, could not be unpleased with her first report card.

Arithmetic and Algebra	Good
English	Good
French	Good
History	Absent from Examination
Geography	Good
Latin	Good
Singing	Good
Attendance	Very Regular
Conduct	Good

In the Michaelmas term (the First Senior Year) Florence added two more languages, German, 'fair', and Italian, 'good'; she continued with Latin, now 'very good', and took Astronomy, 'good', and Geometry, 'excellent', but she abstained from her examination in Geography and her attendance dropped from 'very regular', to 'regular'. By the Lent term of 1878 she was a non-compounder, one who did not take a regular course of study. Her attendance was sporadic and she abstained from examinations. In her last term that summer, she worked again as a non-compounder.[2]

By this time it had dawned upon Florence that the apparent end of her education seemed to amount to the acquisition of knowledge for the purpose of examinations, a phenomenon entirely useless after college, and 'really damaging to the vital apparatus.' And, as far as the intellect went, it was useful for gathering the facts, 'but absurdly misleading when applied to the all-important side of our natures which come under the consideration of the psychologist.' The New Woman felt so inhibited by the well-intentioned institutions of her learning that it took her

quite six years to get out of the shell my education hardened around me. I don't suppose I should ever have spread my own wings if the beak of my destiny had not been stronger than my overwhelming education, so that it succeeded in hammering through that shell at last.[3]

Florence left Queen's College in 1880: 'Good', she wrote, when preparing her horoscope again. By 1882 she had 'failed' in teaching, and, as Joseph Whittall said, was trying her luck on the stage. She was an unusual girl with a beautiful speaking voice and some talent for the piano, but she was quite unprepared for the theatre. True, actors before the 1880's were not as a rule progenies of professional dramatic schools for most had learned their trade behind the footlights. There were exceptions to this: John Ryder taught students privately, and a group, calling themselves the Dramatic Academy was operating from 307 Regent Street. There was a Neville Dramatic School advertising in 1880, and another group named The School of Dramatic Art, which when it opened in 1882 offered classes in fencing, dancing, stage gesture, elocution, lecture and deportment.

The Pagets, no doubt, provided a stimulus for Florence's dramatic ambitions. When the beautiful Henrietta (she was lovelier than Florence) married young Henry Marriott Paget and settled at One The Orchard, Bedford Park, Florence began to experiment there in play-acting. This was a common enough home entertainment in Victorian England especially with the Pagets. The painter was a sophisticated influence; at twenty-five, he had travelled in the Greek Islands, Crete and Athens, studied at the Royal Academy, and shown his first painting 'Enid and Geraint' in 1879. Moreover, he was interested in scene design and took part in the Bedford Park local dramatic club. Henrietta too, had some skill for the dramatisation of stories and so the intimacy of the drawing room, or Paget's studio, which lent itself very well to a stage at one end, became the exciting atmosphere at Chiswick after Florence's journey from Maida Vale.

About July 1882, Florence became a pupil of the actor-manager J. L. Toole at his elegant little playhouse in King William Street. The theatre at Charing Cross had been named the 'Folly' until Toole took up its lease in 1879 whereupon it became known as 'Toole's Folly'. By February 1882 the actor-manager had spent £10,000 on alterations which meant that Florence studied in a 'Raphaelesque' decor under a 'Renaissance' ceiling adjacent to a 'Pompeian' saloon.

For eight months 'Mary Lester' learned Shakespeare and 'step-dancing' and gathered her impressions of Mr. Toole. She thought of his theatre as a product of the old plebian drama, plebian 'because it is the kind of drama that survives revolutions, wars and empires;' it represented the 'low-comedy of life in which all the peoples of the earth have a part.' No-one at the theatre in King William Street ever pretended it was anything else, and nothing and no-one mattered there except J. L. Toole. On Fridays the stage manager rehearsed the apprentices in an old play (although new to the young thespians) and on Saturday they went before the public. Much to their bewilderment, the supporting actors and actresses often found themselves in the same position as the audience since it was the first time for either to see the impressario in the leading role. The cast had a sort of 'scramble through', unheard of in the theatre at the end of the next decade. In effect, it was the remnants of the practice in the 'old stock season "star" method' which Henry Irving had started. Out of necessity Florence had the chance for a 'fresh spontaneous performance', and when in later years she had gained some experience, she compared her training at Toole's to Irving's later methods at the Lyceum. There the 'life was taken out' of a performer by a 'too conscientious' stage-management. 'A month's drilling, arguing and worrying' made a good conception 'automatic and ineffective'. Several actresses confided to Florence that it took quite two weeks to recover from the 'deadening' process of rehearsals. 'Three steps that way', 'to slow music', 'pause', 'lights turned down', groan etc. etc.' were enough to take all the vital force from performances.

Mary Lester, as Florence was first known to Toole became a professional actress before William Farr died. During the weeks of 26 February and 5 March 1883, she played the part of a schoolgirl, Kate Renshaw, in Henry J. Byron's *Uncle Dick's Darling*. As a point of interest, Toole sung the words to a ballad written by the future anti-Ibsenite Clement Scott. Byron's play preceded a musical farce *Mrs. Guffin's Elopement* in which Mary Lester played Mrs. Trundel. On 5 March she played again in the latter play and for the Saturday matinée on 17 March she was 'Marie' in a one-act version of *Robert Macaire*. She repeated the part of Mrs. Guffin on 9 and 16 April (William Farr died 14 April) and once more on 7 May. A month after her father's death, Florence took her own name to appear in the small part of 'Pelham' in an 'original' comedy drama by Byron called *Chained to the Oars*. The occasion on 31 May was a Mrs. Billington's Matinée at the Gaiety which starred one of Toole's favourite actors, John Billington, and an actress, even admired by Florence, Mrs. Billington.

When Florence played at Toole's next she resumed the use of her own name to play Mrs. Trundel once again in the Saturday matinées 15 and 29 December, and 5 January 1884. Then on Thursday 10 January Mary Lester reappeared in Arthur Law's new comedy *A Mint of Money* playing the part of 'Wednesday Flutterby'. On the Saturday matinée 26 January there was a switch to Florence Farr for 'Kate Renshaw' in *Uncle Dick's Darling* and the same for the matinée 26 January for the Wednesday Flutterby part. That day. Florence also appeared as Mrs. Clipper in *The Steeplechase: or, Toole in the Pigskin.* But it is Mary Lester who plays Wednesday Flutterby in the weeks of 28 January and 4 February.[5] Emerging from this bizarre dualism is a pattern in which Florence used her own name for the matinées and Mary Lester for the evening performances.

In 1884, Florence met Edward Emery, a young actor, handsome in an undistinguished kind of way. Edward was the son of the actress Clara Tellet and the well-known performer Samuel Anderson Emery who had gained fame popularising the characters of Dickens. The elder Emery's father had been a comedian before he died in 1882 at seventy-five years of age, and his father Mackle had been part of the Emery tradition on the English stage which traces back to 1746. When Edward was born, Samuel and Clara Emery lived with their daughter Winifred in Russell Square. Plans were subsequently made for Edward to break with the family's stage tradition to train as an army surgeon. These intentions lay fallow when Edward's father died at 3 King William Street 19 July 1881 after a short illness, his burial taking place at Highgate Cemetery on the twenty-third.

A year after his father's death, Edward became a member of the Resident Company at the Royal Princess's Theatre in Glasgow. The following year, he joined the Sadler's Wells Company and after a series of roles[6] was 'resting' until he joined Florence Wade in *Moths.* There was a season with the Wilson Barrett Company in the provinces, some parts at Drury Lane, and toward the winter of 1884, either by chance or by choice, Mr. Edward Emery and Miss Florence Farr were both under contract to W. F. Hawtrey for the provincial tour of *The Private Secretary.* The tour began in October; by April 1885, the Company wound up at the Theatre Royal, Cork. But earlier, during the play's history, Florence and Edward were married in Norman Shaw's grand Church of St. Michael and All Angels in Chiswick. Vicar Alfred Wilson performed the marriage ceremony on 31 December 1884, with H. M. Paget and Frederick Arthur Emery, prominent in English Theatre management, acting as witnesses. Edward gave his address as 51 Park Villas, Regents Park, his age as twenty-four, (he was really twenty-three) and described himself as a bachelor. Florence entered One The Orchard, the Paget address, on the Register.

According to Florence's account of her life, she abstained from the marriage couch until she replaced the harm done to her emotional constitution by the Victorian shiboleths surrounding her education.

Despite her metamorphosis, she made a common blunder in choosing an unsuitable partner and this ill-choice aggravated itself through four years of marriage.

Perhaps she was mistaken, in her own words, by a first (the engagement was obviously not a matter of ardent affection) innocent and valiant love in which the revelation was 'so extraordinary, so unlike anything told by the poets, so absorbing, that it is impossible . . . that the feeling can die out.'

Or, she may have mistaken a 'feeling of gratified vanity and the emotion of a new sensation for love' with a man who happened to make love at the 'propitious moment'.[7] Actually, Florence disliked the rather 'ungraceful gestures' of love-making and it appeared to her, as well, that those who were under contract to each other were privileged to behave without politeness. Even in a good marriage, she suspected that a woman could not hold her attention for a man beyond ten years, and if the relationship remained permanent it was surely founded on mutual contempt. Those who were happy at all were satisfied with a 'very low standard of brilliance' since marriage undoubtedly barred 'the only kind of social intercourse worth having.' And as far as the marriage contract went, it was as indelicate as 'the expectorations from a case of catarrh!' Attempting to find some excuse for women who remained married, Florence decided that 'cruelty, adultery, temporary desertion, every kind of outrage' were acceptable if excitement and interest outweighed their suffering.

For her own part, Florence possessed entirely negative abilities in the home. Besides, housekeeping money was sparse and she often lay in bed all day because she 'found she got less hungry that way than when she was up and about.' Certainly she was able to subsist on the income which her father had protected from the interference of any husband, but it is not likely that Florence wished to live on this with Edward. Not that she expected an average middle-class Englishman who saw married life as a business partnership in which he paid his wife to take care of his material comforts while he devoted himself to business, to golf, to betting, to insure himself from becoming a 'dull' man. It was that she feared man himself for his potential uxoriousness, his innate deceptiveness. That 'dull men' could possibly be all who symbolised the 'quintessence of dust' appalled her. Many years later, Ezra Pound compressed into metaphor her revulsion of that thought—

One dull man, dulling and uxorious
One average mind—with one thought less, each year.

While her marriage deteriorated, Florence became determined to remain emotionally free. No-one came close to her on any occasion or was permitted an abundance of sentimentality. If she confided to anyone it was to Henrietta; yet even Etta never 'trod ground with her' except in the future in some astral light. John Butler Yeats, the poet's father, later agreed to this appraisal by Florence's niece when he spoke of the poetess Susan Mitchell having an 'antipathy' to Florence because she could 'not be cajoled into the most momentary affection.'[1]

Edward Emery meanwhile remained sporadically employed. There was a tour with Cyril Maude (who married Winifred Emery in 1888) in *The Candidate*; *The Tragedy* then came along, and *Why Women Weep* was an appropriate enough title for Edward's last play in England. After the January 1888 production, and after what Florence considered a 'very bad' year in her life, Edward emigrated to America with Florence quite 'content' to forget him. 'Whatever the trouble,' Bernard Shaw later remarked, it was 'not domestic.'

It is questionable whether the trouble was 'not domestic' but it is true that Florence seldom spoke of Edward again except to a future friend and to Winifred and Cyril Maude. Certainly the Pagets never discussed him and it was Dorothy alone who sometimes remembered Uncle 'Ted' as a man of 'weak character, charm, and a love for animals and little children who all responded to him.'

Actually, the profligate did not quite disappear. Rather he was sent away and it was Cyril and Winifred who paid his fare. Away from Florence, Edward became a very well-known and respected actor. When he first travelled out he went with the Wyndham company to play Boston, New York, and the Eastern circuit. Then he worked for the Schuberts playing leading man for Mrs. Minnie Madden Fiske, and Ethel Barrymore. By 1911, he was part of the experiment to 'star the play instead of the actor' by the Chicago Drama players sponsored by Hamlin Garland. There were a variety of leading roles until 1928 when Edward enjoyed his first musical comedy, *Good News.*

The Emerys had never discussed divorce and it is likely that without Bernard Shaw's interference Edward might not have been free to marry the American actress Georgia Waldron. Shaw had urged Florence sometime before 1894 to seek a divorce on the ground that if the marriage was not severed, her estranged husband could 'turn up any moment with very serious legal claims.'[10] It was as unlikely that Edward wanted to return to Florence as she to him but she permitted Shaw (who had other reasons) to persuade her. On 30

July 1894, her brother-in-law H. M. Paget, escorted Florence to Court where she accused Edward of adultery, without naming a Correspondent, and desertion of the Petitioner for 'two years and upwards without reasonable excuse.' Paget confided to William Butler Yeats's father that the proceedings, about which there were so many 'misgivings', lasted for all of seven minutes. There had been some difficulty over the matter of desertion since Edward had really been sent away. Chiefly, Florence despised a law that forbade two people to agree to incompatibility. How inconceivable it was that Society considered a marriage respectable when two people lived together regardless of their suffering; that it could not see their emotional degradation of living side by side never wanting the same thing at the same time. Moreover, she had been forced to reveal in private 'subjects no innocent person would care to mention in private.' Had she her way, it would have been proof of a separation on her first application followed by a decree absolute if she and Edward preferred to maintain a permanent rift.

Two days after the Court procedure, Florence had sufficiently recovered from it all to invite Henrietta, Willie Yeats, and 'some mediumistic chemist's assistant' to her rooms at Dalling Road. All concerned were in the thick of their occult study by then and J. B. Yeats was sure 'wonderful things happened.'[11] The day in Court eventually provoked Florence to write 'Good' in her horoscope as she had done when working out her stars after her broken engagement in 1880.

On 4 February in the following year, Florence received her decree from the Right Honourable Sir Francis Henry James and she and Edward Emery were legally free. Edward's second marriage was a happy one. His wife bore a son John who, when he was seven, made his debut at the Punch and Judy Theatre in New York City. The youngest Emery continued the family tradition in the theatre at first using the name 'Edward' and then 'Ian'. Achieving a list of credits that exceeded any previous member's of the Emery clan on the legitimate stage, John became a film actor as well. In a stage career which claimed over thirty-seven leads in an equal number of successes, including Laertes in John Gielgud's *Hamlet,* his list of film credits included work with Ingrid Bergman and the late Gary Cooper. John had a deep, throaty voice and showed no indication of having studied in the school of naturalism. Friends said, and they were right, that he belonged to the old Barrymore 'profile school' of acting.

'Ted', as he was known to his friends, married and divorced three well-known actresses, Patricia Calvert, Tallulah Bankhead, and Tamara Geva. The second marriage was the most astonishing to the press as well as to the participants. It was an impulsive step for the thirty-five-year-old actress who became attracted to John after seeing him play three roles which included the Earl of Warwick in Bernard Shaw's *Saint Joan*. Tallulah was impressed with the Anglo-American's style and eloquence, and no 'pussyfooting'. As for John, he described the actress only as 'half British, half pickaninny.'

They were married in 'Daddy's' house (William Brockman Bankhead, U.S. House of Representatives) with only immediate members of the family present; the Edward Emerys did not attend. Then, before they dashed for their honeymoon, Tallulah managed a few choice words: 'I've married a man just as dizzy as I am . . . and we're going to New York to raise hell.'[12]

John's role with his second wife was almost too spectacular to endure. Before their divorce on 13 July 1941 (Tallulah pleaded mental cruelty) the Emerys attended a Joe Louis fight. Tallulah was armed with 'a rug, a pair of field glasses, and a flask . . . just in case of snakebite.' When Joe Louis knocked Max Schmelling out cold in the first round, John was obliged to witness his wife scream before seventy thousand people, 'I told you so, you sons . . .'[13]

Edward Emery died while his son was still married to the gravel-voiced actress. On 7 May 1938 he was taken from his apartment at 3 East 77th Street and admitted by Dr. E. P. De Santo at 12.10 p.m. to the Fifth Avenue Hospital. His death occurred the same day from myocarditis, secondary anaemia and inanition.

In 1963, John fell victim to cancer and died after an eighteen month bout with the disease at his home on 8 East 96th Street. He left no immediate surviving relatives except for a cousin in England, Marjorie Maude, but a host of friends mourned him at the funeral services at Campbell's, Madison Avenue.

With John's death in 1964, seven generations of the Emery tradition ended on the stage. It is not too far-fetched to assume that the last owed its life to Bernard Shaw's eager insistence on Florence Emery's divorce.

NOTES

1 *The New Age,* (London, February 7 1895).

2 Searched by Miss Ceridwen Oliver, Archivist, Queen's College.

3 Florence Farr, see *Modern Women: Her Intentions,* (London, 1910).

4 Florence Farr, 'The London Stage', copy, Jeanne Foster-William Murphy Collection, henceforth referred to as Foster-Murphy.

5 Victoria and Albert Museum, Enthoven Collection. Referred to henceforth as VA.

6 Edward Emery played in *The Foundlings or The Ocean of Life, Peep O'Day, Amy Rosbart.*

7 Farr, *op. cit.*

8 'Portrait D'Une Femme'.

9 Courtesy of Michael B. Yeats.

10 Clifford Bax, *Bernard Shaw, W.B. Yeats Letters to Florence Farr,* (London 1946), Preface.

11 Joseph Hone, J.B.Y. *Letters to his Son,* (New York 1946), 56.

12 *Life,* (New York, September 13 1931), 103.

13 Tallulah Bankhead, *Tallulah,* (New York, 1952,), 27.

3

Hammersmith and Bedford Park
1889-1890

Florence Farr calculated that she had lived an 'orthodox married life four years.' She also confessed that having lived previously within a large family until she was twenty-three, she had 'given home and the family as much trial as seemed necessary.'

If her calculations were correct, Bernard Shaw probably came into her life sometime in 1889. (Shaw says the eighteen eighties, at a socialist soirée at the William Morrises.) Of course had Florence studied embroidery with Morris's daughter May earlier than 1889, a meeting with G.B.S. would have occurred. May collected 'charming young ladies' to introduce to Shaw at their evening 'at homes'.

1889, however, gives Florence a scant few months after Edward Emery's departure to acquire the 'Leperello list of a dozen adventures' Shaw attributes to her. As an alternative, Florence may have used the word 'orthodox' in other connotation; or, the goodly sum referred to by Shaw may have been a figment of the divorcée's imagination. By 1894 Shaw has the list up to fourteen, a number that includes himself.

Shaw had gathered a small list on his own account before he met Mrs. Emery and May Morris was vying to be on it. Although she settled for his company at socialist entertainments and lectures she wished for an exchange of more intimate emotions. Still, she played at the fraternal disguise and encouraged frequent evenings at Hammersmith. 'I repeat you must come to us on Thursday—How incomplete were a Social entertainment without the critical smile & quiet sneer of George Bernard Shaw.'[1]

When Shaw played the leprechaun at these events, May ruffled with displeasure—

Why do you pretend that you are so utterly shallow and insincere? This role will begin to pall on your friends after a while. If it makes me impatient who see you but seldom, I wonder how it makes your intimate friends feel, who are no doubt aware of depths in yr. character which you hide with the most insane obstinacy! Self-deprecation is not at all a pretty accomplishment in my eyes.[2]

By July 1885, Shaw was a visiting 'preacher' at Morris's converted coach house on the Mall. Occasionally May summoned him with a letter to confirm a speaking engagement.

As you said that all Sundays were alike to you, you are put down to preach to us the second Sunday in August (9th). I don't know if you are aware that our audiences love you very much. Their faces always broaden with pleasure when we tell them that if they are good Bernard Shaw will be their next teacher.[3]

Shaw noted in his diary on the ninth that he lectured that afternoon on 'Socialism and Scoundrelism'; that Jenny Patterson was there and he had seen her to a bus before returning to Morris's for supper. Slighted, May challenged him:

What a charming lady your friend Mrs. Patterson is! I wonder why you profess to be reluctant to introduce me to her. Did you think I *shd* bore her so much? I mean to find out whether she joined our Branch because a Socialist at heart, or because . . . you persuaded her to 'join first & learn later.[4]

Jane (Jenny) Patterson was more than fifteen years Shaw's senior, and at the time they met in 1882, Jenny, recently widowed, had come to London from Dublin. Shortly after her arrival she began singing lessons with Shaw's mother, Mrs. Lucinda Elizabeth Shaw which threw her into the company of G.B.S. In 1885 he was visiting her rooms until late in the evening, such as the night of 10 February which he jotted down in his diary; attending the Psychical Society with her 26 June, and on 10 July caught in surprise by her visit to him at Osnaburgh Street. Shaw escorted the widow home through the park, had some supper and music in her rooms which were followed by 'curious conversation'. Then came a declaration of passion before Shaw got away by 3 the next morning, 'Virgo intacta still'.[5]

The month of July was almost reckless for Shaw with supper with May Morris on 12 July, a meeting with her on the fourteenth, and Jenny's 'forced caresses' on the eighteenth. A week later G.B.S. celebrated his twenty-ninth birthday with a 'new experience'. What disturbed him nearly as much was 'an old woman next door, whose evil interpretation of the lateness of my departure alarmed us.'

Shaw's escapades in these years included another electrifying ex-

perience before he met Florence Emery. Annie Besant was nine
years older than her would-be lover and in one sense his employer
since G.B.S. contributed to her magazine *Our Corner.* The
Irishman paid his first social visit to Annie on 31 January 1885 and
during the following year they came into close contact during their
work with the Fabians. Toward the end of the year the intimacy
became ' a very close & personal sort, without, however, going
further than a friendship',[6] Shaw felt some relief when he was not
called upon to consummate a relationship and, as if to test this, he
wrote to May for confirmation of their 'mystical' symbiosis. Stalwart,
she answered—

> I am strongly moved to answer of your letter just this: that your
> resolution when we became acquainted not to make love was most
> judicious and worthy of all praise, having, as you say, the most en-
> tirely satisfying results. I don't think our intercourse can have caus-
> ed you more pleasure than it has me. I have always been most im-
> patient of the bourgeois vulgarity of thought and the attendant con-
> vention which almost entirely prevent young men and women from
> holding that frank and friendly intercourse without which life is
> nothing to my mind.
> Let us be comrades by all means.[7]

And comrades they remained until Shaw, smelling a trap sometime
in 1898, abandoned the friendship.

In 1886 then, it was sometimes Jenny and May with Shaw at
Kelmscott House, or calling at 'J. P.'s' on his way to Hammersmith,
and back to Jenny afterwards to find the light out; letter-writing to
May, and by 9 May, a 'violent scene' with Jenny. Shaw decided that
from then out, 'future intercourse must be Platonic', and so it was
until the thirteenth when Jenny called at his rooms and 'there was a
scene & much pathetic kissing & petting' and the widow departed
'comparatively happy'.

The following January the intimacy with Mrs. Besant 'threatened
to become a vulgar intrigue, chiefly through my fault.' Shaw 'roused'
himself in time, but by the end of the year, Jenny was quarrelling
with Shaw about Annie and she had good reason. G.B.S. had started
off harmlessly enough frequenting Annie's house on Monday
evenings to play piano duets, 'mostly Haydn's Symphonies.' Annie,
already married, but convinced that Shaw was serious, had the il-
luminating idea of drawing up a marriage contract of her own design
to snare her fellow Fabian on the side. He, horrified, demanded a
return of letters and after rereading his own, was 'rather disgusted
. . . with the trifling of the last 2 years with women'.[8]

By the time Mrs. Emery entered his life, he was not inexperienced with small harmless intrigues.

When Florence came to the house at Hammersmith to learn embroidery with May, she studied at the same time as Lily Yeats, William Butler Yeats's elder sister. Yeats had been studying French with a group of young socialists at the Coach House when John Butler Yeats prevailed upon his son to take his sisters Lily and Lolly to the lessons. The self-conscious Willie left the group two weeks later but his sisters stayed on and soon Lily began to embroider. She liked the work 'greatly', Yeats wrote to his friend in Ireland Katherine Tynan, and made 'cushion covers without end' for 'about thirteen shillings a week'.

May had considerable talent for her art which she displayed in large pieces in Morris's shop at 449 Oxford Street. John Todhunter, the Irish physician, teacher, and writer who had emigrated to England, wrote to Herbert Horne that May had 'begun where her father has left off.' He spoke of a design 'better than anything of his I have seen'.

a supreme thing of its kind—conventional with all the freedom of nature. It is exquisitely beautiful in harmony and outline, disposition of masses, & what I can only call *revolution* of the decorative idea.[9]

The Yeats family was living at 3 Blenheim Road, Bedford Park by April 1888. John Todhunter had found the dwelling at the request of the poet's father who wanted a house with an efficient boiler for plenty of hot baths. Willie wrote to Katherine Tynan in March that they were moving into 'a fine roomy house, which by good luck we have got very cheap'. He thought Bedford Park was the 'least Londonish' of places, 'a silent tree-filled place where everything is a little idyllic, except the cockroaches that abound there'.[10] Later, he liked Bedford Park even more when in May it was 'at its best, all the trees and flowers in their full dress'.[11]

Bedford Park was the dream 'garden suburb' of a cloth merchant Jonathan T. Carr. Built near the Turnham Green underground station, then thirty minutes from the heart of London, it had all the desirability of location and the satisfying casualness of a country village. None could argue with the 'Ballad of Bedford Park'

> Thus was a village builded
> For all who are aesthete
> Whose precious soul it fill did
> With utter joy complete.[12]

except for the fact the Park was bohemian rather than aesthete, and cheap.

Actors, lawyers, playwrights, doctors, university dons and retired army officers may have been attracted to Bedford Park as much by its cheapness as by the unconventionality for which it quickly became known—the inhabitants had a partiality for fancy-dress balls, walked about in bedroom slippers and met on Saturday mornings for a drink at the Tabard.[13]

G. K. Chesterton, whose wife-to-be lived there in the nineties, describes something more of its 'manufactured quaintness.' Bedford Park resembled exactly what it aspired to,

A colony for artists who were almost aliens; a refuge for persecuted poets and painters hiding in their red-brick catacombs or dying behind their red-brick barricades, when the world should conquer Bedford Park.[14]

Everyone at the Park was neighbourly and Yeats especially enjoyed the Todhunters. He described the Irish physician as a 'tall, sallow, lank, melancholy man, a good scholar and a good intellect.'[15] The Todhunter house struck him as 'charming'. It was more than this, being most elegant in design, and, with number One The Orchard, one of the two largest home sites in the neighbourhood. Yeats was especially pleased with the Morris carpet on the drawing room floor and pictures on the wall painted by his father when he was 'under the influence of Rossetti'.[16] There was much going to and fro between the Todhunters and the Pagets since a fence was all that separated number One from number Three.

The Paget house, on the north side of the Todhunter's, was adjacent to a large garden belonging to the house at the corner of Bedford Road. Built from a design probably under the control of Norman Shaw, number One had an incredible step-gable, two chimneys, and inside, a dramatic stairwell, where, either looking upwards or down, the turns of the staircase made a giddy sight. The drawing room was flooded by light from four sides and across the hall from it was a fairly small dining hall, a bathroom, and an immense kitchen. Upstairs was Paget's studio, an architectural delight with its marvellous North window, (overlooking the neighbour's garden) the only one of its kind in the Park, an exposed beam ceiling, and the little stage that was really a balcony on the level of the second floor. Across the hall was the master bedroom and next to this a bathroom with a splendid Victorian tub covered with sunflowers, marble walls, and a very stately wooden W.C. Emily Farr's bedroom must have been the small room on this floor and on the floor above, off a gallery, were two more bedrooms for the Paget's four children.

When Yeats first knew the artist, Paget had a Samsonian black beard, and a reputation for being the 'strongest' man in the Park. He was also an amateur actor, and a 'voluntary but amateurish' chief of the local Fire Brigade. Not satisfied to express himself totally with a brush, his paintings and drawings exhibited at the Royal Academy were often accompanied by a long text. 'A shortish one', attached to 'Orlando's Adventure with the Fairy Morgana' read:

> Orlando, to deliver his friends from enchantment, enters the garden of Morgana, and finds the fairies dancing and singing to the victims she holds imprisoned in the crystal rock, and proclaiming that the only way to vanquish her is to seize her by the hair which grows from her forehead.[17]

Paget was a romantic, as the titles to his paintings suggest. In 1884, for example, he had shown at the Academy 'Circe Discovered at the Loom by the Companions of Ulysses', 'The Enchanted Princess', 'Reflections', and 'The Poison Flower'.

Willie Yeats spent much time in Paget's studio despite the fact that he had spent his life among painters who 'hated' the Royal Academy. Paget was soon painting his portrait in competition with John Butler Yeats; the latter composition, Willie thought, was 'beyond all comparison the best'.[18] Paget's portrait of Yeats dated 6 April 1889, is now in the Belfast Museum and Art Gallery. Yeats has a moustache and beard and wears a white cravat. At the time of his sitting, he often wore a black tie and Paget questioned his choice. 'To go with my hair and boots of course!' said Willie. On some occasion, the poet infuriated his host by dropping ashes on the studio floor. Paget kept his studio exceptionally tidy and when he referred to Yeats's carelessness, the poet told him arrogantly, 'Why, the world is my ashtray!' Yeats admitted later in those years he was 'arrogant, indolent, excitable'.

There was one other close friend in W. B. Yeats's circle of writers and artists who all abounded in eccentricities. York Powell, he with the 'leonine beard and menacing and misleading eyebrows',[19] lived at 2 Priory Gardens. Powell was the elder Yeats's 'chief friend', a man of genius and unshaped thought to whom John Butler Yeats gave credit for his own philosophy which had been imparted simply by 'looking at him'.[20]

Yeats has remembered the eccentrics of those years; the 'Good Listener', the painter who escaping from his work's boredom made mechanical toys to half-fill his studio—

> a model railway train at intervals puffed its way along the walls, passing several railway stations and signal boxes; and on the floor

lay a camp with attacking and defending soldiers and a fortification that blew up when the attackers fired a pea through a certain window.[21]

(Years later, H. M. Paget told the Yeats's good friend Oliver Edwards that the peas were actually toy metal bullets.)

While Paget trafficked with his trains, John Todhunter played with his own frivolities with a letter-head which read 'Ye Sette of Odd Volumes.' The title represented a Brotherhood which harkened to Benjamin Franklin's creed that 'An Odd Volume of a Set of Books bears not the value of the proportion to the perfect Set'.

A list of contributors who wrote for 'Ye Sette of Odd Volumes', which dates up to 1903, includes the names of Percy Addleshaw, 'Salopian', E. H. Allen, 'Necromancer', Walter Frewen Lord, 'Dominie', H. C. Mariller, 'Knyghte Erraunt', W. Wilsey Martin, 'Laureate', Sir Edwin Sullivan, 'Bookbinder', W. Mort Thompson, 'Histriographer', and Silvannus P. Thompson, 'Magnetizer'.

A Foreword for a volume, composed by John Todhunter, and printed by the Chiswick Press accounts for the way in which the Irish writer spent much of his time when not at the task of writing pastoral plays.

Every genuine Odd Volume, being in the very promise of his title-page a storehouse of pleasant thoughts, will on occasion reveal a text or two of the cryptic scripture within him, for the amusement or instruction of his Brethren in Sette assembled, and their Guests.

Sometimes his voice becomes the gramophone of his soul. Sometimes he confides his maturer wisdom to his pen, for its more exquisite utterances in prose or verse. Now we are grave, now gay; anon we pass lightly from mood to mood, and, in a word, essay to practice that Gentle Art of Playing the Fool which is the relaxation of the wise.[22]

For divertissement, the goodly brothers amused themselves with quatrains, a sample of which is 'A Welcome', put together by Todhunter for the banquet on Ladies' Night 4 December 1891. It was not strictly a quatrain but 'a trifle picked from the highways and hedges' which should sit 'humbly below the salt'.

Eate, drynke, and be merrie, Guest,
A thousand welcomes to our Feast;
And a thousand Welcomes more,
From our Hearte's unstinted store,

To every Ladye here in place,
Who's brighte Eies and whoo's faire Face
Maketh more fayre, maketh more bright
December's Gloom than Junë's light!

> Soe welcome all, feastynge yfere,
> Healthe and good luck, and pleasaunt Cheere!

There were other communal activities among this lot at Bedford Park. A debating club called itself the 'I.D.K.' and a group of 'Dancers' met at the Pagets' house. Florence was responsible for the ladies, who, including Gwendolen Bishop, later Mrs. Clifford Bax, 'gallumpfed' about, throwing oranges into the air with a flagrant disregard for the laws of gravity. Unable to coordinate their feet with their hands, the 'dancers' allowed the oranges to pound to the floor while they 'gallumpfed' with empty hands. Florence directed the show but never participated herself because (despite her training at Toole's) a witness said, 'she couldn't dance.'

It was not the only endeavour of Florence, or 'Follings's' as the Paget children called her, to bring the arts to Bedford Park. She was always organising different, incredible groups for this or the other thing. A little indifferent to her activities, young Geoffrey Paget preferred to pick at the ant-nests in the earth surrounding the young trees on his street. Follings, observing him, thought he was 'well made but odd looking pretty eyes and mouth very fond of fun & most affectionate.'

Yeats had joined the Morris circle before the move to Blenheim Road and became a member of the favoured who joined Morris for supper after the lectures. He found the workmen 'rough of speech and manner', and was told by one of them that he talked 'more nonsense in one evening than he had heard in the whole course of his past life'.[23]

W.B. met Shaw at Hammersmith in February 1888 when G.B.S. was reading the part of a photographer in a play written by the sister of barrister Ernest Radford. The poet found the other Irishman 'very witty'. But 'like most people who have wit rather than humour, his mind is something wanting in depth.'[24] Shaw, on his part, could only remember that he went into supper with 'an Irishman named Yeats?' After this entry in his diary, he added 'Talked about socialism a great deal.' They met again on Sunday, 15 April after a lecture on 'Anarchism.' Yeats and Shaw stayed behind for supper with the painter J. M. Strudwick, Beasley, Sir Emery Walker (associated with Morris in the Kelmscott Press), Sparling (May Morris's future husband) Morris and May.

Shaw was reasonably well acquainted with the Bedford Park set who were just a mile down the river from Kelmscott House. He knew the nihilist Stepniak in 1885, Todhunter in 1886, and spent an evening with E. Heron Allen that September. Allen, he wrote in his diary, had

Above left: 78 Portsdown Road, Maida Vale (left entrance). Above right: Warwick Chambers. Below: Forge Cottage, G.W. Paget's house in Sussex.

Edward Emery, New York.

Florence Farr, c.1890.

Above: The Paget house in Bedford Park. Below: Nora Paget (née Dryhurst) and G.W. Paget, 1971.

Above left: George Bernard Shaw. Above right: W.B. Yeats. Below left: John Quinn. Below right: Edward Emery, New York.

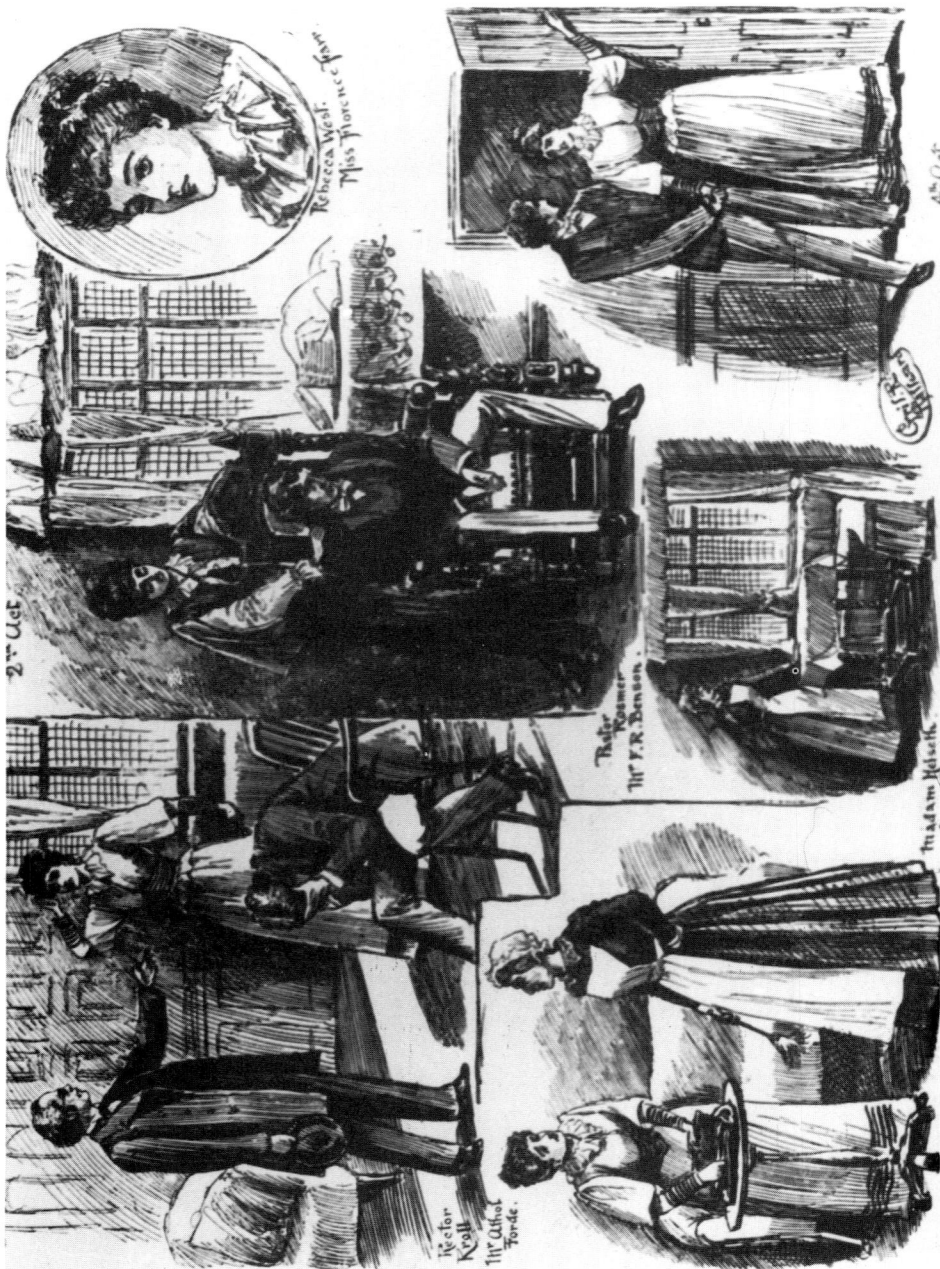

Artist's sketch of scenes from Ibsen's *Rosmersholm*.

**THE BUFFALO FINE ARTS ACADEMY
ALBRIGHT ART GALLERY**

CHARLES M. KURTZ
DIRECTOR

The Buffalo Fine Arts Academy and the Buffalo Society of Artists join in inviting you to attend a Lecture by Miss Florence Farr of London, England, on
"The Chanting of the Greek Chorus"
with illustrations from the translations of Professor Gilbert Murray, at the Albright Art Gallery,

Tuesday Afternoon, April 9th, at four o'clock.

Miss Farr comes highly recommended by Mr. William Archer, Mr. Arthur Symons, Mr. G. K. Chesterton and Professor Gilbert Murray.

Please present this card at the door.   Admission to non-members, 50 cents.

Above: Invitation to Florence Farr's recital in Buffalo, 1907. Below: Artist's sketch of scenes from Shaw's *Widowers' Houses.*

THE INDEPENDENT THEATRE SOCIETY'S NEW PLAY: SCENES FROM "WIDOWERS' HOUSES," BY MR BERNARD SHAW, PRODUCED AT THE ROYALTY THEATRE YESTERDAY. (*See page 10.*)

972

Florence Farr and H.M. Paget in John Todhunter's *Sicilian Idyll*.

Florence Farr and Lily Linfield in *Sicilian Idyll*.

Henrietta Paget.

H.M. Paget.

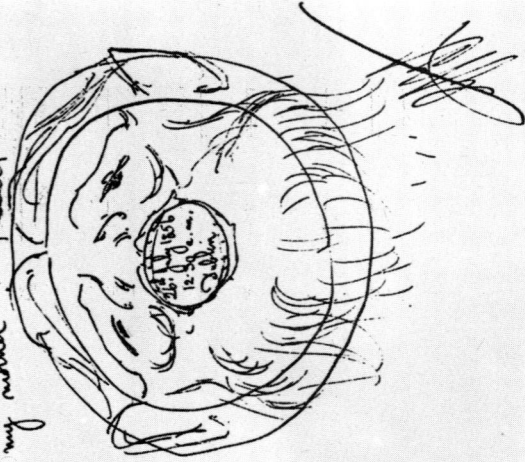

Left: Postcard from Shaw to Florence about Annie Besant's horoscope. Right: Letter from Florence to John Lane about her book, *The Dancing Faun*.

Florence Farr as Louka.

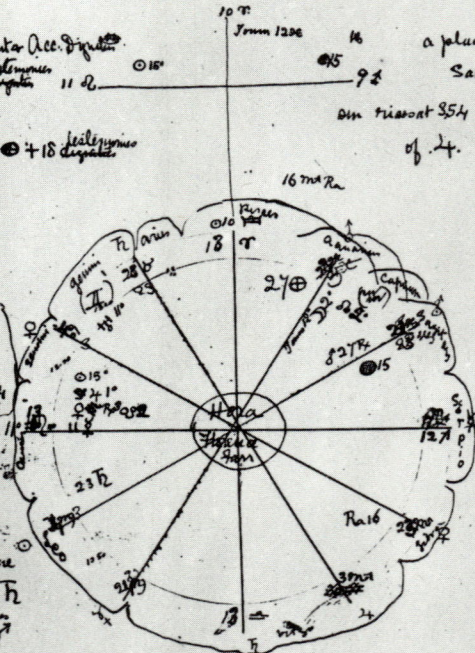

A horoscope prepared by Florence Farr.

Jany 18th 1917

My dear W.B.Yeats. I saw your interview in the
Observer over the Hugh Lane pictures affair. And
was greatly interested in your psychological state, &
point of view. I never got your book which you promised
me, so I suppose you couldn't get anyone to "paper
it up"; or else it has gone to the bottom of the sea.
I much want to read it & have seen very appreciative
reviews. All reviewers seem gentle now a days. I have
not seen even an attack in The Brook Kerith.
Last December I became an Amazon & my
left breast & major pectoral muscle were removed
Now my left side is a beautiful slab of flesh
adorned with a handsome fern pattern made
by a cut & 30 stitches which were put in by
the eminent surgeon of Colombo Dr Paul.

What happened was that I suddenly discovered
I had a sort of piece of rubber in that region
& got shot shooting pains. I saw the local
doctor & was packed off to Colombo & a large
tumour which had spread right under my
arm was removed. It was not malignant so
I don't know whether it would be called Cancer
in England, but that's the name they gave it
here.

It was quite an experience for me as I have
never once been helpless in my life since I was a
baby.

A letter from Florence to W.B. Yeats, 1917.

Florence Farr, in the 1900s.

told his hand 'very successfully.'

Florence, it is certain, knew Yeats before G.B.S. because of the poet's association with the Pagets and the Todhunters; an unassuming friendship must have commenced between them in 1888. It was not, however, based on any socialist credo as was the case with Shaw. When the divorcée came to the Morrises, she attached herself to a syndrome of isms suiting her self-emancipation. William Morris had recently written his paper 'The Society of the Future' licensing the rich to cultivate their garden so long as it was controlled by Morris's aesthetic for beauty. And to the workingman, he held forth a neo-Kiplingesque dream where, one might read, none shall work for the money, and none for the fame, 'But each for the joy of the working . . . Shall draw the Thing as he sees It' . . . etc. 'As he sees it,' really meant in the way Morris saw it, so that the Socialist's Utopia could belong to a very few; those who were fortunate in time or money to cultivate the Morris designs, or those who were game to damn their bellies to find aesthetic salvation more noble than a weekly paycheque.

Florence would have agreed with the Socialist's doctrine for abolishing wedlock. But first, its leader sensibly believed, women must place themselves in an equitable position with men before they unchained the locks of economical slavery. Morris agreed with Shaw that no man was a Socialist who was 'not prepared to admit the equality of women', as far, Morris added, as conditions went. 'Also,' he explained in answer to an article Shaw submitted to him, 'a real marriage is a rare exception and prostitution . . . a kind of legalised rape.'[25]

These were Florence's own sentiments during a century when there was a dearth of working positions available to women. By the time she completed *Modern Women* two decades later, the figures still balanced negatively. A singer was 'delighted' with a thousand pounds a year, an 'average successful' actress with ten pounds a week or five hundred pounds a year; the novelist with three hundred pounds, and the 'average lady doctor with the same.' In a school, a male principal received one thousand pounds compared to the lady superintendent's two hundred pounds. Women found it difficult to find Government positions, Church or law court duties, and the average charwoman made as little as fifteen shillings a week, 'exactly half a man's minimum wage.'

Florence raged intellectually at the hardships imposed upon less fortunate women than herself, and winced at the invincible apathy of a society which tolerated such injustices. It would, however, be stretching the point to suggest, even mildly, that she was an activist. In the year Florence met Shaw it would have been enough for her to agree with him that

> Modern English polite society . . . seems to me as corrupt as con-
> sciousness of culture and absence of honesty can make it. A can-
> ting, lie-loving, fact-hunting, scribbling, chattering, wealth-
> hunting, pleasure-hunting mob, that, having lost the fear of hell,
> and not replaced it by the love of justice, cares for nothing but the
> lion's share of the wealth wrung by the threat of starvation from
> the hands of the classes that create it.[26]

It was Shaw's statement, ostensibly, that 'home is the girl's prison and the woman's workhouse' that cemented his relationship with Florence Emery.

Shaw must have found his newest woman friend quite beautiful. Her heavy-lided eyes were especially significant framed by 'crescent eye-brows' of which he would warn mankind to beware. She had a strong, forward jaw which offset a straight (the Irish writer George Moore called it a big) nose, a shallow forehead and her cheekbones were occasionally set into relief when she was not approaching the square look of the 1890's. She was not a prototype of the Pre-Raphaelite beauty although tradition has it that she is one of the characters in Sir Edward Burne-Jones's painting 'The Golden Stair'. Her hair was cut short in the mode of the New Woman and her natural curls framed a provocative smile. She had two faces; that of the rather saucy, tom-boyish arrogant New Woman, and the poetic, mature countenance revealed in the photographs for the production of her poetic plays. When she was with Shaw, she played the New Woman boldly expressing her dissatisfactions with marriage. Newly released, she might well have told him of her escape from the 'ungraceful antics of love'; that she looked back on the episode of matrimony 'with as much disgust as if she had awakened from a pigsty'.[27] And of sex, she must have startled him with 'It gives us every happiness we know on the condition that we never give way to it in our serious relations. For heirs certainly. For diversion yes. As for "hygienic gymnastic," yes.'[28]

Florence's feigned, or was it born coolness attracted a consummate admirer in Shaw, his ideas on the subject of the limitations of sex not being too disimilar from her own. Moreover, there was no question here of defiling sanctified territory. Besides, even Shaw could notice that she was younger than Jenny Patterson, and certainly less demanding and volatile (as even a quick glance at J.P.'s letters to Shaw reveal). She was not unreasonable or debauched like Annie

Besant (until G.B.S. got her interested in the Theosophists), less pithy than May Morris, and quite willing to admit that women were capable of several love affairs which never inclined him to feel a permanent obligation to her. She confirmed her position in the conglomeration of *fin de siècle* females who believed themselves free from Victorian taboos. They were, of course, no more sexually charged than women had been in any century. They spoke of their amativeness freely, however, and some disguised their vitality beneath an honest passion for the discussion of life so that the 'salt of wit,' Florence said, permitted her to enjoy the 'strongest flavours'. Apart from her bitterness toward her own marriage, in rare moments she shared the Victorian New Woman's wish for an idyllic male relationship

> a rich sense of romance, a passionate desire to make the love of man and woman once more what it was in Eden, a strong sense of the absolute necessity of some significance in human life.[29]

Florence shared other items in common with Shaw beyond sex. G.B.S.'s mother had been singing mistress at the North Collegiate School which had been founded by Mary Buss, an alumna of Queen's. More important though, Shaw had better than a passing interest in the drama. In 1889 he was at work on a play *The Cassone*, (which he never completed) and he and William Archer, a young Scot, were collaborating on a play called *Rheingold*. At the time, Florence was preparing to go on the stage after an absence of several years and Shaw seemed interested in her as an actress.

Dr. Todhunter had invited Paget's sister-in-law to read a new play he expected to produce at the Bedford Park playhouse. His poetic play *Helena in Troas* had been, Yeats said, 'the talk of a London season' in 1886, though 'unactable as it was unreadable.' Select audiences had welcomed the production which ran for six performances at Hengler's Cirque in Argyll Street but the more astute were disappointed with the general 'mumbling' or 'shouting'. William Michael Rossetti took it upon himself to list the actors in order of descending merit. Beerbohm Tree had been fine, sometimes excellent; Chorus still left something to be desired, the something probably not able to be supplied 'save by a couple of generations of similar work.' Mrs. Tree (Florence's alumna from Queen's) was the next in line, or perhaps Vezinn, although 'his elocution did not seem quite stately and abstract enough for a Greek standard.' Miss Alma Murray, fresh from her success as Beatrice in the Shelley Society's *Cenci* at the Grand, Islington, 7 May

I say the same, more strongly of *her* elocution, & her person is not sufficiently beautiful or important but she was intelligent. Please don't give currency to any demur of mine regarding this lady, as she is the Beatrice Cenci of the Shelley Sosc. & as such must command my committee-loyalty.[30]

Yeats, at this time, was impressed with Todhunter as a playwright and since he was also convinced that it should be a 'point of honour' to be content with 'our own little public,' he urged Todhunter to write a pastoral play avoiding the 'oratorical phrase and cadence' of Shelley's *Cenci* and Tennyson's *Beckett*. The physician's response to the challenge was an Arcadian story based on an idyll by the Alexandrian poet Theocritus. By February 1890, Todhunter still lacked a male actor for a role when he thought of 'Ye Sette of Odd Volumes's E. H. Allen who united every month for 'conviviality and mutual admiration.'

I wonder whether you would care to take a part in a little piece I have written, & which I am going to have performed, some time in April, at our little theatre here in Bedford Park, for a local charity. I call it *A Sicilian Idyll*. The scene being laid in the Sicily of Theocritus. There are but 4 characters, two shepherds, & two shepherdesses, & the whole thing is played in an hour. Your part would not be very long (to work) up. It is in blank verse of course. H. M. Paget the artist who played the archer in 'Helena in Troas' is to be one of the two shepherds & I want you for the other. The two shepherdesses will be Mrs. Edward Emery and Mrs. Alfred L. Baldry, both of whom have had some experience on the boards, so I expect it will be well done. Your part requires graceful speaking of the verse, & very few men are so capable of this as yourself, so I hope you will volunteer to help me.
I am going to read it to the company on Sunday week, & hope in any case you will come & hear it. We shall have a cold supper at 8 o'clock sharp, as I want to begin the reading at 9 o'clock. Come if you can.[31]

Yeats went to the reading that evening and wrote to Katherine Tynan, 'Todhunter has written a charming little Arcadian play to be acted in Bedford Park. He read it on Sunday evening. Mrs. Emery and Paget take chief parts.'[32] Florence 'quite surprised' the author at the reading. He thought she would have required some 'coaching' but 'as far as speaking the verses intelligently went, you needed none.' She spoke them 'simply & easily' happily convincing Todhunter that when his lines were badly spoken the fault was not in the lines but in the speaker.[33]

The production became very much of an Emery-Paget collaboration with the artist active in several directions. 'A far glimpse of the Mediterranean' festooned with grapes and vine leaves was the outcome of his design for the set. The painter was also in charge of the properties and the costumes, the latter doing little to offset Florence's generous proportions that year. Alfred Baldry directed Todhunter's players including the director's wife Miss Lily Linfield; Allen came in for Daphnis, Mowbray Marras, the First Shepherd, and W. Herbert Roe, the Second.

A Sicilian Idyll was presented for the first performance 5 May at 9 p.m. at the red-brick Clubhouse on the Avenue (now taken over by C. A. Vandervell & Co. and used for whistdrives). There were two more evening performances on the seventh and the ninth and a matinée on the Friday. Seated with Yeats in the small ballroom (Yeats calls it long) that first evening were amongst others, John Trivett Nettleship, the painter, Selwyn Image, Alma Murray, May Morris, Winifred Emery and Cyril Maude, and Bernard Shaw who arrived an hour too early.

Mowbray Marras's prologue should have particularly appealed to Yeats who had, since he walked the road chanting verses with AE (George Russell), thought of speech as music.

> So, not banished quite
> By Babel and its din, where once she set
> Her buskined feet in triumph, lingers yet
> The Shy Muse in that Thespian bower she ranged
> Singing, ere yet the speech of man was changed
>   For tones unrhythmical.
> O, let none sneer
> If, singing still, she strive to charm your ear
> With vowelled verse, to set before your eyes
> an Idyll . . .

Todhunter's story centres around Amaryllis, a Hellenistic New Woman who, though sworn to forego love, succumbs to the spell of Alcander (H. M. Paget) after rejecting Daphnis (E. Heron Allen). At the same time, Thestyllis (Mrs. Baldry or Lily Linfield) admits to Amaryllis (Florence) her love for Daphnis. Amaryllis with passionate contempt intones:

> Better go cast thy limbs into the fire,
> Or dungeon up thy body from the sun,
> Than scratch thy being in love's bitter flame!
> . . . I have seen
> The tedious tragedies of woman's life

> No poet's tongue dare sing, too mean, too common
> To tread the scene in pomp of tragic words,
> The sullen agonies, the ageing cares,
>
> The dull disease where of poor famished love
> Dies dumbly hour by hour a lingering death.

Surely Florence's damnation of marriage must have inspired some further verses for Amaryllis by Todhunter—

> . . . Ah Thestyllis, wilt thou wed a swarm of cares,
> Slave for a thankless lord, nurse crying babies
> Who, like ungrateful nestlings, quit the nest
> And leave it cold, because a shepherd sighs?

When the curtain fell that first evening, Yeats heard various exclamations of delight from the audience. 'How pretty! . . . How Beautiful' or 'I would not have missed it for the world,' while he was transfixed by the unity of the acting, the scenery, the verse, and most especially, Florence Emery. Such 'grace and power' were incomparable, and the poet's eulogy extended to Heron Allen. While these two were on the stage, 'no-one else could hold an eye or an ear.'

> Their speech was music, the poetry acquired a nobility, a passionate austerity that made it akin for certain moments to the great poetry of the world. [34]

Yeats had been so incensed when any other actor broke the spell by introducing conversational phrasing or intonation into the verses that he listened with 'raging hatred' and muttered 'insulting' phrases a little aloud so that his dissatisfactions would be noticed. The performance brought to the young poet an even greater significance; the realisation that the 'highly cultivated man and woman in certain kinds of drama' could surpass the most accomplished actor who lacked 'culture'. And more, the convictions of the potential power of the poetic drama which could infect an audience into a world of 'renewed insight', and so 'influence the human understanding.'

There were others who capitulated less wholly. John Trivett Nettleship, for one, found the first scene between Florence and Paget 'capitally acted', and Allen 'admirably belied his nature' for Nettleship could not imagine him 'ever sick of love'. But when it came down to the problem of speech, despite Yeats's observations to the contrary, the painter 'missed' or had to 'divine the verse endings'. [35]

The author of this controversial production was so busy with production problems, such as Florence's difficulties with the tripod during an incantation scene, that it was not until 17 May that he sat in the middle of the ballroom to watch the play almost in its entirety. Two scenes had disappointed him before; the libation scene which was 'disgraceful', probably, he thought, for lack of rehearsal on Florence's part, and the scene with the New Womanish speeches. The last had 'never been given its full point', until the seventeenth when it went 'distinctly well'. No-one but Alma Murray could have spoken the verses better; in fact, when Florence spoke at her best, even Miss Murray could not have given her many points. There was also a moment when a touch of passion crept into Florence's voice, and for the first time, she seemed to feel 'I am thy murderer—kill me!' had some meaning '& was capable of being made a dramatic point.' Much to the author's relief, she had finally overcome her tendency to 'coquettishness' and her gestures and facial expressions were 'natural and *vital*'. Her greatest problem, however, still lay in her timing. She had a tendency to top Paget's lines so that if he hesitated for a moment, Florence chopped off the ends of his verses.

> It is all very well to be quick to responding to your cues, but it is possible to be too quick & it is not fair to jump over them . . . I feel your habit of rushing your cues which seem to blind you to the value of a pause between two speeches in a dialogue, spoils the effect of the situation.

Then, she had not learned the value of the pause, for after her passionate scene with Paget

> Wagner would have left you & Alcander facing each other without a movement for 30 bars of an orchestral symphony [an] expression of all that was going on in your mind founded in the Amaryllis motiv the struggle motiv the surrender motiv & half a dozen others.

Yet Todhunter had only asked Florence for ten seconds or so before she moved toward Alcander

> & as I said before I want you to move (as you & Sarah Bernhardt *can* move) toward him as if you were drawn by a spell. I want you to get into his arms before you know where you are, & not say a word for at least ten seconds after you have got there. I want you to emphasize the tragic moment in fact you come to him at once . . . This is not *great* acting & from you I *demand* great acting.[36]

By way of relaxation, Todhunter thought that he should give his protegé a comedy part in his next play. He wanted to see her in a poetic comedy, but first he wanted to play the *Idyll* again on a larger stage. Todhunter had his wish with two performances underwritten by Mrs. Andrew Hart on the first and second of July at St. George's Hall, Holborn. In the new theatre Florence's invocation scene came off to a better advantage but poor Paget 'quite reached the depths of the common-place and mangled his part'. Herman Vezinn said that the 'technical or mechanical faults of elocution were damnable' with the entire cast. As if to make sure he had made his point he asked Todhunter to send him the play, if it was printed, 'so that I may supply the words that failed to reach me at St. George's Hall.'[37]

Yeats no doubt described an idealised and not the actual performance at the Bedford Park Clubhouse. He was, after all, so smitten with Florence Emery's culture (he was very naive in those years) that he may have been blinded to her real worth as an actress. Nevertheless, he soon became a constant visitor to her rooms at Dalling Road and planned for the poetic plays he would 'some day' write for her. Soon, she became the first woman to whom he 'could tell everything'. Writing about this period of time in the 'Four Years', Yeats has magnified Florence's three great gifts; her 'tranquil beauty', her incomparable sense of rhythm and beautiful voice, the 'seeming natural expression of her image'; and her third gift which she was to express through the art of the troubadors. He called this last her peculiar genius, her 'hard burden'; one which in time he would carry with her. But again the question might be asked whether he did not invent this for her and so for himself.

George Yeats, Yeats's widow, implied after Yeats had died that a brief love affair took place during this early association. It may have been a most intense friendship for the poet (and there is none to say nay to the affair) but it was Maud Gonne whom he met that year who stirred his passions in the 'old high way of love.' Several years after their first friendship, Willie complained to Henrietta that he had known Florence for years and they had never once made love. When Henrietta told this to her sister she laughed and said, 'but I'm years older [five] than he is.' Florence supposedly became bored with most men, and one who should know even describes her as asexual. Yeats observed that 'if a man fell in love with her she would notice that she had seen just that movement upon the stage or had heard just that intonation and all seemed unreal'.[38]

Despite Florence's romantic disinterest in Yeats, she became an extraordinary catalyst in his life and surely if she had not become bored, Yeats could have remained emotionally and artistically steadfastly attached.

It was Bernard Shaw who interested Mrs. Emery more imperatively that year. In October he met Florence by appointment at the train and took her to the first Saturday concert of the season at Crystal Palace. Afterwards they both returned to Florence's rooms where what with playing & singing & talking to her about Ibsen (I persuaded her to get up Rosmersholm instead of the Lady From the Sea) I stayed too late to keep my appointment with Pennell.[39]

On 16 October Jenny Patterson became 'angry & jealous about F.E.' and Shaw's day 'ended unpleasantly'. He continued to see Mrs. Emery, however, and on 11 November they spent the evening once more; 'sang a little, talked a little, played a little,' and Shaw managed to catch the last train to town. If there were any romantic overtones they were certainly obscured by Shaw's toothache which became bad during the night 'though I got to sleep at last, after sweating with pain for a while.'[40]

By the fifteenth of November G.B.S. and Mrs. Emery had their 'first really intimate conversation.' There was another evening in Florence's rooms that month, a second concert (Plunket and Paderewski), a family get together with Henrietta and the Dryhursts (Mr. Dryhurst was the Assistant Director of the British Museum and the father of Geoffrey Paget's future wife), and in December, six entries in Shaw's diary for Florence. By then he was losing the last train to town from Ravenscourt Park and spending a 'happy evening'.

1890 ended not unhappily for Florence. She had achieved some recognition by the Bedford Park set at least as an actress. Shaw was a stimulating and attentive companion, and John Todhunter offered hope for a sequel to the *Idyll*. Writing to her on the last day of the year, he expressed his professional regard and a willingness to share household small talk. With typical Victorian politeness which seems to appear even in the most intimate circumstances (and which often makes reading between the lines a hazardous occupation) Dr. Todhunter sent 'Dear Mrs. Emery' a copy of *Alcestis*. Michael Rossetti had confided that Ford Maddox Brown thought of it most highly. The book is inscribed to 'Florence Emery with kind regards from J. Todhunter, Christmas 1890.' The letter reads

I send you 'Alcestis.' It was a case of publish in haste [1879] & repent at leisure. It was written in about three weeks & not sufficiently [worked] for the press . . . hence the various pen & ink corrections of the text. You will find if you get past the cover, & look at the [whole?] of the book I have had some idea of rewriting it in a sort of acting edition which might perhaps be arranged for our little stage here. The scenery could be much simplified. Do you think anything could be made of it, in this way?

We have a pipe burst & the bathroom & kitchen flooded . . . very sea [?] & delightful. Now we have no water in the house except what still keeps percolating through the kitchen ceiling.

Anything further about your coat? It will be January tomorrow, & so a Happy New Year to you,

yours sincerely,

J. Todhunter. [41]

NOTES

1 BM, (June 8 1885).

2 BM, (July 12 1885).

3 BM, (July 21 1885).

4 BM, (August 10? 1885).

5 L.S.E. Diary transcribed by Blanche Patch. Referred to as Diary, henceforth.

6 Diary.

7 BM, (May 5 1886).

8 Diary

9 University of Reading, (December 29 1887).

10 Allan Wade, *The Letters of W.B. Yeats,* (New York 1955), 64.

11 Roger McHugh, ed., *W.B. Yeats Letters to Katherine Tynan,* New York 1953), 96.

12 *St. James Gazette,* (London 1881).

13 T. Affleck Greeves, 'The Making of a Community,' *Country Life,* (December 14 1967), 1602,

14 G.K. Chesterton, *Autobiography,* (London 1937), 139.

15 W.B. Yeats, *The Autobiography of William Butler Yeats,* (New York 1965), 78.

16 Horace Reynolds, ed., *Letters to the New Island,* (Mass. 1934), ix.

17 Greeves, *Artists and Architecture of Bedford Park,* (London 1967 Catalogue).

18 Wade, *op. cit.,* 121.

19 Chesterton, *op. cit.,* 140.

20 Yeats, *op. cit.,* 78

21 *Ibid,* 79.

22 John Todhunter (foreword), *Quatrains,* Opusculum Number Fifty-two of the Sette of Odd Volumes, (Chiswick MDCCCCV).

23 Yeats, *op. cit.*, 94.
24 McHugh, *op. cit.*, 45.
25 BM, (March 18 1885).
26 G. Bernard Shaw, *An Unsocial Socialist*, (New York 1917), 97.
27 Florence Farr, *The Solemnization of Jacklin*, (London 1912), 241.
28 *Ibid*, 78.
29 Chesterton, *op. cit.*, 143.
30 University of Reading, (May 29 1886).
31 VA, Enthoven Collection. (February 22 1890).
32 McHugh, *op. cit.*, 112.
33 The Pennsylvania State University, (May 18 1890).
34 Yeats, *op. cit.*, 80.
35 University of Reading, (May 7 1890).
36 The Pennsylvania State University, (May 18 1890).
37 The University of Reading, (July 7 1890).
38 Yeats, *op. cit.*, 81.
39 Diary.
40 Ibid.
41 Yale University.

4

Bernard Shaw and Florence Farr: The New Drama
1891-1897

Bernard Shaw, at his own admittance, had assumed charge of the campaign for the so-called New Drama in England. That 'figment of the revolutionary imagination', as he alluded to it, took title slowly in the English Theatre if Sir Arthur Wing Pinero's *The Squire* in 1881, and Henry Arthur Jones's *Saints and Sinners* in 1884 are considered part of the new movement. Certainly there was doubt of how far the Theatre had travelled from the Victorian melodrama when at least one of these plays crossed the boards. Playwright Sydney Grundy saw Pinero's *Squire* as an 'amateur piece of work.' The 'very badly painted landscape', he told William Archer, failed to suggest a 'beautiful English setting', and the attempt at verisimilitude had '*not* "got the scent of the hay over the footlights"' but 'the scent of the footlights over the hay.'

> Pinero's bits of characters which are good have nothing to do with the story, his characters which have to do with the story are utterly bad, false & ridiculous . . . His heroine is the most brutal Philistine bitch in literature, & her continual allusions to being in the family way are disgusting: his hero is a feeble-minded snob afraid of his mamma . . . Judgment: Pinero has some knowledge of theatrical effect & is good at superficial character . . . his literary power is only middling.

Shaw, Grundy added, would have the play's title changed to '*Three Months Gone.*'[1]

Although Pinero gave credit to Tom Robertson's *Caste* in 1867 for its influence on the New Drama, it was Henrik Ibsen who stimulated a new vocabulary in the discussion of English Theatre. 'The modern movement . . . the higher drama . . . the new live theatre . . . the era of the problem play . . . the modern realistic drama . . .

the free theatre . . . the modern social drama . . . the new school of thinker-dramatists',[2] were the idioms of the intelligentsia to which Bernard Shaw and Florence Emery lay claim.

Her part in the catastrophe at St. George's Hall withstanding, Shaw still decided to guide Florence's career on the stage. Not long after that mishap, he began work with her on the proofs of Ibsen's *Rosmersholm* translated by Lt. Col. Charles Archer with his brother's assistance. Knowing of Alma Murray's interest in the play, Shaw attempted to coerce her to relinquish the role of Rebecca. 'They tell me', he addressed her

> that you have designs on Rosmersholm. Well, Miss Florence Farr, who lately played in Todhunter's Sicilian Idyll, is going to do Rosmersholm . . . and I am the person who persuaded her thereto.[3]

John Todhunter had promised to back Florence 'on condition' that Miss Murray's rights were not infringed, and that matter settled, Florence began rehearsals at the Vaudeville. Todhunter decided to stage-manage, and A. L. Baldry returned to direct Frank R. Benson as Pastor Rosmer, Athol Forde, Rector Kroll, Charles Hudson, Ulric Brendel, J. Wheatman, Mortensgard, and May Protheroe as Helseth. Under Shaw's private supervision, the New Woman's real work took place in her rooms. G.B.S. coached her on 6 February 1891, and on the eleventh they had a marvellous time playing and singing before Florence tried on her dresses for the show.[4] Afterwards, they rehearsed some more. Florence was relying on G.B.S.'s concept of the 'unwomanly woman' to interpret her role. Since Shaw believed that female sacrifice was the penultimate of the 'idealist abominations that make society pestiferous,' Florence saw Mrs. Rosmer as the 'unwomanly woman',—'a drag, a responsibility, a reproach, an everlasting and unnatural trouble with whom no really strong soul can live'.[5] Rebecca was therefore a 'womanly woman' whose intellectual strength sublimated physical and emotional ardour to spiritual conquest.

With Jenny Patterson off to the East for the winter, Shaw's visits to 123 Dalling Road became a near daily routine. Tea-times were spent at A.B.C. shops, and there were concerts to attend together between rehearsals. The relationship was thriving until four days before the performance of *Rosmersholm* when their dispositions abruptly palled. Both spent the evening of the nineteenth 'in a horrid frame of mind', Shaw jotted in his diary. He was disheartened not only by rehearsals but by the fact that William Archer's reactions to the production were about to prevent him from attending the performance. G.B.S. was admittedly 'terrified' at having 'thrust' Florence on such an enterprise. Two days later he retrieved his nerve for when he arrived at Dalling Road it was in 'high spirits'. [6]

The following Monday, 23 February made Ibsen history on the English-speaking stage. 'White-lipped' men and women, the intelligentsia of the waning century, anxiously awaited the Norwegian's play during a musical entertainment by Ernest Lake.

> Never before at an entertainment for the mentally or physically inflicted . . . at an asylum concert or hospital treat . . . [were there] so many deformed faces; so many men and women pale, sad-looking . . . It was an assemblage of out-patients waiting for the doctor. [7]

Florence appeared on the stage no longer the mature matron of the *Idyll* productions, but a slim, pinched waisted Rebecca with eyes full of New Woman defiance. Throughout her performance she 'scored' with the public and the play 'got through as well as could be expected, & better than in its uncondensed form it deserved.' Frank Benson, 'painfully aware', that he was 'forced' and over-acting, pushed his part along 'as I felt it was touch and go whether the audience would bear with us to the end of the fourth act, perhaps I made a mistake in this, but . . . I did it for the best'. [8]

After the performance, the press asked Shaw's 'womanly woman' what she thought of Rebecca, and G.B.S., of course, appeared behind every word of her answer.

> Rebecca West is attractive just because she is so thoroughly womanly, and if she is not womanly then I give up my claim to womanhood, and proclaim myself an abnormal development at the end of the century. [9]

What a bait to Clement Scott who gleefully accepted the alternative Florence suggested to him!

When the press departed, Florence went with Shaw in a party of four (whom the penurious Shaw had to 'feed') to Gatti's. Later, they 'strolled about the embankment in the fog' until it was time for G.B.S. to take part in a discussion of Ibsen's *Ghosts* at the Playgoer's Club. More celebrating followed at Rulé's before Shaw took Florence to St. James's Park Station for her train to Ravenscourt Park. [10]

As with 'most new sects', the Ibsen appetite was not readily satiated and Todhunter had to promise the Ibsen cultists a second performance of *Rosmersholm*. Florence planned a private rehearsal with Frank Benson the following Monday and a run-through with the entire cast on 2 and 3 March. Meanwhile, she spent her days making efforts to paper the house and rendez-vousing with Shaw. She took tea only while he ate a meal at the Orange Grove in St. Martin's Lane on 25 February. They attended a concert at Crystal Palace three days later; on 3 March Shaw came to Dalling Road, and on 5 March he attended the second performance of *Rosmersholm*.[11] Afterwards, G.B.S. told the actor Charles Charrington that Florence really got by with the 'dint of brains'. Then he counted the receipts. The first performance had brought in ninety pounds, the second, fifty; John Todhunter ended up losing ten pounds, Benson collected twenty guineas, and Florence, 'nothing but her dresses and the kudos'.[12]

Even with Todhunter and Shaw behind her, Florence could not attract a professional, commercial management after her momentary success as Rebecca. Beerbohm Tree offered a guarded promise to consider her; others were 'full up for some time to come'. although George Alexander the actor hoped Florence would care to look him up some evening'.[13] G.B.S. and Archer then pressed J. T. Grein of the Independent Theatre. The Dutchman did meet Florence to 'talk matters over'. and Archer followed up the meeting advising Grein to

produce Bjornson's play *A Gauntlet* & give you [Florence] the leading part, Svava. It is a very strong play, whereas *The Newly-Married Couple* is as mild as milk. Besides, Svava being a social Purity heroine would effectually wash off the stains of Rebecca.[14]

Shaw sustained his mistress's interest in the New Drama, huddling over *Hedda Gabler* after tea at the Strand one afternoon, and continuing his amiability in other ways. There was dinner at a café opposite Victoria Station on 21 March, Dora Bright's concert at the Palace on the twenty-eighth, the 'Dream of Jubal' in April and a concert by Willy Hess and Hugo Becker; a visit to an art gallery, and then, Jenny Patterson returned from the East. On 27 April, Shaw 'went to J.P.'s. Fearful scene about F.E. this being our first meeting since her return from the East. Did not get home until about 3 a.m.'[15]

The following week Shaw went to Dalling Road to discuss the episode with Jenny. No doubt Florence suggested they begin their relationship anew in order to present a less intimate association. If it was 'all over and utterly dead, as if it had never been,' Shaw wrote to Florence the next day, they were really free to begin their attachment over again as they were 'that day at Merton.'

I am a beggar once more; and once more I shall come into my great fortune. I am again an unscrupulous egotist with a remorseless will; and again shall I be moralised and have my backbone sweetly stolen away. We shall even have Rosmersholm again.

That, of course, reminded him of her acting abilities. Not nearly so

naive as Todhunter who merely wished Florence to be another Sarah
Bernhardt. G.B.S. was driven to desperation by her indifference to
her art.

> There is nothing that drives me to utter despair as when I make
> some blundering and unsuccessful attempt to make you see some
> technical point that my mother can teach any idiot in a few
> lessons; and you shrink as if I were disparaging your artistic gifts.
> You do not know the importance of some of these tricks as regards
> health, economy of force, self-containedness and the like. If I break
> in on your artistic vein to urge them, it is because I have an extraor-
> dinary desire to make the most of you—to make effective and visi-
> ble *all* your artistic potentialities . . . And not, observe, merely as
> an actress, but as a woman. Your ability to act must only be a mere
> consequence of your ability to live. You are so real to me as a
> woman that I cannot think of acting being to you anything more
> than a technical accomplishment which I want to see carried to a
> high degree of perfection. For the born actress I have a certain con-
> tempt: for the women who is a consummate artist I have a deep
> fellow-feeling.[16]

Shaw could not suffer the many 'gaps and holes' in Florence's playing but he was enough in love with her, or so he told Charles
Charrington, that even when she 'faded' he was impressed there was
no air of failure in anything she did. He was 'only frightfully afraid'
she would tire of his criticisms.

Florence was relatively unconcerned with Shaw's remarks and
received his impertinences with good grace. The day she received
his letter they attended Eugene Halliday's piano recital at the
Prince's Hall and afterwards took tea and cocoa at an A.B.C. shop in
Piccadilly Circus. Florence even travelled out of her way on the train
with Shaw 'merely to kill time'.[17]

Jenny Patterson was not to be put off lightly by Shaw's attachment
to Florence Emery and on 5 May there was another scene. Two days
thence Florence sat with Shaw at an A.B.C. shop while he soothed
himself with some milk. Somehow he felt honour-bound to appease
the older woman's tantrums so that when he next visited Dalling
Road on 17 May, he only stayed for forty-five minutes 'as I had
promised to go to JP'.[18] Since Florence stated that women were
capable of several love affairs (although she never added
'simultaneously') she did not reveal her pique at Shaw's philandering; any hostility toward him was disguised until it erupted to the
surface in some future writing.

G.B.S. wrote to her in May about the possibilities of the American,
Herman Vezinn, playing *Rosmersholm* with her, the implication

being that Todhunter would put up the money. By the end of the month the physician had changed his mind for on 15 June he backed five performances of his own plays at the Vaudeville. Florence played the leads in *A Sicilian Idyll* again, and a work of 'gloomy character', Yeats called it, *The Poison Flower.*

Florence was terribly depressed by the knowledge of Archer's presence at the opening performance, a fact he rather enjoyed. Pretending amazement at her disturbance he made sure that she was aware that

> the whole performance was not very brilliant, but then (between ourselves) who could possibly do anything with such a play? If you will allow me to say so, I think what you ought chiefly to cultivate is a certain decision of manner—crispness of attack I believe they call it in music—which I now miss in your playing. You are apt to seem a little purposeless at times.[19]

This enigmatic 'gypsy', as the York Powells referred to their friend, exuded little vitality on the stage barely sustaining an optimum level of performance from scene to scene, apart from day to day. Yeats later implied that Florence attempted, perhaps, to break away from the demonstrative style of acting in the period. When he wrote that 'A new school of acting is now growing up under the various attempts to create an intellectual drama, and of changes deeper than that', he included Mrs. Emery 'when she was good,' in the new attempt to seize 'what is distinguished, solitary, proud even'.[20]

Generally, the press commiserated with Todhunter for the plays at the Vaudeville. 'He wanted scenery: he did not get it. He wanted style and *décor* on the stage: he found tawdriness. He wanted music: it was execrable. He needed dancing: it was amateurish to the last degree'. More, the elocution was 'incoherent belonging to the 'worst form of mumbling'.[21]

Yeats blamed the 'meagre and unintelligent' audiences for the disaster, firmly convinced that poetic plays should be kept at Bedford Park where they could meet with the 'praise of . . . equals.' Annoyed that he had to 'hunt up people to fill empty places' he had been called upon twice to review the plays 'only on the chance' of their being printed.

The performances made Shaw painfully aware of those 'gaps' in Florence's interpretations and now he realised there was some deficiency in her articulation. The latter seemed easier to improve and he set upon the task of her schooling. Pleased with their progress, he encouraged her to

> Prithee perservere with the speaking; I found with unspeakable
> delight last time that you were beginning to do it quite beautifully.
> There is much ill usage in store for you, but success is now certain.
> You have reached the stage of the Idiotically Beautiful. There
> remain the stages of the Intelligently Beautiful and finally of the
> Powerfully Beautiful.[22]

And to this end he dedicated the evening of 10 August to 'work on her
dramatic elocution;' the thirteenth, on which he had a 'hard grind'
going over the first half of the third act of *Rosmersholm* and more
lessons the following day.[23] Shaw was 'in love' but he was far from
blind to his lover's true capabilities. 'I tried all I could to work her up
to the point (technically) at which she could pass as an important
leading lady . . . She actually realized greater possibilities than she
had (what a sentence!!)'[24]

G.B.S. remained most faithful to Florence during 1892. He saw her
on at least eleven occasions in January besides purchasing a present
for her 'factotum' Miss Middleditch, a lady who probably forgave his
presence at Dalling Road. Their meetings were less frequent in
February when Florence began her role in *A Breezy Morning,* a
curtain raiser at the Comedy which ran on and off through April. In
March she notified Shaw by telegram of some news about Shelley's
Cenci. The year celebrated the poet's centenary and Shaw, the
previous month, had asked Beerbohm Tree to perform the play for
the Shelley Society and the Independent Theatre productions with
Florence in mind for Beatrice. Apart from a row on 5 March when
Shaw quarreled with Florence 'because she tried to cure a headache
by a spoonful of brandy,' they were happy while they worked on
Shelley's play. By the thirteenth, he had her well enough prepared to
recite to Todhunter and to Grein at Three The Orchard. Nothing was
settled in May when G.B.S. waited for Todhunter at the Wheatsheaf
to discuss the outcome of the audition.[25] But by the following month,
he was stirring up some excitement about a Bedford Park arrangement; 'A gathering of vegetarians and Shelleyites' gathered at the
Wheatsheaf to discuss Shaw's point of view that Shelley the poet was
in danger of overshadowing Shelley the social reformer.[26]

At the end of June the Licenser of plays convinced Grein that if the
Independent Theatre attempted to produce Shelley's play its license
would be revoked; Beerbohm Tree was similarly threatened. It
developed that Florence alone (she having little to lose) was undaunted, Shaw said, and thus proved herself to be the actress *'par
excellence'* for Beatrice Cenci. The project at Bedford Park was
under way but the rehearsals there as well as at the Comedy Theatre

for her part in *The Home Coming* were too much for Florence's limited vitality. On 30 June she fainted during the *Cenci* scenes but 14 July she was well-recovered for the 'odd' celebration at the Clubhouse. In a 'tiny little bonnet of a dungeon,' Florence 'pulled through' the scenes as 'resolutely' as if she were at the Lyceum. John Todhunter, York Powell, Paget and Shaw all 'maintained an honourable gravity' while Ella Dresser, Florence Hunter, Orlando Barnett, Fisher White, Lewin Mannering 'stood up bravely to the limelight . . . much harder on their costumes and venerable make-up,' Shaw wrote in his review, 'than on the white robe and striking beauty of Beatrice'.[27]

On 4 July, *The Home Coming* premiered at the Comedy. Robb Harwood, Harold Constable, Sam Southern, Alice Yorke, and Nina Boucicault helped Florence to present some 'crude conventionality and amateur clumsiness' in an 'irritating' performance.[28] Shaw's 'Rosmersholm Rebecca' was 'honestly buckling-to at six lines in a *lever de rideau* to pay for her lodgings.'[29] Nevertheless, Florence had a steady job until 29 October.

The lovers began to broaden their activities during the summer. They took walks through Regents Park to Hampstead Heath and back across Parliament Hill to Highgate. One day they took a train to Kentish Town to walk through Waterloo Park, and from Highgate to Hampstead taking the Spaniards' Road. In August they went to Hayes and rested on the Heath and sometimes they travelled on the train from Waterloo to Putney to walk along the towpath to Hammersmith. Once they walked through Kew Gardens where Shaw stopped to talk to John Burns and his wife. 'F.E. was left to stroll about alone during all the time we had at our disposal,' which 'quite spoiled the expedition,' Shaw said. In September they managed to see the Buffalo Bill show, and the weather was still pleasant enough by the middle of the month to lie down for a while in Richmond Park before watching the sunset. October was full of daily appointments and on the twentieth, while Shaw waited for Florence to arrive at her rooms, he worked at his play 'which I decided to call Widowers' Houses.' By the twenty-seventh, he was discussing its production with J.T. Grein.[30]

The Dutchman's story has been told so often that it is only necessary to restate here that it took a foreign producer to impress upon England the idea of an experimental theatre for the purpose of bringing the public original drama by native playwrights. Not satisfied to wait for a subsidised theatre that William Archer urged on the English, Grein rented a cheap hall in Tottenham Court Road

and announced a performance of Ibsen's *Ghosts*. Support so exceeded his expectations that he eventually gave the production at the
Royalty Theatre on Dean Street, Soho.

By this year, 1892, Grein also realised that he was left with a list of
productions to his credit, but with an ideal that was not working. He
had not produced a play of worth by a native dramatist. Since Shaw's
dramatic itch was as lively as his enthusiasm for any other artistic
philandering, and since he recognised that he had been the chief
spokesman for the New Drama in England, he 'manufactured the
evidence' for the case he had 'rashly taken up.' Grein's invitation
nudged him to complete the embryonic two acts of *Rheingold*
which left only traces of Archer in the first act. The play was ready
for rehearsal in November when Shaw called on Florence on the
twelfth to coach her for the leading role, a part he once thought he
would bestow upon Alma Murray. On the fourteenth, the first rehearsal took place at the Mona Hotel near the Royalty. The part of Trench
was still not filled, it 'being rejected by all', so that there was no
point to a rehearsal on the twenty-second. The following day,
Florence could not attend because she was due at rehearsals for a
new play at the Comedy. 'Something like a real' rehearsal for Shaw's
play took place on 24 November but there was still no Lickcheese.[31]
At last W. T. Robertson was 'engaged' for Harry Trench (the cast was
never paid) and James Welch was cornered for Lickcheese. The
latter had stuck his head inside the door to see T. Wigney Percival at
rehearsal and Herman de Lange, Shaw's co-director, had called out
'Ecce homo, the very man for Lickcheese.'

Welch accepted the part but never considered he was at work in an
actual 'play'. Even though G.B.S. believed he had a gift of 'fingering'
the stage, Welch said he was a trying director, ignorant of stage-
management. His primary interest was to inject colour when any actor knew, Welch complained, that the first thing to do with a part was
to learn the lines and then apply the colour. Worst of all, when
Florence went over the scene in which she viciously beat her maid,
the entire cast, thinking it grotesque, begged Shaw to delete it.[32] No
doubt with his mistress's encouragement, G.B.S. 'clung' to his directions.

By 7 December 'the rehearsal was so atrociously bad' that Shaw
'could think of nothing else all the rest of the evening.' After writing
letters of complaint to Grein and to his leading lady, in an effort to
quiet his disgust, Shaw visited May Sparling to play a Mozart
quartet.[33]

The following day a wan audience 'plain living and high thinking', one newspaper described it, attended the afternoon dress rehearsal. It was bitter cold in the Royalty, draughtier for sure, those invited remarked, than any widowers' houses. With the opening on the ninth, John Burns wearing his hat, represented the Fabians at the performance, Massingham and Archer in their big fur coats sat in the stalls, and Carl Hentschel as the Playgoer's Club representative sat with horror, yea disgust, while Florence clutched her maid's throat and 'shook the life out of her.' 'Blasting' whatever small reputation she had won elsewhere, Shaw said, she gave a 'painfully amateurish' performance. Bedecked in a series of fetching gowns, one, a scarlet crepon with a long jet fringe, another, a coat of heliotrope velvet worn over a skirt of cachemire in a paler tone, and lastly, a lemon-coloured satin with an overdress of transparent gauze,[34] she had played Shaw's 'Blanche' as a 'female cat . . . a sort of English Hedda Gabler'.[35] By the time Shaw attempted to write about what the press referred to as his 'ridiculous abortion', he had forgotten the day's events. 'I forgot what I did today, except—Oh, I remember. I went over to FE about noon and stayed there for some hours . . . Made a speech at the end of the play.'

Meanwhile, Florence was giving a 'quietly funny' interpretation of an American tourist's wife in *To-day* over at the Comedy. Shaw really did intend to call on her New Year's Eve but since there was no light on in her rooms he concluded she was at the theatre, and, not atypically, 'went straight' to May Sparling.

With the New Year, he corrected the text of the first act of *Widowers' Houses,* read Florence's volume of Browning, 'a lot of Walt Whitman,' and they were both 'very happy', Shaw said. Indeed, the relationship appeared idyllic, and then one evening, very late, Jenny Patterson burst into Florence's rooms. 'There was a most shocking scene; JP. being violent & using atrocious language.' Shaw managed to send Florence out of her rooms after restraining the widow 'by force from attacking her.' It was two hours more before Shaw could get Jenny to leave which he apparently accomplished by escorting her to her lodgings. There, after another two hours of persuading her to write a letter of apology with a promise 'not to annoy F.E. again,' Shaw left. He was 'horribly tired, shocked & upset' but he kept his patience and thought he had behaved neither 'badly nor urgently.' It was 4 a.m. when he got to bed.

The following day, 5 February, Shaw went to May. After dinner they took a quiet walk and it was she who delivered Jenny's letter of apology to Florence. Soothed by his 'mystical' union with May, on the seventh, the philanderer visited her again. This time there was a conversation about 'old times—rather an emotional one'.[36]

In April, Charrington engaged Florence to play in Eugene Scribe's and Ernest Legouve's *Adrienne Lecouvreur* at the Royalty. 'The unspeakable absurdity of that performance', Shaw wrote,

is only surpassed by the unparalleled blastedness of the play . . . . In the first scene you are insufferable. You wave your arms about like a fairy in a transformation scene, obviously pretending to make an impossible toilet . . . . If you decide at any time to do nothing . . . shut your mouth, and compose yourself, and *do* nothing . . . . You should speak a little at least with your lips, and not say 'supposeitisnotformebutforanother' so as to strike the house dumb with its utter want of any intention of meaning. As to the way you tighten your upper lip, and bunch up your back, and stiffen your neck, and hold on by your elbows, that is, I admit, necessary to prevent your falling on your nose, and it is good for the calves and lumbar muscles . . . The sooner the play disappears, the better . . . But you rather score off it; and I advise you to make the most of it while it lasts.[37]

Florence came away from the play aware that Charles Charrington held her talents in poor regard. He had humiliated her efforts when he might have encouraged her, even 'exercised' his cleverness, Shaw said, 'to save her from being crushed'.[38] G.B.S. considered his own criticisms of Florence totally justifiable; besides, they gave him an opportunity to flush his mind. However, his ego did not approve the castigation by others of his mistress's failures.

The New Woman's relationship with Shaw was still flourishing. One time they discovered Perivale Church during one of their long walks '& heard an extraordinary performance by a nightingale' near Ealing on the way to Dalling Road. Since Shaw had complimentary tickets, they still went to the Crystal Palace Concerts, or strolled about Ravenscourt Park 'until the light began to fail.' On 11 May, Florence read to Shaw part of a novel she was writing to be called *The Dancing Faun*.[39] Obviously a satire on her lover's philandering with women, the story ends when the anti-hero is shot, Florence's fantasy of what might have occurred that stormy evening with Jenny Patterson. Amusing simply because of its autobiographical implications, the story centres about George Travers, the dancing faun, half-goat, half-man; clearly an image of G.B.S. superimposed upon Edward Emery. The 'George' certainly fits although 'Travers' had been a character in *The Home Coming*. The faun is also an actor who cheated at cards in his youth and is recently returned from exile in the States. Back in England, he marries the actress Grace Lovell

(Florence). A perfect scoundrel, Travers cheats at cards once more which forces his decision to return to the States. This time, he plans to take his wife to exploit her on the stage. In the interim, he meets and makes advances to a Lady Geraldine who speaks the advanced vernacular of the New Woman. When Travers rejects her, discovering her intention to slip away with him to the States, he dies at her hand, a penalty for his philandering.

During some earlier action in the novel, Grace has a scene with her husband which is provocative enough to suggest a Shaw-Patterson episode unless it implies there was some similar passion between Florence and her faithless lover (Shaw). Travers ends the scene with words used by Yeats elsewhere; 'You appear to think what people say on the stage is real life, and what you see behind the scenes is play-acting'. In a desperate resolve to forget the hideous entanglement of her marriage, Grace resorts to reading aloud—

> something about her voice struck her. She listened, it sounded different, a new beauty had come into it. She read on and on, wondering at the pathos of the tones she uttered . . . it seemed to her some inspired spirit had entered her body and was making use of her voice to reveal to her what life, and love, and divine sorrow meant.
> From that day she settled down to hard work. She heard that some of her words . . . sounded little and thin, and she resolved to work away until she got all alike resonantly beautiful.

Although Shaw believed he was responsible for Florence's technical improvements, and no doubt she permitted him to think this, she was actually referring to the Golden Dawn magic (the Golden Dawn was a Hermetic Society) which had spiritually entered Grace's body.

Florence eventually showed a completed draft of her novel to Edward Carpenter who thought she should play off the publishers against one another. 'If you tell Heinemann that Fisher Unwin thought *Dots* would make a Pseudonym, if altered a little his eyes may grow a little in sweetness and softness'.[40] By January the following year, neither Unwin nor Heinemann had accepted the novel. Instead, John Lane who founded the Bodley Head with Elkin Mathews in 1887, took the MS out of personal friendship to Florence. He had, of course, some hope for its' marketable potential.

> It is always very pleasant to accept the MS of a new riter [sic] but it is a double pleasure when the book happens to be by a friend but when one adds by a women it baffles so poor a creature as a publisher to express adequate delight, but your insight is so great

that I shall feel safe in leaving you to judge of my interest in your book. I am sure you will believe me when I say that nothing has given me greater pleasure since I drifted into publishing than accepting your book The Dancing Faun. [41]

When the novel appeared, it was part of the racy 'Key Note' series for which Aubrey Beardsley was commissioned to design the frontispiece. His drawing turned out to be a faun, a caricature of the painter Whistler [42] posed on a settee embracing his furry leg.

While Florence worked at *The Dancing Faun,* Shaw was completing his play *The Philanderer* which he hoped to put on at the Independent Theatre. The first half of the first act described, more or less, the actual Patterson-Farr-Shaw episode at Dalling Road, 4 February 1893. Shaw presents Florence as Grace as well in his play, 'slight of build . . . proudly set brows, firm chin, and elegant carriage.' Chateris (Shaw) wants to marry her in order to free himself from Julia (Jenny Patterson). In the midst of a discussion between Chateris and Grace on the New Woman and marriage, Julia breaks into the room where follows a violent scene of jealousy.

But of the summer of that year; Jenny was very much out of the way and Shaw was spending his time with Florence still attending concerts or walking in Regents Park. When Florence went off to the country for a month, however, Shaw looked at the sunset with May Sparling and slept at her flat. On Florence's return, he did go right to Dalling Road but shared the evening with Yeats who stayed for a long time chatting.

The New Woman did not appear to be willing to devote herself exclusively to any single male relationship. Her affair with Shaw, therefore, was coincident with her artistic association with Willie Yeats. Then there was her esoteric enchantment with the Golden Dawn. Among the adepts of that society was Annie Horniman, granddaughter of the founder of the tea company, W. H. & J. Horniman, Ltd. After the gentleman died in 1893, Annie was left with a 'substantial' legacy with which, ostensibly, she wished to gratify her curiosity for the theatrical world. There was more to her decision than a wish to become involved with the stage. She was romantically inclined towards Yeats, and the poet needed a theatre for his unwritten plays. Then there was John Todhunter who had joined the Order, 11 February 1892, [43] and lastly Florence, who, by 1894, was to reach the exalted position of Praemonstratrix in the Order. It came about that Annie was to back Florence in a season of plays, one of the first of two practical concepts (the other was Yeats's Irish Theatre) to engender among the fantastic adepts.

Shaw presumably knew nothing of the Golden Dawn's secrets (although on 12 June 1892 he wrote in his diary that Florence told him 'a lot of odd and interesting things about herself') but she did tell him that someone was going to put up some money for her and she persuaded him to write a play. Nothing had been started when they met in August 1893 at the Finchley Road Station for a visit to Hampstead Heath. They bought some fruit and then sat on the ferns not far from the Spaniards' Inn. Shaw found a pencil he had lost the day before there, and then they read the papers, 'talked & dozed' before the romantic one fell asleep. When Shaw awoke

> the sun was setting & there was a bank of clouds on the horizon which were so extremely like mountains with sun on them that I was astonished, & thought for a moment that I was dreaming, & mixing up Switzerland with Hampstead Heath.

By 26 November, a Sunday, Shaw spent the evening 'beginning a new play—a romantic one—for F.E.' Again on the twenty-eighth, waiting for Florence in Ravenscourt Park, he worked on the play until past four.[44] The first act completed, he 'lugged' it to his friend Pakenham Beatty to read it to him. 'Fortunately', Beatty told Michael Field (Miss Bradley) Shaw had only completed one act and he 'actually' expected him to laugh at it.

Around this time Beatty was involved in a correspondence with Michael Field concerning a play she wished to produce. It occurred to him that Shaw and his leading lady might be of use. 'George' was not nearly so bad as his 'Judas coloured' beard made him appear, and Florence had 'eyes that poets dream of. A beautiful soul surely looks out of them.' In subsequent letters Beatty was convinced that Shaw would assist Miss Bradley for had he not passed on the word that Grein thought her play was a 'masterpiece'. In an attempt to influence Florence to play the lead (she would have jumped at the chance to do anything that was offered to her) he had written a 'very beautiful lyric—straight from my heart' entitled 'Prayer'. Since 'discretion is the better part of poesy', he sent the poem to Shaw.

> Forgive Love, sweet; that has no skill to say
> How sweet you are!
> The hair that strung Apollo's lute is grey O Florence Farr!
> Yet I must love thee, by my being's law most best; Do thou
> Shrink from the sacriligeous eyes of Shaw
> The Brazen Brow!
> O white warm breast more balmy than the south,
> Art nor afeared
> Of that trite [?] heart? O tender mouth,
> Wilt kiss *That Beard*?

As love's watch sees in unillumined skies
His faint first star,
My soul sees heaven's light in your lyric eyes,
Sweet Florence Farr!
And feels earth drearier, seeing heaven so near,
And with hushed awe
Prays softly: If you will not love me dear,
Please Don't Love Shaw! [45]

During Christmas time of 1893, Florence brought Yeats to the Pagets' Christmas party and asked him to write a one-act play for her niece Dorothy Paget. Eleven then, Dorothy was very keen on acting especially in her mother's dramatisations of fairy stories with 'marvellous invention' by H. M. Paget. Knowing nothing of children, 'but with an abundant mind when Mary Bruin was, for I knew an Irish woman whose unrest troubled me,' Yeats set about his task in 'some discomfort'. Florence needed the play for her season to be backed by Annie Horniman and by January she was looking around for a suitable theatre. She had already asked Aubrey Beardsley to design a poster for her and he was held up in the lettering until Florence decided on the Avenue Theatre by the Thames Embankment. Shaw had disappointed her by not finishing his play and so she wrote to him reproaching him 'vigorously' for not working at it. Instead, she was obliged to rehearse a new work by John Todhunter. Fresh from his disaster at the Independent Theatre with the *Black Cat* on 8 December, he had

> converted the stage into a dissecting-room and treated the weird but scanty audience of long-haired atheists, sexless socialists, agnostics, Ibsenites, Anarchists, and egoists to a demonstration in morbid anatomy so appalling and sickening as to delight their carrion-loving souls. [46]

The physician's new play was similarly received. Written as 'an experiment on the taste of the British public', that is a play that developed character and dialogue rather than plot and 'sensational situations', Todhunted wondered if it would be tolerated. It was not; perhaps, he suspected, because it was 'too audaciously conceived' or 'too carelessly conducted, by both author and management.' The press yelled 'Ibsenism again,' nay worse, 'Dodoism, Sarah-Grandism, Keynotism . . . For had I not impudently exhibited The Modern Woman upon it?' [47]

Once again, Florence's influence had penetrated this normally poetic individual so that she, playing the lead Lady Brandon asked:

'Why should a girl be persecuted into marriage before she has had time to live?' or, speaking to the character Mrs. Chillingworth, 'Didn't you find marriage a rather horrid experience when it came?' and 'Don't you think a man's love is rather hard to bear?'[48]

The opening night was indeed a fiasco although Yeats's little play came off well enough. Shaw was there and wrote mildly in his diary that Todhunter's *A Comedy of Sighs* 'failed rather badly . . . owing to a lot of unlucky circumstances.' Actually he was horrified at Florence's performance and in an effort to console himself for her inadequacies wrote immediately to Elizabeth Robins.

> Oh my Saint Elizabeth, holy and consoling, have you ever seen so horrible a portent on the stage as this transformation of an amiable, clever sort of woman into a nightmare, a Medusa, a cold, loathly, terrifying, gray, callous, sexless devil? What madness led Todhunter to write a part like that?—What idiocy has led me to do virtually the same thing in the play which I have written to help her in this hellish enterprise? Did you hear those damns and devils, meant to be pretty—did they not sound like the blasphemes of a fiend? Had she been able to give full effect to herself, the audience would have torn her to pieces.[49]

After Florence read the reviews, she telegraphed Shaw to come to the Avenue. He arrived to find her and the ostensible manager, C. T. H. Helmsley, mulling over a copy of *Widowers' Houses.* Shaw dissuaded them from their intentions to produce the play and after some discussion proceeded to the Embankment Gardens to finish the 'romantic' piece he had lugged to Pakenham Beatty. When he had finished, he dropped it off at the Avenue to be typed and with complete aplomb went home to write an article for *The World.* Sometime that night he wrote to Alma Murray telling her of the Avenue catastrophe and of his new play in which there were two young women's parts. Contrary to his intentions when he began the script he was going to persuade Florence to play the part of the servant 'without any sacrifice to her dignity', and 'to crown her maganimity' in so doing 'by allowing' Alma Murray to play the lead.[50] The agreement arranged, The Avenue Theatre became a holocaust in the wake of his thunder.

Yeats, meanwhile, was acknowledging with modesty his own small success which ran with Todhunter's play until 13 February. No account of him at the theatre is complete without George Moore's reminiscences in *Ave;* how the little play struck him as an 'offensive trifle'. Yeats striding to and fro at the back of the dress circle, a long black cloak dropping from his shoulders, a soft black sombrero on his head, a voluminous black tie flowing from his collar, loose black trousers dragging untidily over his long heavy feet . . . an Irish parody of the poetry I had seen all my life strutting its rhythmic way in the alleys of the Luxembourg Gardens.[51]

Yeats had invited Paget to go with him to the upper circle on the opening night to see how the play went. The cavalier playwright sat 'unceasingly blowing his nose—trumpeting loudly.' Presently he asked Paget whether he could hear the actors all right. 'Perfectly,' Paget replied, 'if you would stop blowing your nose.'

Annie Horniman must have doubted whether Shaw's play would save her investment for on 20 April, the *Times* announced the availability of the theatre on 10 May. Shaw's cast, meanwhile, had only a week to prepare; on the sixteenth the rehearsal went from 11 to 7 p.m., on the nineteenth there was a dress rehearsal at 6.30, and 20 April a run-through with words only. That evening there was another dress rehearsal at 7. In between, Shaw attended a Fabian Committee meeting at 4.30 and an Executive meeting an hour later. *Arms and The Man* opened the following day, its author having attended a 3 p.m. concert beforehand.[52]

After the opening performance, there was no doubt that Shaw had saved the Avenue adventure and that his play was a success. Years, years later, Dorothy Paget remembers her mother taking her around to the front after her own performance in Yeats's one-act. Shaw's play having been performed, he was on the stage making his historical speech. Dorothy was fascinated by the fact that the footlights made G.B.S.'s hair very red and his skin light green so that he looked just like a carrot!

Shaw's play ran for over eleven weeks[53] with Florence playing the 'enigmatic' Louka. It put G.B.S. 'in possession of some spare money' and he opened a bank account for the first time in his life. Strangely, he was unaware of the identity of Florence's backer for many years even though he met Annie at the Pagets on occasion and she assisted him in the copyrighting of many of his future plays. It was not until 1905, when Florence was living at 107½ Holland Road, Kensington, that she revealed the Avenue secret to Shaw. Annie had written that she could now divulge the whole affair—

My circumstances in life have now so changed that secrecy is no longer necessary. Any credit in the matter is certainly yours [Florence's] I simply had an idea and paid the money.
I do not intend to *tell* people, but it can come out now.[54]

Then Florence wrote to Shaw

> it is genuinely a relief because after she turned disagreeable [over a matter in the Golden Dawn] it was horrid to feel we were at open warfare with a secret obligation. Now the warfare is over as far as active antagonism goes and we are absolutely polite and charming when we meet for a few minutes. And at last I can acknowledge the obligation.
>
> She was wonderful about the money really and just gave it to me to do anything I liked with the way of advertising myself. I might have played Lady Macbeth & Camille etc. etc., but of course I felt I must do something for the stage when I had the opportunity. As you remember to discuss Todisscuss [Todhunter's] 'Black Cat' was the 'last word' at the moment. I secured him you and Yeats & Beardsley's poster. And I'm afraid poor Todhunter is the only person connected with the affair that appears as a ridiculous failure.[55]

It wasn't until 22 June 1907 that Annie wrote to Shaw herself telling him he was making too much about her connection with the Avenue. 'I only gave the money to carry out my idea. I did nothing else for it, because I feared to do harm'.[56]

The Dancing Faun was published during the summer of 1894 and Florence wrote to John Lane to enquire whether it would not be worthwhile to advertise the novel to boost its sale. She was constantly being asked 'how it is to be got etc. and it seems to me not to be going at all'.[57] There had been some good reviews in the *Athenaeum* and *The Liverpool Daily Post* (the former had been minimally affirmative, the kindest comment being 'Miss Farr might not have been so effective if she had been more intelligible') which seemed to Florence 'as if they would quote well.' She excluded mention of the July *Bookman* which compared her to the 'weaker fibred writers' with the 'hysterical desire to be accounted wicked' reminding the reviewer of 'weak minded patients who craved the notoriety of the criminals.' Her dialogue was 'cheap', leading into a story that was 'weak, malformed, ugly,' its strongest effect being one of profound depression.

When Christmas approached, Florence hoped the book would have a chance of selling. She was displeased that Smith's catalogue had printed her name Florence 'Parr' so that it 'lost all the benefit in that direction.' Undaunted by poor sales and adverse criticism, she called on Lane sometime afterwards to discuss with him an 'epoch making work' of 120,000 words 'calculated to make anybody's hair stand on end.' The work was divided into three parts, 'Hell,' 'Purgatory,' and 'The Gates of Paradise,' and was a more serious undertaking than

The Dancing Faun which she had written 'more or less' as a joke.[58]

In February 1895, Florence's divorce from Edward Emery became final. If she believed when Shaw encouraged her to file that he had more reason than legal prudence, she was surely dismayed. By May she was writing to him of his avoidance of her. When they met by appointment he 'chatted and chatted', and Florence 'laughed and laughed'. They ate at the Swiss café before going to Henrietta's house and Florence spoke of her bicycling and flippantly mentioned the quarter million pounds that was available to her. Annie Horniman did not have that amount, so that Florence was having fun at Shaw's expense, attempting to keep him interested, or using the statement as a palliative for what she knew Shaw considered her apathy toward her profession. More pleasant company, Shaw told Janet Achurch of their meeting, 'one could not desire.' Florence was 'good humoured, adaptable, no trouble, easily amused (frightfully easy), beautiful grey eyes and so on.' But what was it, he asked, that was lacking in her, and in the other women of her 'class'.

> Not brains: she is a clever woman. Not knowledge: it is impossible to mention anything she does not know. Not affection: she would respond gratefully enough to any tenderness shewn her. Why then, the frightful vacuity, the levity, the shallowness, the vulgarity, the pointlessness that makes me wish, in Richmond Park, that I could have half an hour with the trees, and the earth and the sky over the Thames Valley.[59]

Perhaps, pondered Shaw, it was her lack of 'religion', meaning her direction in life. In May he was using Florence as bait to whet Janet Achurch's regard for him. If the latter would not communicate, Florence, G.B.S. wrote, 'shall be Mrs. Bernard Shaw at the earliest date thereafter permitted by statute.' By the second week of May, Florence was not Mrs. Shaw but Esther in Tom Robertson's *Caste* in which she was giving an 'excellent portrayal' in Orlando Barnett's Company at the Theatre Royal in Jersey.

Back in London in September, Florence worked on her MS *Modern Woman,* although at the time she called it *New Woman.* Richard Le Gallienne, of some account in literary circles, arranged to have the 'reader people' look it over. They thought it 'very clever,' he said, but were inclined not to print it. *The Newest Woman* and *The New Woman* were titles of plays too fresh in the memory; 'they say, death on the New Woman & all her work.'[60]

An opportunity arose in October for Florence to co-direct the Independent Theatre. Grein was retiring to devote his time to the

London representation of Wellenstein, Krause & Co., Dutch East India Merchants, and Dorothy Leighton (co-founder of the Independent
with Grein) had four hundred pounds left in the till for a new season.
Shaw suggested Charles Charrington for the position with Elizabeth
Robins or Florence as alternatives. There wasn't an inkling in his
mind that Florence Emery would ever be considered. To his amazement, Grein favoured her nomination and when Shaw heard this, he
was convinced that the Dutchman made the choice believing her
pliant enough to bend to his will. Florence was not finally involved
and any disappointment, in fact, all disappointments by then, were
sublimated in magical tracts for the Theosophical Society; her
'unreality', Shaw called it. He could not sympathise with her 'phrase
and a shilling's worth of exoteric Egyptology' and he was weary of
her wandering away from work and theatre. He had, he told her, 'the
greatest regard' but now she made him 'frightfully unhappy'. When
she questioned the direction of their relationship, he compared it
only to the North Pole from the South. 'Forgive me; but you have
driven me to utter desperation: I can no longer be satisfied to suffer
and shake my fist at the stars.'[61]

It must have been a bitter disappointment to the 'womenly'
women with whom Florence prided herself in belonging to be jilted
when affairs were over as if they belonged to the tired cult of
'unwomanly' women. Their idealism had forced them to practice the
art of abstinence in passion and possessiveness but they were often
left simply holding a theory. Therefore, in spite of Florence Farr's
New Woman ethics, she was unwilling to let go (for so it must appear
from Shaw's letter). 'You are incorrigible', he wrote, 'Have I not
tried and tried, lectured, protested, warned, implored? Do you want
me *for ever* greedy one?' And on the following day,

> Serve you right! I hereby warn mankind to beware of women with
> large eyes, and crescent eyebrows, and a smile, and a love of
> miracles and moonshees. I warn them against all who like intellec-
> tual pastimes; who prefer liberty to happiness and irresponsibility
> to care, suffering and life; who live for and in themselves in stead
> of for and in the world; who reject the deep universal material of
> human relationship and select only the luxuries of love, friendship
> and amusing conversation.
>
> I declare before creation that you are an idiot, and that there
> never has been, is not now, nor in any yet discovered fourth dimen-
> sion of time ever shall be, so desperate and irreclaimable an idiot,
> or one whom Destiny mocked with greater opportunities.[62]

There are some, and Hesketh Pearson is one, who subscribe to the idea that Shaw's letters to various women have an identical ring and might be addressed to any one of whom with a mere exchange in salutation. Even with Florence, Shaw basks in innate self-esteem, but the woman he describes, beautiful, artistic, introspective, un-remorseless, indolent, is Florence singularly, and fathomed out of as generous perception as she would know. Only Ezra Pound in later years[63] equals Shaw's written portrait of this plastic, liquid personality, the mermaid of the 'Sargasso Sea'.

Shaw was in his forties when he released Florence from a love af-fair that had been for him no second childhood play. Tradition has it that he was not a man of passion; yet, whatever quantity of that characteristic he possessed belonged to Florence had she but known how to preserve it. Fortunately for Shaw the pragmatic side of his nature detached itself from an entanglement that might well have resembled a life-long voyage on a roller-coaster. Besides, the 'green-eyed millionairess' Charlotte Payne-Townsend was 'in love' with him, and he was not resisting. Unlike the poetic 'gypsy', she was a woman of remarkable determination, an irresistible quality to Shaw.

If Florence mourned for G.B.S. it was unapparent to her family; they knew she was 'fond' of him but she remained busy, untidy, as was her custom, and restive.

Another chance to perform in an Ibsen play came for Florence in October 1896. Elizabeth Robins negotiated by letter for her to play in the first performance of *Little Eyolf* at the Avenue. It was the climax to a silly turn of events which began at the end of 1894. The in-cident involved Shaw, William Archer, Miss Robins, and Florence. They were all playing a sort of blind man's buff with 'Little Whatshisname' as Shaw referred to Ibsen's play. Secret information concerning its presence in a translated script in London had been im-parted to Florence. Purportedly, Archer was the culprit and whatever facts he gave her, she disclosed to Shaw. When Archer heard rumours that the play was being discussed, he accused Elizabeth Robins of the leak; she in turn accused Florence. Thereupon the latter turned upon Shaw 'in the most injurious and destructive manner', and Shaw laid the blame where it belonged, with Archer.[64]

It was Elizabeth Robins who became the victor. Ten pounds, she told Florence, was all she could offer for four performances.[65] The Avenue was licensed to Charles Hawtrey although Shaw suggested to Miss Robins that Helmsley might do or even Florence 'might be of use. She can't act; but she is an intelligent woman of business and honourable in money matters.' He also warned Elizabeth Robins of

Janet Achurch's dispositions and cautioned the judicious insurance of an understudy. The play opened with a matinée performance by subscription on 23 November. Florence was not in the cast but she was the obvious understudy and sat with William Archer during the rehearsals. Much higher by then in his regard, he transmitted to Courtney Thorpe that Florence thought he should be paler in the second act 'and I'm not sure but that she is right'.[66]

Janet Achurch stayed with the cast until 6 December and then Mrs. Patrick Campbell who had played the Rat Wife was given a day's notice to replace her. She practically read the part at the first performance, the book tied to her waist.[67] At that time, Florence came in for the Rat Wife.

It was some time in March 1897 when Florence met Shaw, not having seen him for several months. 'She was horrified', and told him he looked his age. Then she pointed out that his 'moustache and two great tufts of his beard were grey'. But it was Florence who was taking notice of the years. At thirty-seven she felt discouraged. She had spent her better years with Shaw with the idea, no doubt, that she might one day have a permanent relationship with him. She had wanted to be a representative actress in the New Drama, and she had had her chances. Yet with all of the opportunities offered to her she had received no lasting recognition, nor come close to the success of Alma Murray, Elizabeth Robins, or Janet Achurch. Certainly she had not touched the stardom of her ex-sister-in-law ·Winifred Emery, or the younger Mrs. Patrick Campbell. Even the French observer of the English Theatre, Augustin Filon, did not include her name with those who with 'faith, passion, and courage' had given themselves to the work of Ibsen.

Perhaps it is not difficult now to think of Florence Farr as a dilettante. She, however, believed firmly in herself as an actress, seeing her failures, the failure of others. G.B.S. is not always mentioned by name but he hovers behind every complaint. Shaw who had the capacity to instruct and to mould her was, in their dissimilarity of goals, her nemesis, a 'fiend' who 'damned all acting of temperament.' Mrs. Emery must of course be questioned for the degree of that quality she brought to the stage.

By 1897, unable to succeed in popular theatre, not wilful enough to pursue her role in the New Drama, not dynamic enough to capture the public in poetic theatre, Florence Farr came to the end of her career playing a paradigm of Shaw's 'womanly' woman. Quite possibly the Victorian audience preferred the unintellectual, seductive femininity of the 'unwomanly' woman. So, if Shaw is to be believed, Florence detached herself effortlessly from his unyielding demands to support her dignity as an artist in the world of poetry and magic. In September, aware of her restiveness, G.B.S. pontificated, 'Wait for the usual fifteen years or so and you will fit yourself in somewhere.' For all his tidy but superficial impatience with magical thought, he was being strangely prophetic.

NOTES

1 BM, (January 1 1882).
2 Carl M. Selle, ed., *The New Drama,* (Miami 1963), 2.
3 Dan H. Laurence, ed., *Collected Letters 1874-1897,* (New York 1965), 272.
4 Made for her by Claude of Welbeck Street, W.1.
5 Bernard Shaw, *The Quintessence of Ibsenism,* (New York 1925), 34, 36.
6 Diary.
7 The *Illustrated Sporting and Dramatic News,* (London March 7 1891), 36.
8 University Of London, (February 27 1891). Henceforth UL.
9 'The Playhouses', *The Illustrated London News,* (London February 28 1891).
10 Diary.
11 Diary.
12 Laurence, *op. cit.,* 288.
13 UL, (March 17 1891).
14 UL, (March 30 1891).
15 Diary.
16 Clifford Bax, *Letters* 1-2.
17 Diary.
18 Diary.
19 UL, (June 18 1891).
20 Dorothy Wellesley, *Letters on Poetry From W.B. Yeats to Dorothy Wellesley,* (New York 1940), 475.
21 *Illustrated London News,* (June 20 1891).
22 Bax, *op. cit.,* 5.
23 Diary.
24 Autograph note from G.B.S. to Clifford Bax, Academic Centre, University of Texas.

25 Diary.
26 *The Daily Chronicle,* (London June 27 1892), 3.
27 *The Daily Chronicle.* (London July 16 1892), 3.
28 *Era,* (July 19 1892).
29 Laurence, *op. cit.,* 349.
30 Diary
31 Diary.
32 *Star.* (London December 17 1892).
33 Diary.
34 *Star,* (London December 8 1892).
35 *Sunday Sun.* (London December 11 1892).
36 Diary.
37 Bax, *op. cit.,* 8.
38 Laurence, *op. cit.,* 603.
39 Diary.
40 UL, (Agust 17 1893).
41 UL, (January 29 1894).
42 Stanley Weintraub, *Beardsley,* (New York 1967), 52.
43 Courtesy of Ellic Howe.
44 Diary.
45 BM.
46 William Archer, *The Theatrical World of 1893,* (London)
47 John Todhunter, *The Black Cat,* (London 1895), *viii.*
48 University of Reading, TS.
49 University of Cornell.
50 Laurence, *op. cit.,* 422.
51 (New York 1923) 5-6.
52 Diary
53 The London production brought Shaw £90.0s.9½d. Courtesy of Dan Laurence.
54 BM, (December 5 1905).
55 *Ibid.*
56 BM, (June 22 1907).
57 Bodleian.
58 Bodleian.
59 Laurence, *Letters,* 504
60 UL, (September 23 1895).
61 Bax, *op. cit.,* 11
62 *Ibid,.* 12.
63 'Portrait D'Une Femme'.
64 Fales, New York University.
65 UL, (October 28 1896).
66 VA.
67 Mrs. Patrick Campbell,ed., *Mrs. Patrick Campbell, My Life and Some Letters.* (New York 1922), 152.

5

The Golden Dawn and Other Mysteries

1890-1904

'Wound in mind's wandering
As mummies in the mummy-cloth are wound.'

So large a part of the myth Florence wove, ensued from her obsession with the occult. Bound fast to her hermetic enquiries it was often a question of whether she was an 'eccentric fake . . . madwoman or saint,' even the poet, perhaps, 'in pursuit of the ineffable or the mystic in communion with God'.[1]

In an account of his early friendship with Florence Emery, Yeats has described her contempt for the phenomenal world. Reality or 'actual things' were spoken of with 'cold wit or under the strain of paradox'. And personal dissatisfactions were, no doubt, sublimated by countless hours in the British Museum reading room, where, Yeats said, Florence became 'erudite in many heterogeneous studies moved by an insatiable curiosity.' Immersed, in particular, in an absorption with antiquities, the walls of her rooms at Dalling Road were soon 'covered with musical instruments, pieces of oriental drapery, and Egyptian gods and goddesses painted by herself in the British Museum'.[2]

The humour and good-nature that Shaw described to Janet Achurch in 1895 are seldom apparent during Florence's early and even later association with the poet. Her worst moods, in fact, reduced him to rage. Often erratic and irritable, she reminded Yeats of the game of 'Spillikins' known to him in his childhood. Much like the player who cautiously manipulates little pieces of bone, Florence was 'a bundle of ones' instead of 'Demeter's golden sheaf!' Although their companionship was often beset by such moods, Yeats shared

Florence Emery's intellectual curiosity. In 1888, through an introduction from Charles Johnston in Ireland, he joined Madame Helena Petrovna Blavatsky's Theosophical Lodge in London. During October 1889 he wrote in a penny exercise book printed by the Acton Post Office in Bedford Park: 'about Xmas 1888 I joined the esoteric section of TS. The pledges gave me no trouble except two—promise to work for theosophy & promise of obedience to HPB in all theosophical matters.'

Yeats consulted with Madame Blavatsky to explain that if he signed the pledge it must be 'on condition that I myself was to be the judge as to what theosophy is;' especially since he considered his work on Blake 'a wholly adequate keeping of this clause.' Of the promise of obedience, HPB explained that it only referred to 'things concerning occult practice if such should be called for.' After a 'private meeting of London esotericists' on Sunday, 24 October 1889, Yeats still doubted 'as to whether I could sign this second clause'

(1) We believe in HPB.
(2) We believe in her teach[ing].
(3) We will defend her, subject to our own conscience.[3]

Yeats was anxious, obviously, for a more autonomous position in a Hermetic Society by the time he became acquainted with Samuel Liddell Mathers in the British Museum. A Freemason and occultist, Mathers was one of the three founder-members of the Isis-Urania Temple in London, a terrestrial manifestation of the Golden Dawn. That Society's history, so brilliantly related by Ellic Howe,[4] requires the briefest passage here.

Sometime in the eighteen eighties, Dr. William Wynn Westcott, Freeman, retired physician and practicing London Coroner, came into the possession of certain cypher manuscripts. In due course, he invited S. L. Mathers to interpret and expand the hermetic rituals contained in the cypher MS. Whereas the former occultist delighted in fantasies, the latter leaned towards highly creative but later, meglomaniac aspirations. Compatible for the while, the two developed five rituals suitable for a system of occult study for Lodge work. With a mind to protect his brain-child, Westcott subsequently concocted a secret personage to sanction the Order's work as well as his undisputable authority. To this end, he manufactured the identity of a Fräulein Anna Sprengel of Nurenburg. In a carefully faked correspondence, this ficticious character allegedly recognised the Golden Dawn and ordained three Chiefs, Westcott, Mathers, and a second retired physician, Dr. W. R. Woodman to dispense its divine wisdom. The Order was thereby totally *bone fide,* or so its future members believed. At the time, Westcott and Mathers were too inspired to realise their complicity in a spirited but colossal fraud and the devilish truth of their quackery did not come out for years.

When Yeats met Mathers, he was enormously impressed that the occultist had translated *The Kabbala Unveiled* and shortly joined his Order. By June 1890 he had brought Mrs. Emery into the Golden Dawn. The Society permitted both sexes to membership so that theoretically, progression and authority were accessible to all who qualified by examination. Ascendency relied upon a system of grades which corresponded in their heirarchy to the abstract principles of the Tree of Life. Identification with the hebraic mythical Tree and its growth in *Ain Soph Aour,* the Infinite or Boundless Light, was the nucleus of Order teaching, 'Long hast thou dwelt in darkness. Quit the Night and seek the Day'.[5]

Florence and Yeats were not atypical in their search for spiritual significance outside the doctrines of the Christian Church. G. K. Chesterton wrote that among the educated as well as the eccentric there was, in those years, a conserted movement toward 'unbelief' in organised Western religion; a movement as definite as the Elizabethan's 'demand for uniformity in belief'.[6] (James Webb in *The Flight From Reason* describes this rebellion in greater depth). Chesterton's explanation, however, simplifies the position of Florence Emery and Yeats. The poet would have required a spiritual as well as an occult mythology in any age to engender his flights of the imagination. For Florence, Magic was, above all, a necessary anodyne for her often troubled, searching personality.

The initiation of the Neophytes occurred at a ceremony in Mark Mason's Hall in Euston Street. Not a distinct grade in itself, Florence described it thus:

> In the 0=0 Ceremony the principles most insisted on are Secrecy and Brotherly Love. Apart entirely from the practical necessity for secrecy in our Order, it is the fact that Silence is in itself a tremendous aid in the search for Occult powers. In darkness and stillness the Archetypal forms are conceived and the forces of nature germinated . . . I may mention that the 0=0 of the Grade of Neophyte has a deep significance as a symbol; a 0 means nothing to the world—to the Initiate in the form of a circle it means *all,* and the aspiration of the Neophyte should be 'In myself I am nothing in Thee I am all; oh bring me to that self, which is in Thee.[7]

'Thee' represented the initiate's poetic or dramatic image of God, one that was within his own Soul.

The grades proper corresponded to the enumerations of the Sephiroth (the branches of the Tree) with *Malkuth,* Earth, the first step of ascension. Thus, 1=10 applied to the first rung of the ladder with its identification of the tenth Sephirah and its call of Zelator. A Neophyte proceeded from 0=0 to Zelator, and thence to Theoricus (Yesod), 2=9, to Practicus (Hod), 3=8, and to Philosophus (Netzach), 4=7. The first grade of the Second or Inner Order was Adeptus Minor (Tiphareth), 5=6; beyond this, none could travel except the three Chiefs. Later on, Mathers by far out-fantasied Westcott and became the Chief Adept of the Second Order, 'Ambassador of those Secret and Unknown Magi who are the concealed Rulers of the Wisdom of the True Rosicrucian Magic of Light'.

It is not possible to recreate here the drama, the pageantry, or the complicated learning procedures attached to the system of grades. But from the time the Neophyte assumed his secret motto, Florence's was S.S.D.D. (*Sapientia Sapienti Dono Data,* wisdom is given to the wise as a gift), to his symbolic crucifixion before spiritual resurrection in 5=6, he worked on transforming his lower nature into his higher. Epiphany, then, lay in his exalted realisation that man's root, one with the Boundless Light, was the source of his own Divinity.

By 1892, Florence had brought John Todhunter and Henrietta Paget into the Order. Since the Farr girls told the story of their descent from a famous gypsy, and Lolly Yeats said there *was* something of the gypsy in both sisters,[8] it was not too remarkable that Henrietta shared Folling's credulity for the occult. Etta was not quite as enthusiastic in her study and her attendance at the Order's Headquarters, but she was also less questioning in her search for 'reality'. She did keep a dressing-room off the front bedroom as her 'secret room' (not unlike Yeats's small sanctuary at Thoor Ballylee) when she moved to 76 Park Hill Road at Hampstead. Presumably her robes and magical implements were locked away here from the aroused curiosity of her children. It was an absolute necessity, a G.D. member wrote, to perform the rituals where 'proper precaution against disturbances' could be enforced for the spirits to gather peacefully.

For much of the last decade in the century, Florence merely flirted with the stage; that is, in contrast to her devotion to her hermetic studies. It was a fact that caused G.B.S. to shake his fist at the stars. On 10 November, for example, while Florence prepared for her role as Blanche in *Widowers' Houses,* she and an Adept, Mrs. Hamilton, shared a Spirit Vision.

Example of Mode
of
Attaining to Spirit Vision
and
What was seen by Two Adepti
S.S.D.D. Fidelis; 5=6
on
November 10th 1892

Secure for an hour or for longer absolute freedom from interruption. Then alone, or with one or two Adepti, enter the Vault, or a private chamber. Remain in silence and contemplation for several minutes.

Rise and perform the Qabalistic Cross and prayer. Then proceed to contemplation of some object, say a Tarot trump: either by placing it before you and gazing at it, until you seem to see into it; or by placing it against your forehead or elsewhere, and then keeping the eyes closed; in this case you should have given previous study to the Card as to its symbolism, colouring, analogies, etc. In either case you should then deeply sink into the abstract ideal of the card; being in entire indifference to your surroundings. If the mind wanders to anything disconnected with the card, no beginner will succeed in seeing anything spiritually.

Consider all the symbols of the Tarot Card, then all that is implied by its letters, number, and situation, and the Paths connected therewith.

The Vision may begin by the concentration passing into a state of reverie; of with a distinct sense of change, something allied in sensation to a faint, with a feeling urging you to resist, but if you are highly inspired, fear not, do not resist, let yourself go; and then the Vision may pass over you.

If you have anything occur to disturb you, you will come to readily enough—or as from a doze; otherwise the Vision ends of itself, or some can check it by will, at any stage, others can not at first, at any rate.

Example

The Tarot Trump, The Empress,7, was taken; placed before the persons, and contemplated upon, spiritualised, heightened in colouring, purified in design and idealised.

In vibrating manner pronounced Daleth. Then the spirit saw a greenish-blue distant landscape, suggestive of mediaeval tapestry. Effort to ascend was then made; and rising to the planes; seemed to pass up through Clouds, and then appeared a pale green landscape and in the midst a Gothic Temple of ghostly outlines marked with light. [Tennyson and William Morris's poetic influence seem to creep in here.] Approached it, and found the Temple gained in definiteness and was concrete, and seemed a solid structure. Giving the sign of the Netzach Grade (because of Venus) was able to enter: giving also Portal signs [The Portal Ceremony preceded the 5=6 and introduced, as Yeats might have said, the knowledge of truth without its embodiment] and 5=6 signs in thought form. Opposite the entrance perceived a Cross with three bars and a dove upon it; and besides this, were steps leading downwards into the Dark, by a dark passage. Here was met a beautiful Green Dragon, who moved aside, meaning no harm, and the Spirit Vision passed on. Turning a corner and still passing on in the dark emerged from the darkness on to a Marble Terrace brilliantly white, and a Garden beyond, with flowers, whose foliage was of a delicate green kind, and the leaves seemed to have a white velvety surface beneath. Here, there appeared a Woman of heroic proportions, clothed in Green with a jewelled girdle, a crown of Stars on her head, in her hand a sceptre of Gold, at the apex a lustrously white closed Lotus flower; in her left hand an orb bearing a Cross . . . . She smiled proudly, and as the human Spirit sought her name, replied:—

'I am the mighty Mother Isis; most powerful of all the world, I am she who fights not but is always victorious, I am that Sleeping Beauty whom men have sought, for all time; and the paths which lead to my castle are beset with danger and illusionary influence—I am lifted up on high, and do draw men unto me, I am the World's Desire, but few there be who find me. When my Secret is told, it is the Secret of the Holy Grail.' Asking to learn it, replied:—

'Come with me, but first clothe in white garments, put on your insignia, and with bared feet follow where I shall lead'.

Arriving at length at a Marble Wall, pressed a sacred spring, and entered a small compartment, where the Spirit seemed to ascend through a dense vapour, and emerged upon a Turret of a Building. Perceived some object in the midst of the place, but was forbidden to look at it until permission was accorded. Stretched out the arms and Bowed the head to the **O** which was rising a golden Orb in the East. Then turning, knelt with the face toward the centre, and being permitted to raise the eye beheld a Cup with a Heart, and the sun shining upon these. There seemed a clear ruby coloured fluid in the Cup. Then the 'Lady Venus' said 'This is love, I have plucked out my Heart and given it to the World; that is my strength. [Yeats's *Countess Cathleen* must come to mind here.]

Love is the mother of Man—God, giving the Quintessence of her life to save mankind from destruction, and to show forth the Path to the Life Eternal. Love is the Mother of the Christ Spirit, and this Christ is the highest love, the heart of the Great Mother

Isis—the Isis of Nature. He is the expression of her Power—She is the Holy Grail, and He is the Life Blood of Spirit, that is found in this Cup.'

After this, being told that Man's hope lay in following her example, we solemnly gave our hearts to the keeping of the Grail; then instead of feeling death, as our human imaginations led us to expect, we felt an influx of the highest courage and power, for our own hearts were to be henceforth in touch with Hers,—the strongest Force in all the world.

So then we went away, feeling glad we had learned that, 'He who gives away his life, shall gain it.' For *that* Love which is Power is given unto him,—who hath given away his all, for the good of others.

Small wonder that Shaw discovered 'gaps' in Florence's dramatic roles. Had the New Woman concentrated on her characterizations as devotedly as her Hermetic studies, she might have developed into the technical artist G.B.S. attempted to create. On this subject, it is perhaps interesting to place her activities in the Order into the context of her relationship with Shaw. When S.S.D.D. became a 5=6 on 2 August 1891 (the 20th name on the Second Order's membership roll), the Second Order premises were at Thavies Inn until after July 1892 when they moved to Clipstone Street, a small street east of Great Portland Street. This was a sizeable distance from Florence's rooms but a stone's throw from Shaw in Fitzroy Square.

In 1892, for instance, while Florence was very much engaged with G.B.S., she made twenty-one visits to Clipstone Street. Entries in the records from May to December were:

Monday 9 May	SSDD called at 7
Monday 16 May	She called & left letters for SA [Westcott]
Friday 27 May	SSDD has taken Vault key to FER [Annie Horniman. The Vault was a seven-sided replica of the allegorical Father Christian Rosencreutz's resting place.]
Saturday 16 July	SSDD signed in
Wednesday 20 July	SSDD called
Wednesday 14 Sept	SSDD in afternoon
Saturday 17 Sept	There with SA, SRMD [Mathers]
Tuesday 20 September	At consecration of Vault
Friday 30 September	SSDD called at 8
Friday 7 October	There with VNR [Mrs Mathers], SRMD, SA and LO [P. W. Bullock]

Friday 14 October	SSDD there in evening
Wednesday 19 October	SSDD called at 9.30
Sunday 30 October	SSDD called
Tuesday 1 November	SSDD called at 7.30
Wednesday 9 November	SSDD called and Fidelis
Monday 14 November	SSDD called at 6
Tuesday 8 December	SSDD looked in about 7
Saturday 17 December	SSDD, SA 6 o'clock
Wednesday 21 December	SSDD called at 2
Thursday 29 December	SSDD called at 2
Saturday 31 December	SSDD called at 1 o'clock [10]

Only four of these visits coincided on the days that Florence met Shaw. In 1893, there were seventy visits recorded. Glancing at those entries which account for specific events, there is a notation for 21 January when Florence lectured on the Enochian system; one for the thirty-first when she skipped out to tea. Thursday 9 March, she was making invocations in the Vault (no doubt producing her 'resonantly beautiful' vocal tones); Friday 17 March, 'SSDD gone out to buy matches.' 24 March, Florence was there from 6 to 10 p.m. for a meeting of Instruction for the Neophytes. On Thursday 20 April, she left a parcel for Annie Horniman and word that she would be engaged in the evening until Wednesday, six days ahead. Tuesday 30 May, there was a Council of the Adepts, Westcott, Florence, Mrs. Hamilton, Annie Horniman and Yeats. Saturday 4 November, Florence came to meet Annie at 11.30. She waited until the 'little clock' was at 2.15 but Florence imagined it to be only 1.30 and went outdoors to check.

Not unlike the previous year, the visits to Headquarters usually alternated with the dates of Florence's meetings with Shaw. Clipstone Street on 9 January, for example, was sandwiched between G.B.S. on the eighth and the tenth. Florence did not see the neophyte playwright again until the twenty-fifth because she was busy at Clipstone Street 12, 18, 20, 21 January. After reading Whitman with Shaw and being 'very happy' on the twenty-sixth, she played with magic on 28, 29, and 31 January.

Florence was absent from the Second Order premises in February, the month of the violent scene with Jenny Patterson. Perhaps she was unable to reconcile the shock to her Aura, the Sphere of Sensation! But she was very much present on 2, 9, 11, 13, 14, 17, 18, 24 March, a month that shows bare in Shaw's diaries. In April, Florence met Mrs. Hamilton on the fifteenth at Clipstone Street, and on the same day she attended Sauret's first violin recital with Shaw before taking tea at the Orange Grove. There was a 'conflict' of interests again on 27 April when Florence met Westcott and then saw G.B.S. in the evening. On 29 April, she had been to Headquarters before Shaw visited her at Dalling Road and there 'caught a regular cold.' SSDD enjoyed both of her interests on 6 May, and 29 May it was 'Regulus Martis' at Headquarters and going through *Rosmersholm* with Shaw; 'a long job', because Elizabeth Robins was afraid of becoming ill at the Opera Comique and wanted Florence to be prepared.

When Florence met Shaw on 5 June at Regents Park, it was because of its short distance from Clipstone Street. S.S.D.D. was expected there while the philanderer escorted May Morris to *Hedda Gabler*. On the eighth it was Clipstone Street again, on the ninth Florence was with Shaw after he telegraphed her to join him. Then she was in the country until 13 July, the date that Shaw and W. B. Yeats were together at Dalling Road. The New Woman spent much of her time at Headquarters during the following month until the eighteenth when after a visit to Clipstone Street, she spent the evening with Shaw attending the Earl's Court Exhibition and 'coming down "The Chute" '.

A date coincides on 22 November. Florence was unable to attend to her Golden Dawn activities until eight in the evening because she was at the Albert Hall with Shaw for 'Israel in Egypt'. After 'The Lord is a Man of War', G.B.S. 'put her into a bus'. The concert was three days after he had gone to the Charringtons to talk over 'their scheme of doing a professional tour with F.E. on the strength of the money that has been promised to her for theatrical purposes'. On 28 November Shaw worked on *Arms And The Man* for Florence and the following day, S.S.D.D. waited unprofitably for her meeting with Annie Horniman at Clipstone Street.

By 1894, Florence had published the first of her philosophical tracts, An Introduction and Notes to *A Short Enquiry concerning the Hermetic Art by a Lover of Philalethes*. The five page Introduction was an affirmation of her 'religion' rooted in the alchemical belief that

> the man who is content with anything,
> who does not feel in his most successful moments, during the most sacred earthly joys, a keen sense of want and disappointment can never hope to find the Stone of the Wise.

The passage illuminates a passing anecdote by Yeats in the *Autobiography*:

Florence Farr once said to me; 'If we could say to ourselves, with sincerity, "This passing moment is as good as any I shall ever know," we would die upon the instant, or be united to God.' Desire would have ceased, and logic the feet of desire.[11]

Desire, S.S.D.D. continued, was the superior expression of the Imagination; the force that manipulates series of images into an act of Will. This concept, and a passage from Dr. Israel Regardie's *The Golden Dawn* bring an additional perspective to Mary Bruin in Yeats's *Land of Heart's Desire*. Regardie writes: 'so far as the nature of the environment and the creative power of the personal self permits,' the task of the Initiate is to reassemble his physical and mental phenomena to 'remould them nearer to the heart's desire.' In Yeats's play, the faery child incites Mary Bruin to permit her imagination to soar into a supreme act of will. Her symbolic death, therefore, is the ultimate gesture that frees her from the chains of the phenomenal world. See, in passing, how the poet has mastered Amaryllis's New Womanish lines in the *Idyll*. The Child recites:

> Stay and come with me, newly-married bride,
> For if you hear him [Father Hart] you grow like the rest;
> Bear children, cook, and bend over the churn,
> And wrangle over butter, fowl and eggs,
> Until at last, grown old and bitter of tongue,
> You're crouching there and shivering at the grave

Instead—

> . . . I can lead you, newly-married bride,
> Where nobody gets old and crafty and wise,
> Where nobody gets old and godly and grave,
> Where nobody gets old and bitter of tongue,
> And where kind tongues bring no captivity;
> For we are but obedient to the thoughts
> That drift into the mind at a wink of the eye.

The faery child will summon the images that transform the dross into gold which is Yeats's simile for transmuting life into art.

In the closing paragraph of her tract, Florence admitted her withdrawal from 'reality', that quality of vagueness so disturbing to Shaw. '*In* the world Adepts may be, but not *of* it' implied that magical work required total absorption; that little effort could be allowed for perishable commodities.

This particular New Woman's uniqueness lay in the paradox that while she was having fun with the *Dancing Faun* she could still work at her serious sermons. But this is, of course, the reason for G.B.S. saying a decade thence:

if you want to write popular books, write them; if you want to
write mystic gospels, write them: but in the name of commonsense
don't try to popularise your mysticism or mystify your popular
readers. If preachee, preachee; if floggee floggee; but no preachee
floggee too.[12]

Then Florence tore off the rest of his remarks. In another instance,
when Shaw was being his most profound, she wrote alchemical signs
on the opposite side of a letter[13] which began: 'Miserable ill-starred
woman'.

By 1895, Florence was Praemonstratrix in the Golden Dawn, a
position of immense responsibility that had come about when the
Matherses moved to Paris in the Spring of 1892 (Mrs. Mathers was
the sister of the French philosopher, Henri Bergson). After Florence
returned from her tour in *Caste,* not as 'Mrs. Bernard Shaw', as
G.B.S. threatened in his letter to Janet Achurch, she issued an edict
to the Order that 'Wednesday evenings will be discontinued, and instead:—S.S.D.D. will attend on Thursdays at 6.45 p.m. for ritual
study.'[14]

The spiritual and social intercourse in the Golden Dawn could, in
part, supplant Shaw's romantic affections. Florence could, for example, busy herself with chores for G.D. acquaintances. That year,
Frederick Leigh Gardner, a founder member of the Ananda Lodge in
the Esoteric section of the Theosophical Society, asked her to paint
four figures for him. They were to resemble the Egyptian figures
which the Outer Order members used in their ceremonies at Mark
Mason's Hall. Florence could not promise this for she was unable to
execute two figures alike. Moreover, she intended to charge only for
her time and materials, 'not as an artist, because an artist owes it to
his profession to "stick it on".'[15] In July the following year, S.S.D.D.
acknowledged Gardner's cheque for what appears to be a different
attempt at some embroidery. Believing the handiwork to be 'better
and stronger' than any previous efforts, she commented 'but what
would be the use of all our struggles if we didn't progress?'[16]

By this year, Florence completed two additional texts for the
Theosophical Publishing Society, Volume VII, *A Commentary on
Euphrates, or The Waters of the East,* and Volume VIII,
Egyptian Magic. The Commentary on Thomas Vaughan in the
former justified Shaw's remark to Janet Achurch the previous year;
'. . . knowledge: it is impossible to mention anything she does not
know.' Florence had transcribed and reconciled the seventeenth century Qabalist's post-Reformation reflections on Alchemy into contemporary Theosophical concepts and to nineteenth century scien-

tific data. The results indicated an inordinate quantity of metaphysical enquiry. But it was *Egyptian Magic,* the final straw that drove Shaw from Florence into the North Pole or the South, that encouraged G.B.S. to rail at the New Woman for not believing in his doctrine of

> not working at some reality every day; but you none the less worked every day at your unreality. And now you think to undo the work of all these years by a phrase and a shilling's worth of exoteric Egyptology.[17]

It was indicative of Florence's restiveness in the Order, as well as a reflection of her personal crotchets, that some time in 1896 she wrote to Gardner telling him to inform Westcott she was 'thinking of chucking the whole thing.' But in another letter; 'When things are bad, it is the moment for work not for the moment for sitting idle. I have to constantly be helping things occultly. Then the foreshadowing of later events: 'But I do not work on G.D. lines & I am only keeping on until I have seen one or two more people through 5=6'.[18]

That year Mathers expelled Annie Horniman from the Isis-Urania Temple after a number of unpleasant confrontations. In turn, she withdrew the financial support that had enabled him to comfortably practice Magic for several years. These events directly affected Florence and Yeats. Their fondness for FER was questionable, but she did have money and the autonomy to dispense it. Not only had she been the most important accessory to the Avenue Season, but there were plans for an Irish Theatre. In 1897, Gardner composed an appeal to reinstate Annie. Florence did not especially care for his wording, but still in FER's debt, she, as well as Henrietta, decided to co-operate and sign. The appeal eventually showed several signatures but never reached Mathers. At any rate, Annie stayed out of the Order for another three years.

By 1897, Westcott was out of the Order as well which put Mathers very much in the position of King of Heaven. This particular resignation was tremendously important to Florence since it made her Mathers's Representative in London and, therefore, Chief of the Isis-Urania Temple. Presently in a role which she assumed with occasional outrageous officiousness, her added work and responsibilities inclined her to agree with Shaw; if she applied herself to the profitable as hard as she worked at the unprofitable, she would soon be rich. The admission was to Gardner and not to G.B.S.; the former had proposed to round up some G.D. clients for her embroidery. Generous as his sentiments appeared, Florence believed it was not a good idea for her to make 'a practice of doing work for members of the Order unless it is quite a spontaneous necessity on their part. Especially I would not like them to think I wanted them to give me work to do.'[19]

It was not as if she was in actual want, she explained, since she could obtain money from her father's trustees to keep her for a year to come, but 'naturally one does not like to spend all one's capital.' At work on another tract, she hoped for sixpence profit per copy on its sale. Egyptologist Sir W. M. Flinders Petrie, to whom she submitted the paper for comment, thought the British Public would hardly 'swallow' its 'doses' but 'so be it, and good luck'.[20]

After Annie Horniman cut off the Matherses' allowance in 1896, the Chief was barely able to 'jog on from day to day.' Upset at his predicament, Florence collected twenty pounds for him in May 1897 before calling a meeting for the night of the fifth. She wanted to 'lay the case before the 5=6's.' In order to keep Mathers going, she planned to increase the fee for Outer Order members. (The fee in 1896 had been two pounds or guineas, Florence forgot which; a pound if the person was not well off and a poverty clause for the very poor. There was also an annual subscription of twelve shillings and sixpence.) Gardner had already lent money to Mathers which Florence asked him to 'let . . . lie a little longer in peace' until regular contributions could be collected. Generous when he chose, on 18 May he also sent Florence a cheque for the amount of seven pounds in payment for 'copper brocade curtain 22ft. by 17ft.' In August she wrote to him about a buyer for her Townsend bicycle. She had won a new 'machine' in a prize competition. 22 August, her correspondence took on a new tone.

> With much regret I have to tell you as Superintendent of Ritual I cannot recommend you for further official position in Isis-Urania Temple, for the following reasons:—
>
> 1. While you were attending ritual classes I repeatedly warned you that dignity must at least be aimed at by an official. Your movements were and are much too boisterous, and your voice too uncontrolled.
>
> 2. Your manner to candidates, and those below you in the Order is intolerably rude; and I have over and over again received considerable complaints from those who have been pained by your want of consideration for their feelings and your own dignity.
>
> 3. I had hoped that the office of Hegemon would have produced some beneficial effect on you but I hear that it is quite painful to be present at ceremonies, and see the rites celebrated by one who

seems to consider that he is a drill master in a board school.

The tone of your letters to those who have undertaken work for the Order in general is that of one who is employing and paying wages to those he is addressing, and I must ask you to adopt a different attitude.[21]

It never occurred to Florence that she was behaving other in a dutiful manner and she reminded Gardner there was nothing personal in her complaints. It was simply that having assumed authority in such matters a year before, she had no intention of being 'bullied into doing what I don't think is for the general good.' After all, she continued four days later, 'You don't suppose that I can let my personal friends spoil the effect of ceremonies just because I get on well with them, do you?[22] She offered small hope for his return to an officiating position in the Order. Certainly the Hegemon (leader) office had not pulled him together; the Hierus (priest) would only accentuate his faults, and the 'Hierophant [head of the Eleusinian cult] is impossible.' Gardner questioned her decision and SSDD remained relentless. After all, when she had asked him to whisper at ceremonies, he either told the Candidates much too loudly to 'step up', or treated them as if he were driving a lot of sheep to shambles. 'Well, I call that sort of thing abominably rude! You may not; but I do. I don't want any further correspondence on the matter.'[23]

The rift continued, Gardner was ousted from the Isis-Urania Temple into the Horus at Bradford, and the Order prepared for mightier events which were to be triggered off by Aleister Crowley.

The well-to-do young man believed himself to have been the mystic Eliphas Lévi in another incarnation. During a climbing expedition in Switzerland in 1898, Crowley met Julian Baker, an analytical chemist, and a member of the Golden Dawn. Since Crowley expressed his desire to pursue the art of Magic, Baker introduced him to another chemist in the Order, George Cecil Jones, and it was he who brought him into the Golden Dawn. Crowley was well-read in Magic and ripe for the teaching of the Order. In revolt against formal Judeo-Christian religion, he 'did not hate God or Christ, but merely the God or Christ of the people whom I hated . . . The sum of the matter is that Judaism is a savage, and Christianity a fiendish superstition.'[24]

The new Initiate found the G.D. group 'muddled middle class mediocrities', an assemblage as 'vulgar and commonplace as any set of average people.' There were exceptions; Jones and Baker, and later, Allan Bennett. He found one literary light, 'W. B. Yeats, a lank, dishevelled demonologist' who might have taken more pains with his dress 'without incurring the reproach of dandyism.' Yeats received further dishonour in *Moonchild* as the 'lean, cadaverous Protestant-Irishman' named Gates:

> tall, with the scholar's stoop. He possessed real original talent, with now and then a flash of insight which came close to genius. But though his intellect was keen and fine, it was in some way confused; and there was a lack of virility in his make-up. His hair was long, lank and unkempt; his teeth were neglected; and he had a habit of physical dirt which was so obvious as to be repulsive even to a stranger.[25]

There was considerable jealousy on Crowley's part for what he considered Yeats's dim genius. He once wrote to George Moore.

> You write of Yeats as 'a poet in search of a pedigree'— but who told you he was a poet?
> Read ME![26]

For Mrs. Emery, Crowley had an 'affectionate respect tempered by a feeling of compassion' since her abilities were inferior to her aspirations. No proof has been offered for the myth that he had physical intercourse with her on 'at least one occasion'.[27] Crowley was fifteen years younger than his superior and very egocentric. He considered his masculinity above normal but his body of 'certain well-marked characteristics'; his limbs as slight and graceful as a girl's and his breasts developed to an abnormal degree. 'This sort of hermaphroditism' prepared him, he thought, to understand women unusually well so that he could beat them at their own game and 'emerge from the battle of sex triumphant and scatheless.'

There is no doubt that Florence and 'The Beast', as he was later called, shared some sort of rapport for a short while; passages from their writing imply as least a measure of intellectual exchange. Crowley wrote:

> It is monstrous for a man to pretend to be devoted to securing his wife's happiness and yet to deprive her of a woman's supreme joy: that of bearing a child to the man she desires sexually, and is therefore indicated by nature as the proper father, though he may be utterly unsuitable as a husband.[28]

And Florence—

> If a girl were free to choose according to her inclination, there is practically no doubt that she would choose the right father for her child, however badly she might choose a life-long companion for herself.[29]

By the year Crowley had advanced to Portal he had alienated the regard of several Order members. His increased familiarity with

Mathers also appeared to some as a collusion of sorts. Then there was the matter of his excessive eccentricities. The London hierarchy refused to initiate him in the Vault Ceremony and Crowley, infuriated, crossed to Paris. On 16 January 1900, Mathers had initiated him as a 5=6 at the Ahathoor Temple. The new Adept then returned to London and asked the acting secretary for the documents to which he was entitled.

Florence did not take Mathers's slight to her authority kindly; he had flagrantly disregarded her wishes by performing the ceremony for Crowley; yet, she attempted to suppress her own feelings to search for a diplomatic solution to repair the diminishing respect for the Chief within the Order. Unable to resolve her problems, she decided to resign.

Mathers met her decision head-on. Wary that she might create a schism in the Order with the idea of working secretly with Westcott (a prevailing fear with Mathers), he dealt a deadly blow. Sapere Aude, he wrote, was only under the impression he had received an Epitome of the School of the Second Order work from Anna Sprengel. Moreover, Westcott had

NEVER been at any time in personal or written communication with the Secret Chiefs of the Order, he having either himself forged or procured to be forged the professional correspondence between them, and my tongue having been tied all these years by a Previous Oath of Secrecy to him, demanded from me, before showing me what he had either done or caused to be done or both.[30]

The Chief stressed that 'every atom' of the Order knowledge had come from him alone and that only he had been in communication with the Secret Chiefs.

As Crowley wrote, the letter 'struck at the very heart of the moral basis' of Florence's conduct. The revelation, if it were true, caused her to face the reality that for years she had initiated people under false pretences. Now she was being asked not to leave the Order or to consult with others. Utterly dismayed, she decided to visit Bromley, the scene of her childhood, to sort out her thoughts. There she came to a decision to share the contents of Mathers's letter with the Second Order.

A correspondence between Florence and the Chief followed while she formed a Committee to pursue a formal investigation of the foundation of the Order. Mathers's refusal to recognise such a committee and his eventual removal of Florence as his Representative in London brought the following letter from her.

I saw that if I kept silence, I should become a party to a fraud . . . We sent you repeated messages, couched in most respectful terms, pointing out as delicately as possible the impressions conveyed by your letter. You refused to recognise the friendly Committee, so the only thing to be done was to get the Committee appointed by the Second Order Council of the Adepts. This has been done, and neither I nor anyone else have the power to prevent the matter being carried to its legal conclusion.[31]

By 2 April Mathers announced 'I *annul* the Committee and I *annul* the Resolutions passed at the meeting.' The prevailing disaster, he claimed, could only compare to the trials in the Theosophical Society after Madame Blavatsky died. After prophesising even greater tribulations for the G.D. and unable to threaten its members further, he deputised Crowley to take possession of the Second Order premises. Crowley then forced his way into the rooms which were presently situated at Blythe Road, Hammersmith, and ordered all present to appear at Headquarters (Paris) at 11.45 on the twentieth. The following day, Yeats and Mrs. Hunter called upon Mr. Wilkinson, the landlord at Blythe Road, to enquire why he had permitted Crowley to break in. Florence, the landlord said, had failed to put in writing that she wished the rooms closed, and his clerk had failed to transmit to him her verbal orders. Since she was the nominal owner of the premises, Florence gave Yeats and Mrs. Hunter a letter authorising them to change the locks on the door, and this they carried out.

The following day, Crowley arrived again attired in Highland dress and black mask. Forewarned this time of his approach, Yeats called a constable and the masquerade was aborted. Unable to scare the London group from further action, Mathers attempted to save face:

In giving these persons so great a knowledge, I have not also been able to give them brains and intelligence to comprehend it, for this miracle the Gods have not granted me the power to perform. You had better address your reproaches to the Gods rather than to me . . . You say 'am I to understand that there is never to be any truth and light let in upon this Order.' I tell you there has been too much light let in upon these rebellious children of clay, and it has blinded them![32]

J. M. Watkins in St. Martin's Lane came out that year with F. Farr Emery's *The Way of Wisdom*; it was an ill-timed title in view of the unbelievable behaviour in the Order and their almost child-like naïveté.

By April, Yeats had been elected Imperator of the Outer Order's Isis-Urania Temple and by May, Second Order members were aware that it had been 'unanimously resolved' that Mathers was no longer recognised as their Chief. From then out, dispositions continued to deteriorate despite a new hierarchy and their attempt to perform Magic as if nothing was rotten in the Golden Dawn.

Florence, meanwhile, resumed a business relationship with Gardner; in fact, there had been a negotiation of ten Home and Colonial shares which he appears to have purchased for her. This did not stop him from 'smarting' for her dismissal of his official duties in 1897.

> Dear Madam,
> I have for several years smarted under a sense of injustice to my having been degraded among my friends and finally removed from my membership of the Isis Temple. I hold a letter from you in which you say that you alone caused my degradation with its consequent results, and that the Chief Adept had nothing to do with it. I never believed you!!! but until recently I have never been able to disprove your statement.

It appears that Mathers had informed Gardner that it was he who had authorised Florence for his dismissal and

> while he had never thought you capable of acting dishonourably towards Members of the Order, your conduct has since shewn him that you have few scruples where your Ambition or Self Interest are concerned.[33]

Gardner retaliated in sorts in 1900 when either out of the goodness of her heart, or for some monetary remuneration. Florence took care of a very elderly G.D. member, the Reverend William Alexander Ayton. The arrangement ended with Florence 'circulating' a report that Gardner was the 'means of inducing' Ayton to 'dismiss her' from his household. Gardner complained about Florence spreading this rumour and the clergyman answered: 'It is inconceivable to me that she should have so said. Is it not possible that some evil-disposed person has circulated the report to make mischief?'[34]

Florence was away from her lodgings again that year. Presently with her good friends Lady and Sir Edward Colvile, she wrote to Annie Horniman (who had been reinstated as Scribe) from Lightwater, Bagshot of a new candidate. The Neophyte was Princess Aribert of Anhalt, granddaughter of Queen Victoria, whom Florence wished to initiate under private circumstances. The previous year the former Princess Marie Louise had written to her from Cumberland Lodge, Windsor that she wished

> more than ever I could see you but all my plans have been upset

[her unsatisfactory marriage to a German Prince and her brother's service in Natal] and I am forced to return to London on the 17th for a night at Buckingham Palace . . . My mother not feeling very happy about my health made me consult a doctor a few days ago. Strange to say the cure he prescribed besides the usual impossible remedy of utter rest and absence of mental worry . . . was 4 months in Egypt. Alas I cannot always do what I should like to—but I will leave it to a higher power and am convinced if I am far enough advanced I shall return there—I say return—though I have never been there during this present life—I have often had the impression that I know those scenes well—

Perhaps if we can meet you will allow me to ask you about different things.

Presently in the role of *confidante,* Florence's letter to Annie Horniman therefore read:

I have a new Candidate but I want to get her initiated privately . . . because her social position makes it impossible for her to come to Mark Mason's Hall . . . she has a kind of nature that the G.D. course would help tremendously. I have had many serious talks with her since Saturday but have not spoken of the Order because of the difficulty in the way of her going to M.M. Hall etc. However as she is to be separated from her husband and will take a home near London by the time she is ready for 5=6 she will be able to go to Headquarters. The 5 introducers could be arranged thus.

> Lady Colvile propose her.
> Sir Henry Colvile interview her as a man.
> I interview her as a woman.
> and anyone you like for astral exam.[36]

|Annie Horniman obviously made up the fifth|.

Around this time, Annie began to use the office of Scribe to vent the malcontent of several years. Upon digging into Orders records, she discovered that Florence was sloppy in her record-keeping as well as her rules for examinations. Always innovative, as early as 1896, SSDD gave

the Examining Adept full power to *tell the Candidate facts* that he does not remember. Of course making a note [to] the effect as a few marks would be gained by those who do remember facts.

But I want especially to be able to judge the synthesizing facts of the 4=7's and if the facts are not put right before the inferences are made the whole scheme will be useless.[37]

More aggravating to Annie than Florence's stretching of the rules were the private organizations within the Order. It seemed to her as if these must work against messages being sent from the Secret Invisible Chiefs. Florence's 'Sphere' annoyed her in particular. At Annie's asking, Yeats advised SSDD to open the 'Sphere' to any 5=6 who wished to join. Florence ostensibly complied but with the qualification that it was up to the Council to determine whether secret organizations were not invaluable to the spiritual welfare of the Golden Dawn and therefore valid and legal. Yeats reacted strongly. He had, no doubt, compromised himself with Annie in demanding an agreement of compliance from Florence. SSDD had got around her part in the matter by extrapolating from the Council authority to continue with the 'Sphere'. The Imperator now realised that nothing short of total capitulation on Florence's part would appease Annie Horniman. From 18 Woburn Buildings, he wrote to SSDD, dictating the first part of his letter to Annie. There were strong demands for Florence to undo the work of the Council, and if the majority would not agree to this, to resign.

> I shall await your reply with considerable anxiety as much will depend on it. If you will keep faith with me—and I cannot suppose that you mean to do anything else—we can do much work together. The G.D. is only a part of a much greater work—work that may bring you greater opportunities.

The poet referred to the Irish Literary Theatre which had, by this time, enjoyed its first modest success with *The Countess Cathleen*. The remainder of the letter, of which the following is part, was in Yeats's hand.

> We can make a great movement and in more than magical things, but I assure you that if (through weak vitality, through forgetfulness or through any other cause) you make it difficult for us to rely upon one another perfectly you make everything impossible. [38]

Machinations withstanding, Florence still embarked on astral journeys. Here is a cloudy description of a vision shared with Reena Fulham-Hughes. (Mrs. Hughes was one of the seven Adepti Litterati elected when 'A New Constitution' came into power in 1900.)

> 'Used yachad as password' . . .
> yawningly for Snake and Serpent in its tail. It yawned & we walked into centre. A revolving stone tipped up & snake told us to go down . . . We went down steps 'to come to the Book of Thoth.' At the bottom there were 5 passages with recesses at the ends . . . We brought offerings to each shrine & received spiritual gift from each. From (1) we received ruby wine the choice is shall it fall into ferment or be exalted into yellow flame of the intelligible life. (2) Yellow oil the [?] of the head of the fire which can be generated from the

spirit of the wine. (3) A secret name written on a papyrus roll, name is enclosed in a cartouch & stamped on forehead & lips. The name taught has ineffable power over the material body which must obey its mandate . . . (4) . . . around it an auriol in a rain of manna like soft feathers gently buffetting the body & establishing it . . . (5) . . . Uraeus Immortal form complete and white robe 15 yds of stuff kilted [Mathers's Highland influence?] & twisted etc. . . . serpent says next time you must enter in Adytum of Isis.

As far as I can remember we went to the water side & found there the Mystery of the Cow and analogous to milk butter curd and whey etc. And fire a parafin spring & the wonderful coal tar products—as we know it now in . . . tin etc.

The following year, still fired by esoteric fever, Florence had written and produced two one-act plays in collaboration with Yeats's intimate friend, Mrs. Olivia Shakespear. It is difficult to decide what part each contributed to the remoulding of the magical tales of Egypt. Olivia Shakespear had written several novels; her style was less direct than Florence's, more decorative, and her subject matter rather more romantic.

The argument for each piece preceded the text. In *The Beloved of Hather,*

> Aahmes, beloved of Hathor, has for many years been watched over by his High Priestess, in order that through him the great spiritual kingdom of Egypt might be restored. His final choice is between this great destiny and the mere splendour of material victory.

The action in the second play develops in a cave on Mount Bakhua, near Sinai, c.4000 B.C.

> Gebuel, the Magican of Fire and Metals, makes a talisman to Heru in the form of a golden Hawk, in the hope of overwhelming the power of Zozer, King of Egypt, builder of the Step-pyramid at Sakhara. Zozer finds this out, and sends his daughter who is skilled in the sombre mysteries of Isis, to win for Egypt the Golden Hawk, giver of exultation of heart.

A note written after the 'curtain' of the above, and reading very much as from Florence's hand, included a small sermon. The author pointed out that just as the modern world had come to think of heaven as a state instead of a place, so did the ancient Egyptians know that the gods were states and not persons.

Casting for both plays revived the family collaboration of Florence and the Pagets. In *The Beloved of Hathor,* Florence played the *'femme serieuse',* Ranoutet with force, Sidney Paget (H. M.'s brother), showed as a 'massive and magnificent' Aahmes, and Sylvia Dryhurst (sister of Geoffrey Paget's future wife), as a refined and inaudible Ouny. Dorothy Paget, eight years older than when she played Yeats's faery child was presently a 'naughty' Nouferou wearing clinging costumes and 'no petticoats to speak of while she induced Aahmes to recline on a couch 'softly walk[ing] around . . . doing a wild skirt dance.' Yeats, reviewing her in the *Star* on 23 January 1902, described her playing as picturesque, and, it must have occurred to him, not unlike Florence's performance in the *Idyll* over a decade before. 'Often she was filled with sweetness and gravity, and always with that beauty of voice, which becomes the essential thing in a play.'

Still, he thought she was lacking a little in maturity, that she had the beauty of extreme youth and a fluent charm as one who had put on womanhood and not yet put off childhood.

Dorothy Paget was the only member of the family to play in the second one-act performing the part of the Ka, the small figure, the text explained, who walked behind the king or queen in ancient frescoes. Dorothy presented the 'subtle body' (or Yeats's the 'wine breath') whose presence supported and gave strength to the material body.

Florence was extremely pleased that her innovative stage design had kept the production cost to less than £30. There were no flats but 'pale sienna hangings' so arranged 'that the figures of the actors, moving across the stage may reproduce the effect of the ancient frescoes or illuminated papyri'.

In all, one reviewer wrote, nothing as bizarre in dramatic art had ever been performed before. Some found the plays a religious experience, and Yeats, rituals 'of a beautiful forgotten worship.' The actors spoke with so great a religious fervour, 'with so high an ecstasy, that one could not but doubt . . . their Christian orthodoxy.'

Neither play stirred in the poet a 'strictly dramatic interest', yet they must have contributed to the conception of his dance plays; these, perceived many years before his introduction to the Noh, were foreshadowed in 1904 by the production of the *Shadowy Waters*. At the Egyptian Hall Yeats was caught up with 'one final dramatic moment when a priestess, who has just been shirking in terror before her god . . . dances in ecstasy'.

1902 is also the year that Florence, tired of the accusations against the secret groups, severed her association with the Golden Dawn. John Todhunter and Henrietta Paget resigned as well. Fragments of a sort of mystical stream of consciousness jotted down by Florence in diary-like form, and letters from the Bedford Park circle describe and recreate the New Woman's personal unrest. In January, the month of the plays at the Egyptian Hall, York Powell wrote to John Butler Yeats that he had seen Mrs. Emery 4 January.

She made some excellent coffee in a frying pan, just like the gypsy she is. She watches a fire like an old Tent-Dweller, and does not let time interfere with her will. She plays with her life like a child with a toy, but she's a good pal and a brave woman.[39]

About the third week in June, Florence joined the Theosophical Society in London. She made a note that

1902 July 8th. I joined the Theosophical about a fortnight ago. Meade was saying Christ was interested in the movement going on to Theosophise Christianity. (1) What place has the being they call Christ in the Hierarchy of Adepts?(2) How are the different adepts connected (3) if the Theosophists have a right to force this movement as Meade spoke of. Forcing why not sweep away by will force the veil of Maya at once & have no more fuss. (4) Why should we go on with all this worry of existence at all?

The impression must be that Florence was 'sick to death of life altogether,' an admission she later made to a New York friend.
Then

(1) The Being they call Christ arises at certain intervals from an age long trance. He is a Mamanakya which has been active during the last three years or so. He is working through Ramanathan & many others. His message is not for you, (2)   The different Beings who retain the Khu body [?] to function at Will upon earth have all attained the realisation of Unity but the different forms of the Khu body involving as the differences or difference of thought & colour make them less in sympathy with one than with another. Your colour is green but the colour of the Christ is blue & pink. You should be most attracted by a pink ray & you will get into touch with that after the Realisation of Unity has been attained . . . Ruby pink is your need.
(3)   Will force will sweep away Maya as soon as it is forceful enough to overcome the Will force that creates Maya. They are forever ebbing & flowing alternating.
(4) The worry should not exist it is only folly that causes worry. Nothing is really necessaryly [sic] unpleasant. All you desire is yours the instant that you consider that it is yours . . . Heaven be with you. Remember the Ruby. ('The great illusion which turns all one looks at through it into gold. It transforms & transfigures making me take interest in follies.')
    The same evening. Please show me exactly what I should define as my aim in manifestation. I know my aim is to become One with the Nebrazer the Limitless Wholeness—but I suppose I should work at something definite also? Now as things are I no sooner settle on one thing than another forces itself upon me. May I see my path clearly?
For the present think of nothing but the sentence

Bb   CDbC   Db   Eb   Bb   DbEbDbBb BbC Bb
I am the one Without Motion; giving motion to all things.
Whenever you are alone or working at mechanical work that you
can do without devoting attention to it repeat to this tune . . . Is
that the right mantram? Very nearly you must use the Tinyest [sic]
intervals. . . .

There is most likely a connection between a journey to Ceylon by a
member of the Golden Dawn and the meeting between Florence and
Ceylon's Ponnambalam Ramanathan who is mentioned in the diary
extract. Allan Bennett, Crowley's friend in the Golden Dawn, had
suffered in England from spasmodic asthma which he could relieve
only by a cycle of drugs. He took opium for a month, morphine next,
and then switched to cocaine before finally, chloroform. Either
Bennett or Crowley decided that the former must seek a warmer
climate for survival, but it was the latter who slept with the wife of a
British Colonel stationed in India in order to collect the fare. Bennett
then went off to Ceylon. In time, the Honourable P. Ramanathan
hired him to tutor his young sons. Crowley met the Guru when he
visited his friend and described him as a man of 'charming personality, wide culture, and profound religious knowledge . . . eminent as a
Yogi of the Shavite sect of Hindus'.[40]

It is perhaps through Bennett's association with Ramanathan that
the future Tamil parliamentarian became acquainted with the London circle of ex G.D. Adepts and practicing Theosophists. Lady
Ramanathan, the second, Australian-born wife of the Guru, recalled
in 1947 that her husband went to London on a business trip about the
year 1902. While there he was invited to speak to a group interested
in Eastern thought. Present among those at the gathering, Florence
Farr appeared greatly impressed with the Easterner's teaching as
well as his educational plans for his country. After listening to him
speak, she committed herself to help him whenever he consummated
his plans for a college.

Florence seemed to be in deadly earnest about leaving England,
but, whatever her feelings, she tucked them away for several years.
Immersed very shortly in Eastern meditations and the study of
pamphlets written by Ramanathan, she embarked on a series of
dialogues between her phenomenal self and soul, occasionally
reminiscent of Yeats's 'Ego Dominus Tuus'. On 23 March 1903, she
wrote:

May I see more clearly now? Oh how long is it that you will wander
about with every wind that blows. Fixed meditation is *the* only

way. All wisdom of the world is useless in words it must be known in its manifest. Go back to the root of being. Do not be deluded into thinking anything else matters.

In August she was meditating on colours and having 'enough of the red I should think; what do I need. I should advise a course of severe reading of the Vashista & Bhgavat. You have never given enough time to the study of those books'.   Still searching for the ineffable she later wrote: 'Be silent and still wait. Ask no advice from any human being. It is sacriledge to do so when I have taken up the work'.

An entry on Sunday 15 May in the following year, 1904, at last reflects some peace.

I wonder if I should not define my state more clearly to myself now? There is no longer any necessity to divide yourself into Questioner and Answerer. It is best to keep United as was said the last time you wrote. Now the right formula is as follows.
In my name of Narayana I declare that the way is entered and the goal is in sight. Work as you are doing in the vehicles that are dedicated to me. So finding Truth remain in the centre of all things & focus the light to the dark. So is the Union of man & God symbolised.

Several pages of a diary commencing on Monday 21 November 1904 are a vital inclusion in the surrounding biographical data. Not only does the writing reveal how important Florence must have been to Yeats's understanding of the nature of the soul (although she found his interpretation of it as well as Shaw's 'half-baked') but also, how grippingly entwined were the two halves of her paradox. Much in the following lines reappears in 1907 in the more didactic essays which found their way into the *New Age*.

I have had a day of Peace and Meditations after months of disturbed life in the exterior. I can not even make this statement without telling countless untruths for Time & change are both false ideas inhering in the vain thought of separateness.
I am unchangeable & the wholeness containing every thought and action but not contained by them as I vainly imagine when I do not take heed in my expression. What is my expression? My expression is not myself but my will to manifest—I never change but I appear & disappear. I am neither light nor darkness but contain all pairs of opposites. I am the creator of the visible universe and when I pay attention to it I become one with it, I have no vehicle or name or form but the indrawing of my breath creates an illusion of separate life in the dust of the earth . . .
I appear & disappear because the Illusions of Time Space &

Causality inherent in subjectivity have found a means of deluding me by flattering my vanity & making me think it is a fine thing to manifest & think & speak & 'stamp myself upon the age.' The illusion is born because I want to touch hear see taste smell it because I want to speak to it grasp it move about on it, get rid of it, & increase it, pour myself into it. I want in a word to enter into relations with it. I want to separate myself from my settled convictions that I am everything & prove to myself by argument reason speech sensation . . . at present I have the illusion that I am a kind of 4 limbed creature of inconceivable smallness occupying myself exclusively with the destiniy of a race of parasites . . . I look around & see many of these parasites have quite a clear idea of their relative unimportance but they are filled to the brain with the illusion that their mutual relations are of the utmost interest & importance & they slave & struggle to maintain themselves as if they really were going to rescue the universe from the laws of manifestation & attain a state in which there shall be light without darkness & goodness without badness & consciousness without matter. Some of them think that by much talk they can persuade the parasites to temperance & social benevolence. They talk of the one life that animates the human race & hope that by so doing they will induce the Parasites to unite into a kind of large Being conscious of itself as a whole & without need of food or digestive processes disinclined to propogate its species because the usual methods of doing so offend modesty & occasion various individuals concerned grave inconvenience. A kind of Static White State is imagined in which the highly involved Being who has by inconceivable efforts surmounted all the natural instincts . . . & other laws of nature shall rule other less evolved vortexes & try to reduce them to the same condition. The object seems to be to regularise illusion & say this vortex might be improved upon it changes perpetually it must be made static then it will be a wholly virtuous vortex & may become capable of lasting for ever & ever & that will be grand.

All the while there is absolutely no occasion for any struggle at all. Everything is a play in my real being & we've only all got to realise we are doing this to amuse ourselves by experimenting with our playthings, Space Time & Casuality to escape from the illusion that we are only parts of ourselves.

After an accident we sometimes think very much of our crushed leg but when it is well we forget it. So let us forget this accidental illusion & know we really do not suffer do or exist that these are only verbs and nouns we use to play games with.

Then comes a practical parasite & he says rubbish my foolish dreamer see me what happens to me when I work & believe in the reality of my senses & use my mind to gratify them & help forward the race. See how my heap of possessions increase: see how the other parasites crowd around me & listen to everything I say. See how I construct useful things why I can send my workmen from one end of this old globule to the other in 3 months. I can make my voice heard all over it in 3 minutes. I dig tunnels & I shall soon fly all over the place.

Then the dreamer says but you cannot get rid of your master which gnaws your vitals unless you give it food. You cannot get rid of your master which makes you cringe before the beauty of women. You cannot get rid of your master which makes you fear to die. The practical man says I don't want to. I get myself enough food to spare by starving my fellow creatures. I buy women whenever I need aleasure feast. I die when I am ashamed of my life, very often by my own hand; who says I have not courage. Besides I give employment to hundreds of otherwise useless parasites. The dreamer says I too have known the enslavement of these things & I have only one desire to be freed from slavery & in my dreams I have seen the way.

The wise man comes forward & says we have seen the way also my friend & teach it' to all who seek in the schools of philosophy.

The dreamer replies There is more power in the liberation of one human Being than in all the words of all the prophets and teachers that ever spoke.

The wise man said That is Truth but what is Liberation?

The Dreamer answered To know certainly that Here & Now This inmost Seer who perceives the wholeness in Itself is the unchangeable jewel we call God.

TAKE HEED LEST YE FORGET

To be the Self & begin once more to contemplate the self.
Later the same day.
After Tea. Why do I eat?
Because you are full of illusion you could Be all things if you had not separated yourself in order to select some & reject others.

The teaching is to say Oh it is my body that eats I do not do so. I do nothing.

It is your most solid illusion that performs the violent action called eating but it is only a verb devouring a noun after all in essence Action using up Energy. If the actions of your solid body are to manifest solidly you continually give off & take in solid matter otherwise solid energy . . .

Now the best attitude toward life is this—You are conscious of characteristics which do not vary these are your connection with the general illusion which rules this part of your real being. It is silly to dignify these rulers by calling them by names associated with God because they are all limited & it is no better to be limited on a large scale than it is on a small scale. Illusion has its law & your root illusion has a law you call the law of your being which gives you all your characteristics tastes.

Behind law is liberation & liberation implies your being has no law but desires nothing desire is law & binds more firmly than chains desire nothing & you are unborn.

Will nothing & you are all things in the twinkling of an eye. Desire is always for what we are not, have not, cannot do. If we can do all, have all, be all, we desire nothing . . .

The truth seems that a sense of humour has caused the human race to develop a capacity for looking on at itself & judging itself as it were dispassionately & from the outsider it is to some extent aware of its grotesque pretentions & its absurd performances. It notices its awkwardness; its ugliness; its screaching voices, like a chorus of starlings . . . Then it laughs & shrugs its shoulders & writes a comic song . . . God to think I belong to this race of fools! . . . I see all its absurdity I laugh at myself for my vanities—yet I let them seize me & carry me down the stream of Time instead of remaining in the Lake of Eternity. I become a phantom & think I exist as a miserable little puppet—and I do all this because I have a silly fatheaded thought somewhere in the background that I should get lost somehow if I abandoned it. I should not get lost—I am lost & the only way to get found is to abandon it. There is the whole glory of God waiting for me to put out my feeble candle so that I may see it & yet I don't. I hear a postman now & I think I'll go see if there is a letter for me. I expect nothing—I am a rather elderly woman with no prospect of anything more than a momentary gratification & yet I labour & toil instead of leading a peaceful life as I might quite easily on £50 a year. I think I can do something in the world—I've tried to get people to speak beautifully but not a soul sees the truth any clearer for all I have said & written. I cannot see it myself clearly enough. Half baked people like Yeats & Shaw have tremendous influence & yet they only tell half truths.

They are thorough as far as they go & I see further than I can be thorough. Mrs. Besant is thorough.

But if I was thorough I shouldn't exist in this place at all.

If you feel that cease to exist on this plane & you will fulfil the law of your being. You are not sincere.

Oh yes I am—I never pretend to be better than I am.

You are too versatile.

Rubbish, one can't be too versatile.

Versatility & wit are the gifts of the most advanced souls.

Wit is only an artificial juxtaposition of the incongrous. It is a poor sport very easy to practise.

Versatility is the result of want of thoroughness & the want of the faculty of mastering your means of expression.

I don't believe in all this becoming.
Then don't become. Being never changes.
Sit still & watch the Gods Become Struggle & Achieve.
They are your faculties let them work.
They are your Wisdoms let them know.
They are your Beauties let them perfect.
You are unchangeable. We are what? . . .
I'd better leave off I don't think I'm getting any good now.
Farewell.

NOTES

1 Jayanta Padmanabha, 'In Memorium Florence Farr Emery', *The Ceylon Daily News,* (April 30 1947).
2 W.B. Yeats, *Autobiographies,* 81, 82.
3 National Library, Dublin.
4 Ellic Howe, *The Magicians of the Golden Dawn,* (London 1972). Mr. Howe graciously permitted me to work from his proof copy. I am, therefore, unable to quote page numbers.
5 See Israel Regardie, *The Golden Dawn,* (Wisconsin 1970).
6 Chesterton, *Autobiography,* 144-45.
7 Francis King, *Astral Projection Magic and Alchemy,* (London 1971), 149-50
8 Note from Lolly Yeats attached to a programme of *The Countess Cathleen,* courtesy Michael B. Yeats.
9 Collection of Gerald Yorke and courtesy of Ellic Howe. Hereafter, information obtained from the MSS of Mr. Yorke will be listed as GY. These documents were passed on to me by way of Mr. Howe.
10 GY.
11 Yeats, *op. cit.,* 349.
12 Bax, *op. cit.,* 118.
13 Academic Centre, University of Texas.
14 GY.
15 GY.
16 GY.
17 Bax, *op. cit.,* 10.
18 GY.
19 GY.
20 UL, (August 5 1897).
21 GY.

22 GY.
23 GY.
24 Aleister Crowley, *The Confessions of Aleister Crowley,* Vol.
One, (London 1929).
25 Crowley, *Moonchild,* (London 1929), 152
26 Autograph Inscription.
27 King, *Ritual Magic in England,* (London 1970), 202.
28 Crowley, *Confessions,* 138-39.
29 Farr, *Modern Woman,* 29-30.
30 Crowley, *op. cit.,* 279.
31 GY.
32 GY.
33 GY.
34 GY.
35 The Pennsylvania State University, (1899).
36 GY.
37 GY.
38 Courtesy of John Kelly, Eric Domville and Sir Rupert Hart-Davis.
39 Courtesy William M. Murphy.
40 *Equinox,* (London), I, no. 8. 61.
41 Padmanabha, *op. cit.*

6

The Music of Speech
1890-1906

The proud and careless notes live on,
But bless our hands that ebb away.[1]

The friendship did not end when Bernard Shaw abandoned his love affair with Florence but her neglect of the Drama for magic and her collaboration with Willie Yeats in a 'New Art' never ceased to arouse his annoyance.

Not long after the first performance of the *Idyll* at Bedford Park, Yeats became enchanted with making his poetry a garden for magical thought. With Florence his chosen instrument, he embarked upon a life-time of mingling musical notes with words 'So artfully that all the Art's but Speech/Delighted with its own music'.[2] His idea was to revive the lost art of speaking instead of silent reading of poetry and to put its audiences into trance-like states, much in the way of the invocations and intonements in the Golden Dawn ceremonies.

During Florence's first attempts with Yeats to provide a renaissance in poetry speaking, Maud Gonne listened to her 'strange chants'[3] in the poet's rooms. There were many occasions when a circle of ladies sat on the floor there while Yeats held court and Florence plucked at a single string of a crude instrument, seemingly designed by the poet.[4] But he being tone-deaf, and she merely an amateur musician, the neophytes soon

> wandered into the wood of error; we tried speaking through music in the ordinary way under I know not whose evil influence, until we got to hate the two competing tunes and rhythms that were so often at discord with one another, the tune and rhythm of the verse and the tune and rhythm of the music.[5]

Aware of their lack of proficiency, Yeats and Florence found their way in the second part of the 1890's to Arnold Dolmetsch, a performer of old English music and a restorer of ancient musical instruments. A coterie of artists and writers, Arthur Symons, Swinburne, Sturge Moore, Laurence Binyon brought their ideas to the musician and he became 'capable of illustrating their words with sympathetic music, or rather of crystallizing the latent music enshrined in them'.[6]

Yeats and his 'muse', as Mabel Dolmetsch, the musician's third wife referred to Florence, were frequent visitors to Dolmetsch's Sunday night concerts at Charlotte Street. There their trials ended when he described to them an instrument, 'half-lyre half-psaltery', Yeats called it, for the monodic accompaniment of verse. Soon, Dolmetsch designed for Florence the 'first modern psaltery' and she and the poet came to him often thereafter for instruction. Yeats was concerned with quarter notes believing them to be comparable to the natural inflections of the speaking voice, but Dolmetsch tuned the thirteen strings to semi-tones. Florence was urged to pitch her 'golden voice,' Dolmetsch called it, to a chromatic scale and to use the vibrating strings to subtly complement her rich, low vocal tones. At first she spoke her notes to the stave of the old C clef in which the central line as it is written today corresponds to the middle C of the piano. Before long, she worked in another way.

> Within the limits of an octave of semitones I set to work to discover and write down the inherent melody of a number of poems. I reduced everything connected with the art to the simplest possible terms, and used letters to indicate the notes of my scale, G indicating below and .G above the central C. I then spoke the first line of a poem in the most impressive way that occurred to me, and immediately after sang and wrote down the notes I found I had used as starting points for the spoken word . . . I do not chant . . . or use the singing voice except in refrains . . . I simply speak as I would without music, and having discovered the drift of my voice in the phrase, indicate that on the psaltery.[7]

Her early work, without rhythmic stress or definite melodic patterns seem almost weird to a Western ear sensitive to rhythmic and tonal resolutions. Yeats, who yearned for a little more dash, often questioned the monotony of the music's schematic void. Yet, the simplicity of her inflexible system of notations, inflexible because once set the notes could never vary with an added insight of interpretation to a poem, held a promise for him that speakers of his poetry would learn the notes with the poems. Careless readers would then lose their license to ignore the inherent melody in his verses and to speak them with the inflections of daily, extraneous common speech. The young poet pretended to individual sensibility within the dogmatic structure but in essence, the Art demanded from its interpreters an adherence to style more than to sense. This is of course what the Magicians preferred.

Matter, concerns us for a little time but style concerns us for all time. And style is the appreciation of phrases as melodies, not merely as the expression of thought. The Vedantists tell us that sound is the elemental correspondence of etheric spaces, the root of measurable things. And our hearing and our speech, the part of the mind that receives impression, can all be resolved into the element of sound—the strange grey world of sound, flashing or detonating; imperceptibly subduing and mastering, or roaring maledictions upon us, gasping in ecstasy or choking in death, thousand-tongued.

The mystery of sound is made manifest in words and in music . . . we are overwhelmed by the chatter of those who profane it, and the din of the traffic of the restless disturbs the peace of those who are listening for the old magic, and watching till the new creation is heralded by the sound of the new word.[8]

The idée fixé belonged to Florence but the message it contained moulded Yeats's concept for a literary theatre. One of the prime elements in his excitement for the poetic drama was this absorption with sound, and by 1898 he was to see some fulfillment for the New Art. That year the Irish Literary Theatre had been consummated with his *Countess Cathleen* slotted for the first production. Uppermost in the society's programme was the production each year of 'one or two plays dealing with Irish subjects, or reflecting Irish ideas and sentiments'. Use of the word 'literary' implied that the theatre was to be without commercial objectives; fostering the 'higher intellectual and artistic interests in the country'.[9]   Several years had elapsed since Yeats's visits to Dalling Road when he promised himself to write poetic plays for Florence. Presently, his production in limbo, he was able to appoint her general stage manager for the Society. There were several members or Patrons she had not encountered in the formative years of the theatre's organization in London. One of these was Edward Martyn, an Irish landlord and playwright of independent means who planned to place his *Heather Field* on the same bill with the *Countess Cathleen*. Yeats arranged to introduce him to Florence with W.B.'s friend Lady Gregory joining the discussion. Then, in early 1899, plans were made for the stage manager to meet formally Martyn's friend George Moore, an ostensible promoter and sponsor in the young theatre. 'It was very amusing', W.B.Y. informed Lady Gregory from Paris:

> Moore began with hostility but softened so remarkably that he kept urging her to come to dinner with him to discuss the thing, and she kept suggesting that Martyn might be asked too — not thinking a dinner alone with Moore desirable — and he kept saying 'I tell you he knows no more about managing a theatre than a turbot from the North Pole.' That dinner will not come off. Moore used to be always abusing Mrs. Emery and her acting. He called her 'the woman with the big nose,' she says.[10]

The production imminent, Yeats changed his plans for Florence to train Irish amateurs how to speak his verses. They had been over to Dublin, more than likely to look over potential performers, and Florence was left with the opinion that 'there are none or very few pretty girls in Dublin compared with London.'[11] John Butler Yeats said that his son and Florence imagined 'London is crowded with beautiful actresses and capable actors, the supply far exceeding the demand, so that if they only search they cannot fail to find suitable people'.[12] Florence was spare in her estimation of Ireland. After one particular visit, J.B.Y. said she was only impressed by a 'round tower and some ancient eaves. These Londoners have no eyes for natural beauties'.[13]

Much to Florence's displeasure, the rehearsals in London for Yeats's *Countess Cathleen* were satirised in later years by George Moore in *Ave*. Throughout his commentary, he confuses her identity with 'Miss Vernon', a deliberate slight to Florence and to Yeats's intimate friend Olivia Shakespear. (Yeats wrote of her as Diana Vernon.) Moore's account has Martyn rushing to him to solicit professional guidance. Rehearsals for the *Heather Field* were going poorly and he was frankly fearful that Yeats's play would come off to greater advantage. Moore, reluctant to associate himself with the poet and Martyn, 'the queer pair, united for a moment in a common cause', was affronted that the actors rehearsed at the Bijou, rather than at a more fashionable theatre. Nevertheless, Martyn prevailed upon his friend to take some definite action. Rushing him to Bayswater, they found the two collaborators in the bun shop instead of the theatre 'talking continually of the speaking of verse.' It was not long before Moore took control and engaged May Whitty to play the Countess Cathleen, the part Yeats had written for Maud Gonne. Dorothy Paget had been especially taken out of school by her parents to join the company and now Moore quickly relieved her of her lines. He insisted that one of the fairies would do for her instead remarking, 'You'll look enchanting in a blue veil.'

The rehearsals eventually moved to the Strand where Yeats and Florence held up progress by their illustrations of The Music of Speech. Worse, the 'lady in the green cloak' sat on the floor plucking her stringed instrument muttering, 'cover it up with a lonely tune.' May Whitty 'walked to and fro like a pantheress' waiting for Florence to produce some practical stage directions but the latter could never interpret her own notes. Miss Whitty watched in contempt while Florence evaded the issue of the stage directions and lay on the floor again speaking through the cracks. She explained that her dramatic intention was to evoke hell, but she looked for all the world, Moore said, as if she were 'trying to catch cockroaches.'

Martyn's and Yeats's plays opened at the Antient Concert Rooms in Brunswick Street, Yeats's play to run 8, 12, 13 May with a matinée on the tenth, and Martyn's 9, 10 May and a matinée on the thirteenth. Lollie Yeats came to Dublin for a week to see the performances and later made a note about Florence.

> Aleil was played by Mrs. Emery, i.e. Florence Farr...When we knew Florence first she was then Mrs. Emery. Her husband was out of the story. He was a very bad hat — brother in law [a mistake] of Winifred Emery well known actress.[14]

The reviews of Yeats's play are now a familiar story. Denounced in *The Irish Times* on 9 May as a failure in dramatic action, characterization, and plot, the elocution was cited as being far from satisfactory. Yeats had managed to speak to the *Irish Daily Independent's* critic before the production so that the latter found the New Art worked well.

> The great charm of the acting was the manner in which the music of the poem was preserved. The rhythmic beat and cadence of the verse stole on the ears like music sweetly played . . .Miss Florence Farr was a charming Aleel. Her's is the best delivery of verse that we have heard upon the modern stage; and Miss Dorothy Paget, who was the Sheogue, also spoke the prologue tastefully.

(Lionel Johnson, Olivia Shakespear's cousin, had written the prologue for the opening performance and Dorothy had been partially reinstated.)

There were attacks elsewhere on Yeats's use of blasphemous language in the dialogue and his seeming denial of patriotism, but the venture was successful enough to plan a future production; the young playwright looked forward to producing the *Shadowy Waters* in London in the Autumn. His wish to do a little play that could be 'acted and half chanted' betrayed his near obsession with the occult and its influence on his work. 'This is really a magical revolution; for the magical word is the chanted word. The new Shadowy Waters could be acted on two big tables in a drawing room' he expressed to A.E. [15]

By July the Irish Literary Theatre decided that its second production would be in Dublin. Edward Martyn informed Florence from Tillyra Castle, Ardrahan, County Galway that an agreement had been made to use the Gaiety Theatre. George Coffey, a barrister and guarantor of the Literary Theatre, had looked into the contract and foresaw no liability on the part of the Society unless it failed to meet its responsibilities. Martyn was seeking Florence's signature as the I.L.T. representative.

I think you are the proper person to sign and enter into an agreement as you are a professional & manager of . . . concern. On the other hand I agree to hold you free from all liability as regards those £200 if you should be liable to pay them . . . At the same time I would ask you not to sign this agreement until such time as they force us to definitely settle about the theatre. At present the date is only pencilled. And you had better keep it like that as long as you can. We have not yet got in any of those plays that have been promised to us, nor shall we until I think September. Of course I have two plays *Maeve* and *The Tale of a Town* but I dread the experience of *Maeve*.[16]

Yeats looked forward to the production at the Gaiety with discontent. Since he and George Moore were rewriting Martyn's *A Tale of the Town* he was especially anxious to shape the mind of the press. The original author had been carelessly abusing the play in public conversation and word had reached Florence via Coffey. Fearful that Martyn's opinion was just, the problem was 'depressing her energy', Yeats wrote to Lady Gregory. On account of it, she was depressing others. Abetting her bleak spirits were the fractious 'children of clay' in the Golden Dawn and soon after the production of *The Bending of the Bough* (Martyn's play was retitled and Moore actually appeared as the author) on 19 February 1900, she was involved in the Golden Dawn schism. Then came Yeats's desperate attempts to set matters right between S.S.D.D. and Annie Horniman. His sentiments for Florence were now secondary to his desire for Annie's financial support.

I tell you now, in strict confidence, that I have been approached by a group of artists and writers with a view to a theatre of art. . . I know through long experience that practical work is an endless waste of time, unless everybody carries out their promise, in serious matters, with the most scrupulous care for the letter and spirit alike.[17]

The disagreement between Yeats and his stage manager seemed barely to affect their continued collaboration in the New Art to which they were virtually addicted. In all fairness to Yeats for his devoted interest in Florence, it is also reasonable to realise that he took every opportunity in their lectures and performances together to promote the Irish Theatre. The following letter is not dated but it is probably during those cavalier years of the Literary Theatre's emergence that the poet asked Florence to come to Dublin for a lecture. 'Please answer at once—How much could you come for?'

The Nat. Literary Society asked me to lecture on the Psaltery, & bring you over. I do not want to lecture on it again in Dublin & they have accepted my offer to lecture on the following subject 'The ideal of Manhood in heroic and folk literature.'

You would chant the Emer lamentations perhaps the Morte d'Arthur lament. One or two joyful bits of heroic poetry which I will find you.

Mrs. Coffey, wife of the barrister, was going to put Florence up which brought from Yeats some mild sarcasm concerning the condescending attitude of the group. 'Isn't this civil & humble on the part of the Nat. Lit. Society?'[18]

In October of 1901, Arnold Dolmetsch completed a new psaltery for Florence that she and W.B.Y. had ordered to be made especially for her 'rather low' speaking voice. By then she had moved to 67 The Grove, Hammersmith, an abundantly tree-lined street with a massive holly bush in the front garden of 67. It was a cheerful, decorative, four storey house with wrought iron balconies and trim; one of several, identical structures on the pleasant road. Dolmetsch wrote to Florence here from the complex of small cottages where he had moved his entourage from Charlotte Street After 'many tribulations', the psaltery was perfectly satisfactory, and he wanted to have a 'long talk' about it. Florence evidently went to Boveney, near Windsor to pick up her instrument with Elodie, the Frenchman's current wife, fetching her from the station by pony.[19]

Dolmetsch had spent ten pounds on the psaltery whereas Florence thought it would only cost four. Unsure how she would pay the sum, Yeats decided to write an article for a review and to prepare a lecture to get her out of the difficulty. In November, Florence paid 'part of the money by performance of a very amateurish Egyptian play rather nicely.'

By then, Arnold Dolmetsch had given his approval of Florence's 'chanting'. Joyously, Yeats wrote to Lady Gregory that he could now make a perfect record of Florence's work. In 1902 he made good his promise in an essay entitled 'Speaking to the Psaltery'. It would be a considerable addition to the new edition of *The Celtic Twilight,* he told Lady Gregory, 'but in any case a necessity that I may launch Mrs. Emery.' The article appeared first in the *Monthly Review* in May and later became part of a four page collection of *Lectures by Mr. W.B.Yeats on poetry and the Living Voice Illustrated by Miss Florence Farr,* printed by Farncombe & Son, Croydon.

Yeats's words may strike a reader as if he had that instant discovered a new art. Instead, they represent an idea that had taken over a decade to perfect.

> I have just heard a poem spoken with so delicate a sense of its rhythm, with so perfect respect for its meaning, that if I were a wise man and could persuade a few people to learn the art, I would never open a book of verses again. . . I, at any rate, from this out mean to write all my longer poems for the stage, and all my shorter ones for the psaltery, if only some strong angel keep me to my resolution.[20]

That year, private and public audiences gathered at Clifford's Inn in Fleet Street for the Westminster Lectures. In May, three lectures were announced: Tuesday 5 May at 8.45 p.m. 'Recording the Music of Speech', 'Heroic and Folk Literature', Tuesday 12 May at the same time; and Friday 29 May at 5 p.m. 'Poetry and The Living Voice'.

William Archer, Arthur Symons, Laurence Binyon, Charles Ricketts, Charles Shannon, Granville Barker, and Bernard Shaw were among those who listened to Yeats extoll his theories of recitation. Florence then chanted poems by Shakespeare, Shelley, Keats, Blake, Rossetti, Walt Whitman, Lionel Johnson, Robert Louis Stevenson while she and Dorothy Paget and her sister Gladys played their psalteries.

On Tuesday 10 June at 8.45, Yeats delivered a new lecture, 'Speaking to Musical Notes'. When Florence asked Swinburne if she might perform scenes from his *Atalanta in Calydon* that day, the poet replied, 'No compliment could be more gratifying. It is not for me to give leave but to return thanks'.[21]

For the most part, the critics present at these gatherings were close friends and so obliged Yeats by their reviews. They argued between themselves whether there was structure or symmetry to Florence's system, whether it was not the poetry 'buoyed up' which had been more effective than the poetry itself. Yet, Archer admitted that Florence had possibly 'hit on something very like a new art.'[22] Arthur Symons thought that Mr. Yeats's method was useful in teaching a reader to 'unlearn something and to learn something more, but not for making verse live on the stage'.[23]   The general attitude of recognition by the critics annoyed Bernard Shaw. A firm believer in 'athletic articulation', he stuck to the adage 'take care of the consonants and the vowels will take care of themselves'. Although in 1891 he had encouraged his amorata to 'prithee persevere with the speaking', in 1902 he refused to involve himself with her 'cantilationary polemics'. Thoroughly disgusted that Yeats was 'heaping fresh artificialities and irrelevances. . .' Shaw reminded Florence he had been unable to 'knock enough articulation' into her during their teaching bouts.

Her final consonants 'withered,' and worse, the sense of her readings disappeared while she attended to the mechanics of the psaltery; at such moments, G.B.S. felt moved to throw things at her. Athletic articulation and intellectual conviction were the only rules, he said, for making speech tolerable.

> Without it cantilation can do nothing except intensify ordinary twadling into a nerve destroying crooning like the maunderings of an idiot-banshee. Remember that even in singing, it is an Irish defect to lose grip and interest by neglecting the music. Cats do the same thing when they are serenading one another; but the genuineness of their emotion gives them poignancy.[24]

Yeats called the lectures a 'great success'; people standing and many who could not get into the Inn. £22 worth of tickets went on one occasion and more might have been sold if there had been courage between the collaborators to rent a larger hall. Florence spent the proceeds on new psalteries 'and on charming dresses for our troubadors to speak in.'

Because the emotional relationship between Florence and Willie Yeats was not always commensurate with their small success, his 'muse', on occasion, could make the poet extremely piqued. Early in 1903 he invited friends of the Terrys' to Woburn Buildings who wanted to hear Florence at her best, 'and out of sheer laziness she gave the worst performance on the psaltery I have ever heard. There are times when she makes me despair of the whole thing'.[25]

G.K. Chesterton provided a dubious send-off for a lecture Florence proposed to deliver with Yeats in Manchester in May. W.B. was always careful in the future to delete certain remarks from the article, but Florence, I think, quite enjoyed them. If, G.K. wrote, Yeats believed that poetry should be recited again for the multitude as in the days of yore, let Florence take her 'shawn or sackbut . . . into third class carriages and combine ecstasy with emolument.' Moreover, let Yeats 'go and intone in public houses,' where anything would be appreciated with a 'lilt.'

Florence and the poet arrived in the North 18 May for 'The Speaking of Poetry to Musical Notes.' At Whitworth Hall in Owens College, the performers met with an audience who questioned the relevancy of reviving a primitive art in a sophisticated age. After a generally 'mournful' performance by Florence the poet confirmed their method by his wish for poetry to leave its 'dead words upon dead paper.' Then came his true *raison d'etre,* that the 'poetic spirit [will] not give peace on earth, but a sword fitter than a plough for the hand of the Celtic aristocracy which shall revive and keep alive the heroic traditions of the race'[26] — a blunt admission when, ostensibly, he planned a National Theatre for a hypothetical, democratic audience.

There was an amusing aftermath to the lecture which may not have been known to its participants. Their engagement occured in the same week as an eminent German professor speaking on the Daltonian Atomic Theory. A child attending school in Brunswick Street

a pool wherein the heavens of Owens College find reflection . . . was asked if she knew what the Atomic Theory was:—'O, yes: we know! It is speaking to music or something of that kind. Miss Farr does it.'

Herein the associative psychologist may find mental nourishment.[27]

Back in London, in pocket for her share of the £20 for the lecture, Shaw asked Florence to copyright his *Man and Superman.* It was 'frightfully long, the first and third acts longer than *Hamlet.* 'Cutting is permissable provided enough is performed to leave the unperformed parts useless to pirates.' Florence sent the text to the Examiner of plays, George Alexander Redford to read before its performance at the Bijou in Bayswater. Recently returned from taking the waters in Bourne, he had hoped, he wrote Florence, to find a haven of rest at his hotel (Grand Central) in London,

but Mr. Bernard Shaw's flood of words (very witty and entertaining no doubt) threatens to overwhelm me. I should require a fortnight on a high mountain to fairly master 'Man and Superman'. I have already devoted a few of my precious hours (I am paying two house rents, and a hotel bill) in an endeavour to satisfy myself that at least the piece does not belong in the 'unpleasant' series. I have had to skip the very lengthy, but most entertaining stage directions, and perhaps by judicious skimming of the dialogue, which I should greatly enjoy on the top of Snowden, I may be able before Thursday to send the usual informal letter to Victoria Hall. But life is really too short and certainly the 'at least 7 days' is not long enough, and you cut me short of my allowance.[28]

Toward the end of 1903, Yeats left for an American lecture tour largely through the encouragement of the Irish-American lawyer, John Quinn. The poet's visit coincided with rehearsals of *The King's Threshold* for a National Theatre Society performance. In a tribute to Florence and to her New Art, and to the local Dublin actor Frank Fay 'the most beautiful verse speaker I know—at least you and Mrs. Emery compete together. . .' the play opened with the verses

> I welcome you that have the mastery
> Of the two kinds of Music: the one kind
> Being like a woman, the other like a man
> Both you that understand stringed instruments,
> And how to mingle words and notes together
> So artfully that all the Art's but Speech
> Delighted with its own music;. . .

Florence had written the music for *Cathleen ni Houlihan* which was to appear on the same programme with *The King's Threshold*. In the States in December, Yeats wrote to Lady Gregory from Bryn Mawr asking her to urge Florence to write a note on the way to speak the poems in the play. 'Please revise her style — she won't mind.' The note was prepared for Bullen's edition of Yeats's plays but the publisher decided against using it. Yeats wrote in the following January that it didn't matter; 'indeed the note has disappointed me; it is too meagre to mean anything. . .'

A letter from Bernard Shaw to Florence in April 1904 makes it clear she was anxious to establish the New Art on a more permanent basis than the lectures with Yeats permitted. Shaw, always practical as far as Florence's livelihood was concerned, harped on his old notion that she should study phonetics and then associate herself with Sir Herbert Tree (a model, later, for his Professor Higgins) in his new school of drama. G.B.S. really debunked the 'Dramatic School stuff' in favour of 'scientific training for actors', but he was sure that if Tree's experiment turned into something of permanence, Florence, with the proper background, could 'make an original and solid and lasting place' as a teacher of phonetics. Florence's personal regard for the actor-manager was ambivalent but her opinion of his work is valuable. The contents of the following are especially germane to an account of the years when she was speaking to the psaltery, as well as their reflection of her growing sensivity toward the Dramatic Art. Without any doubt, they show how Yeats's dramatic version fed from her own.

Now I enjoy magnificence and wealth and every kind of grandeur as much as an Asiatic does; but I don't want to bother with European poetry at the same time. I may not be sufficiently complex but while I am enjoying a spectacle I cannot listen to literature enough to appreciate it. Instead of poetry I should like to hear weird musical instruments. I should like to see a dumb show of diabolical wickedness and intolerable sorrow in magnificent surroundings. But I do not want to listen to the music of a violin or the music of the poets or to any great literature in the midst of lights and constant music. . . . As a matter of temperament my whole attention must be concentrated on one perfect art and not scattered on a thousand luxurious details if I am to feel any keen aesthetic emotion . . . The Tree Tradition seems to me a little too continuously magnificent. As a room with patterns on the walls, on the carpets, on the ceilings and the curtains, makes us long for a plain space, a stretch of polished wood or white washed wall; so I long for dim shadows and for more of the famous black velvet curtains Mr. Tree provided as the background of Hades, when, as Ulysees, Mr. Tree visited that region. . . .I do not think Mr. Tree, and those producers of comic opera who try to follow in his footsteps, realise the value of the plain and the simple as a contrast to the ornate pattern. Just as the decoration of India pleases us less than the decoration of Japan because the Japanese recognise the power of deprivation in contrast to satiety, so Mr. Tree's sumptuous productions please us less than they would if he took a hint from Japan and gave us a contrast such as voices unaccompanied by visions every now and again.[29]

Florence did not become a teacher of phonetics with Tree. Shaw's proposal would have involved a two year confinement with Henry Sweet at Oxford who, Shaw said, had 'a genius for making everything impossible for himself and everybody else'.

In May, Florence had her first opportunity since the Egyptian plays in 1902 to apply her New Art to the London stage. Granville Barker, a young man of the theatre, was directing Gilbert Murray's translation of *The Hippolytus of Euripides* for The New Century Theatre at the Lyric. Florence composed the music for the play and led the Chorus in another effort to 'tickle the palate of the play-house gourmet with what is caviare' to the general public. William Archer who attended the dress rehearsal thought Florence's compositions were 'strikingly beautiful', but he did wish for a little more firmness of attack in your pupils. Your own voice comes out beautifully in the solo passages. Once or twice it seemed to me, when you were not doing anything, as if you let your attention wander & were not *in* the scene.

Perhaps it was 'merely due to the hundred distractions of a dress-rehearsal', but Florence wore 'an almost indefinable matter of expression'.[30]

Yeats probably attended the last of the four matinées on Friday 3 June with Lady Gregory. He suggested meeting her at the box office 'about 2.40 or 2.45. Do not take a ticket as I will try to change my 7/6 ticket for two 5/- seats'.[31]

The production at the Lyric foreshadowed the burgeoning of yet another young theatre of ideas which was to give Florence an opportunity to practice the New Art. This new venture at the Court Theatre was dedicated to audiences not expecting to find the 'austere dignity' of the Lyceum, or the 'fat laughs and easy tears at Toole's'. Instead, Florence said, its objective was to make the most 'inveterate woolgatherer' come to an opinion or two 'even if it had to turn him upside down and shake him in order to do so.' She was aware that her own efforts in similar theatres of ideas had failed because, as Archer put it, ventures like the Ibsen Campaign, The Independent, the Avenue, etc., attempted to interest 'clever people' but never got in touch with the public, Then came along Granville Barker. No-one, Florence remembered, worked as hard as this young man during the first years at the Court. He rehearsed from 11 to 3, saw to production details from 4 till 7, acted from 8 to 11, and often in three matinées a week. He even wrote plays at odd moments. 'The clever young man produced plays for clever people, found out clever authors, and with the clever assistance of Mr. Vedrenne, collected clever audiences'.[32]

The season at the Court opened with Shaw's *Candida* in April and May, 1904. In October, Barker's productions continued with a second run of Gilbert Murray's *Hippolytus*. Actually the tiny stage at the Court robbed the production of the 'solemn aloofness' it had achieved at the larger Lyric. As for Florence's Chorus:

the words were undoubtedly better heard — largely — no doubt because the Court is so small . . . [Florence's] art of speaking to natural notes of a phrase is I think so difficult & delicate as to be apparently incommunicable. As you do it you make it beautiful and poignant — when the rest attempt it I feel doubtful as to the whole technique & I begin to doubt also whether it is the magic of your voice that allures me.[33]

At another time, Jane Ellen Harrison, Fellow and Lecturer in

Classical Archaeology at Newnham College, Cambridge wondered if Florence's method was 'speech half asleep or song half awake', and where she dreamed and wavered, her Chorus fumbled and blundered 'in sheer ineptitude'. The obvious failure to place her work in the main-stream of art forced Florence to confess in her diary: 'I've tried to get people to speak beautifully but not a soul sees the truth any clearer for all I have said and written'.

Florence, however, thought the play at the Court succeeded to 'a certain extent'. The Chorus might have shown to better advantage if someone had thought to place them in the orchestra stalls and if the cost to remove them were not prohibitive. Neither, she regretted, had anyone dreamed of engaging Isadora Duncan to lead the dance songs. She thought very highly of the American dancer and although Florence was generally 'indifferent to gossip', she was 'expedient' enough to think it was 'stupid' of Miss Duncan to keep speaking about her illegitimate children when 'society was trying to take her up.' But if the play at the Court had failed it was really because there was not enough 'homespun' in the 'clever people' producing the Greek tragedy.

> When they take to the antique they forget that time has rubbed the paint off the statues; but for all that they had plenty of colour originally and were by no means of such pure white marble as the shepherds of our minds would have us believe.[34]

Shaw's *John Bull's Other Island* followed *Hippolytus* in November and it was the turning point, Florence said, for real success at the Court. Yeats had asked G.B.S. to write the play for his Irish Theatre, and it was almost as if the piece, it seemed to Florence, answered all the Anglo-Irish problems.

> The Irish had been annoying Londoners for a number of years; nobody quite knew why they made themselves unpleasant; but after seeing Mr. Shaw's play they felt the whole thing was most satisfactorily explained for all parties concerned. After that success was certain at the Court Theatre for anything Mr. Shaw liked to write.[35]

As far as Yeats was concerned, it was 'fundamentally ugly and shapeless', and since he was an advocate of the short play, far too long; it began at 2.30 and did not end till 6 p.m.

Following Shaw's success, Florence played in the fourth Vedrenne-Barker production, Maeterlinck's *Aglavaine and Selysette*. Presented at 2.30 matinées 15, 17, 18, 22, 24, and 25 November, Walter Hampden played the singular male role and Florence, Meligraine. It was 'curious, unreal, mystical, very well acted.'

How typical that when Florence might have been vitally absorbed in her role at the Court, in the middle of the run she wrote the passage in her diary:

I have had a day of Peace and Meditation after months of disturbed life in the exterior. . . . I hear a postman now and I think I'll go and see if there is a letter for me. I expect nothing — I am rather an elderly woman with no great prospect of anything in the world that could give me more than a momentary gratification. . .

In 1905, Florence was busy with a production of her own, a masque she copyrighted in August 1904 with Shaw's *How He Lied To Her Husband*.[36] On 17 January she booked the Albert Hall for a 'very curious' programme. At 5 p.m. she read from Carmen Sylva, Dr. Douglas Hyde, Gilbert Murray, and Dante Rossetti. The Masque, *The Mystery of Time* followed. Borrowing from G.B.S.'s method of dramaturgy, which she really despised, Florence had written a lengthy preface to her play explaining the gist of her introspections.

I suppose that there are thousands of people in England and as many elsewhere, who are trying in one way or another, to learn that ancient art, taught by the wise from the beginning of recorded time, the Art of Guiding the Mind. And those who study it, from whatever point of view, find that it gradually absorbs the very life of the Devotee, so that he lives in it alone.
I have imagined a discipline in which the struggle has been to fix the mind on that imperceptible point of Time called The Present . . . and I have imagined personification of those two attributes of human consciousness (The Past and the Future) to be terrified because they see the mind of the Devotee melting into the state beyond Mind in which the Past and the Future have no part.
That state I have endeavoured to suggest by the words:—'I stood naked in a bleak and dark eternity and filled it with my exaltation.'

Satisfying her concept of a theatre of suggestion which she initiated in the Egyptian plays, Florence avoided any stage setting beyond a single throne. It was an additional opportunity for Yeats to visualise the sort of symbolic theatre he had put into words in 1899: a theatre of 'austere and grave costumes and scenery, that we may appeal to the imagination alone'.
Lewis Casson, Sybil Thorndike's husband, played the Present, Archibald McLean, the Past, Gwendolen Bishop, the Future, and Gwendolen Paget, the wife of one of H.M. Paget's brothers, provided the 'too modern' music. The dialogue certainly betrayed the whole matter of its author's dilemma.

| The Present | The supreme desire is to be without desire. . . Seek the imperishable while the tides of life are on the flood. Then they carry you beyond all mortal hope. For those who wait for the dark time of feeble will can only sink and drown. |

The Past   Is the goal Truth?

The Present   She is burned up in Being. The Gods may labour in the fields of Time but I remain. The ten winds may sweep through Space, but the dust returns to its own place.

The Past and The Future   What is this Mystery.

The Present   The smallest of the small is the greatest of the great.

The Past   What is the smallest thing that is so wonderful.

The Present   That smallest thing is NOW, for eternity is found in it . . . Where I am there is no Fear. All life is mine; all possession is a burden; for I see time as it is and am at Peace.

During the third part of the programme, Florence recited poems by Yeats before doing some of Shaw's maxims. The playwright's presentation copy to her of *Man and Superman* has, in Florence's writing, notations above the maxims on pages 242 and 243. These are very likely the ones she used to provide a marvellous spoof of Shaw and to adhere to her own maxim that 'Apollo's lyre should be alternated with the pipes of Dionysus and the rollicking fun of nymphs and satyrs.' From the Revolutionist's Handbook:

G   B   D
The reformer for whom the world is not good enough finds himself
  Eb   D   Bb
shoulder to shoulder with him that is not good enough for the
  G
world.
  D   Db   D
Every man over forty is a scoundrel
(Common chords from G)
  G   F Eb   D   C   G   C
Youth which is forgiven everything, forgives itself nothing;
  Ab   Eb   D   C
Age, which forgives itself everything, is forgiven nothing.[38]
  The month after the Albert Hall programme, and sometime before

or after Florence lectured with Yeats at Leeds and Liverpool, Shaw communicated with her about the 'Philanderer affair'. He was under the impression it was to be put on for some charity, and instead, it was turning out to be a 'sort of Junior Stage Society'. Florence was scheduled to stage-manage; 'so much the better', Shaw wrote, 'I will go down with you and start the affair — arrange the business etc'.[39] The 'Junior Stage Society' was actually The New Stage Club which produced Shaw's play on Monday night, 20 February at the Cripplegate Institute, Golden Lane. Gwendolen Bishop was presently cast as Grace Tranfield, the character modelled on Florence, and Louise Salom on Julia or Jenny Patterson. Millicent Murby played Julia's sister, Sylvia Craven. What the real-life protagonists experienced during the retelling of that bizarre episode is, unfortunately, unrecorded.

Before April, Florence was busy with the New Art once more in her compositions for Gilbert Murray's translation of Euripides' *Trojan Woman* for the Court. Be 'very discreet' in the use of 'modern fashionable discords', Shaw warned her. In the *Hippolytus* she had rambled up and down staircases of minor thirds in a deplorable fashion.'[40] When the play opened on 11 April to run for eight matinees, Florence was working with a small chorus, divided into groups of three who alternated between reciting and intoning her 'plaintive' music. Uncharmed by the production, she thought the 'unmitigated tragedy was more than the people could bear.' How different it would have been, she said,

> if the chorus describing the taking of Troy could have been chanted as the explanation of a wild dumb show, symbolic of the Trojans over their fancied deliverance, followed by the music and dance of the festival and the grotesque horror of the final tableaux accompanied by the sound of trumpet and carnage. Instead of this the limitation of the resources obliged these deeds to become more matters of narrative recitation like the rest of the play.[41]

In what was a year of extraordinary professional accomplishment, and what must give the lie to an earlier description of her indolence, Florence began work directly after the Court production for Oscar Wilde's *Salomé*. Presently to be put on by The New Stage Club, Wilde's play for some years had met with the refusal of the Examiner of plays. Angered by its rejection, he wrote to William Rothenstein that Edward F. Smyth Pigott instead 'panders to the vulgarity and hypocrisy of the English people, by licensing every low farce and vulgar melodrama.'[42] Florence rounded up the same actors from *The Philanderer* for her cast; Mrs. Bishop, Miss Salom, and Miss

Murby who played Salome. Here was a part, Oscar Wilde told publisher Leonard Smithers, that should only be played by Sarah Bernhardt, that "serpent of the old Nile," older than the pyramids'.

Aubrey Beardsley, who had pictured *Salomé* over a decade before, was in a sense represented after his death in 1898 at the memorable production by Florence. Mabel Beardsley wrote from 48 Charlotte Street, Belgrave Road to apply for her membership of 14/6 entrance fee, 6/- subscription, and 6/- for an additional seat for a friend.

The performances, the first of *Salomé* in England, were a great success. Sturge Moore offered ecstatic congratulations for the best representation of modern life he had seen in English.

> It seems to me a veritable triumph when I consider how narrow your resources must have been. I am more especially happy in having this opportunity of expressing my sincere admiration to you as too often I have been unable in the past to add my voice to those that praised some production for which you were responsible and could not help feeling that my inability was a poor return for all your generous kindness & aid to me on various occasions.
>
> My gratitude for your production of Salome is in proportion to the keen pleasure and admiration which I felt last night and so I write to thank you with all my heart.[44]

Florence had moved to 107a Holland Road, not nearly so charming a residence as 67, The Grove, Hammersmith by the time she went into rehearsal for her next play, Yeats's *Shadowy Waters*. It was to be sponsored by the Theosophical Society for their convention on 8 July, W.B.Y. told John Quinn, and 'the Theosophists were paying the piper.' That, he made it clear, did not identify him with them in any way. (Yeats, at the time, was a member of the Stella Matutina.) Florence was playing Dectora, which the poet expected her to do very beautifully, and Robert Farquharson who had played Herod so well in *Salomé* was cast as Forgael. Yeats's rehearsal techniques were little changed since the *Countess Cathleen* and he itched to correct Farquharson's vocal tricks of running up and down the scale. Yeats was totally dissatisfied, indeed, with the whole production, his writing, the acting, in fact, all except the set constructed after a model designed by H.M. Paget. There was one encouraging comment for Florence made by a friend of the poet's after the performance: 'it was worth while having the play done, well worth while, because Mrs. Emery was a delight.'

After seeing the play in production Yeats rewrote the script and Florence's prompt copy shows how extensively both she and the poet rewrote the dialogue and stage directions even as rehearsals had progressed.[45] Plans were soon initiated for Florence to perform *The Shadowy Waters* again; this time Yeats wished her to replace Farquharson with a good speaker of verse. He thought the actor impossible as an artist and Olivia Shakespear noticed he was extremely offensive to Florence personally. Farquharson was the kind of man, Yeats remarked, whose vulgarity constantly demanded explanation. Not a little jealous, the tirade was continued to Arthur Symons with the poet explaining that the play had turned into an 'execrable' affair except for Florence and another. There was probably more said to his friend in magic about her 'marionette', as Florence referred to Farquharson, but since she preserved his letters to her it is unlikely she ceded to Yeats. A euphuistic correspondent, Farquharson gushed like a veritable geyser. For many reasons it is unlikely that there was a romantic attachment to his co-star at the Court and if the Count de la Condamine (R.F.) ever imagined himself to be a lover in life it was in Michael Field's (Miss Bradley's) company he chose to spend 'beautiful hours . . . for always your Herod.'[46]

Sometime before the end of 1905, the ever restive Florence moved again, this time to 21 Warwick Chambers, Pater Road (now Pater Street), Kensington. Pater Street is a small road between Earls Court on its right, and Abingdon Road on the left. Number 21 is in an old brick block of flats numbered from 19 to 28, the first of three attached units near to the public-house on the corner of Earls Court Road. Unchanged since Florence leased it, 21 is to the left of the staircase going up; it has a small bedroom, sitting-room, W.C., bathroom, and kitchen, with the window of the sitting-room in the rear overlooking a small garden. Sadly neglected today, the little plot of ground as well as Warwick Chambers, were probably a little jollier in 1905.

Florence was holidaying at the Staither in Bournemouth in December where Shaw's letter of the first of the month was forwarded. It contained for the most part the news that Annie Horniman had confessed the Avenue secret. On 5 December, Florence replied telling Shaw that she had arranged to associate herself in the organization of a new little theatre of poetry. Not surprisingly, after his letter of congratulations to her, Sturge Moore as well as Charles Ricketts were to be her collaborators. Her niece Dorothy Paget was off to the States on a stage tour and Florence who had planned to accompany her there had cancelled these plans in favour of the new theatre. In February, having decided to produce *Salomé* again, she wrote to

Robert Ross, the executor of Oscar Wilde's estate, to question the copyright status of the play.

While the new Literary Theatre planned for its debut, Florence briefly forsook the Music of Speech to finish a preface and an end chapter for her *Life Among The Supermen*, not published, and extant only in a small closing paragraph.

> end of Life among the Supermen.
> 'Work Wisdom & Devotion and the greatest of these three is devotion,' said Mrs. Moffet, 'We must all go our separate ways as I said the other day. I cannot close the eye of my mind so I must watch & Madeline must work & wait while you attain.'
> 'You see Devotion is like Charity. It covers a multitude of sins,' he said as he held open the door.
> 'Yes,' she replied, 'and Wisdom is a gift given to the wise.'

THE END

Life Among The Supermen was probably an autobiography in disguise, Mrs. Moffet being S.S.D.D. (Wisdom is a gift given to the wise) and possibly Bernard Shaw is the 'he'.

Ever since she quit the Golden Dawn and its drain on her energies, Florence was undergoing a sort of artistic renaissance. By March she was appearing again at the Court as the Nurse in the Vedrenne-Barker production of Gilbert Murray's *Hippolytus*. Obviously impotent as a character actress, Florence's interpretation drove Yeats to exasperation.

> 'Why do you play the part with a bent back and a squeak in your voice? How can you be a character actor, you, who hate all our life, you, who belong to a life that is a vision?' But the argument was no use, and some nurse in Euripides must be played with all an old woman's infirmities and not as I would have it, with all a Sybil's majesty, because 'it is no use doing what nobody wants' or because she would show that she 'could do what others did.'[47]

During the two week run at the Court Florence also played Phaedra on 1 April in a production for her poetic theatre with Sturge Moore. Sixteen years after the *Idyll* John Todhunter was among those who still struggled to hear her words. Truly magnificent though she looked in her gown designed by Charles Ricketts

> at first when you came on I (being in the gallery) found it difficult to follow you in your lines as I missed several words. It was as if 'the unavoidable nervousness' of a first performance had got hold of even such a mistress of your human machine as you! . . .

occasionally I felt that in the abrupt changes of intonation . . .
you did not quite do justice to the more beautiful tones of your
voice . . . I imagine you found your Hippolytus rather difficult to
play up to — for he did not seem a very fascinating young hero,
not merely because of his insensibility to your wooing but in his
personality. But you carried the weight of the play on your
shoulders with a fine authority & made your personality felt
more as the helpless wanton.[48]

The taskmaster went to Sturge Moore's production; generous in
his derogation, he thought it full of absurdities with the stage
business not fitting the lines. There had been something to
Florence's Phaedra but she was still inaudible and relaxing her grip,
going out of character until she 'felt interested enough to have
another turn.' Someone needed to whip her constantly and Gilbert
Murray had asked him whether she had not a mother with a big stick
to keep her awake. Even Barker had given up, Shaw plied her. It
pained him still that Florence positively liked doing things feebly
when with her looks, her voice, and her intelligence she should never
lack for work.[49] A decade later his exasperation had not lessened
from the year 1896 when he wrote 'I declare before creation. . . that
there never has been, is not now, nor in any yet to be discovered
fourth dimension of time ever shall be,. . . one whom destiny mocked
with greater opportunities.'

A showing of *Salomé* was next on the boards for the new poetic
theatre with Florence playing the part of Herodias. Ricketts ordered
black and gold tissue for her cloak asking her to be sure to note that
the gold was to shine through the black. He also found 'this heavenly
tissue' for Herodias's hood which would require strengthening with
wires or chain before it was spotted with coral.[50]

Wilde's play by the Literary Theatre Club produced an 'ebulition of
rancour', Robert Ross said, but it was a remarkable attempt in spite
of the 'deliberate misrepresentation' on the part of the critics.
Charles Rickett's setting and costumes were magnificent and the
results well worth the obloquy the stage pioneers shared with Wilde.
Little impressed with Florence's production at the Bijou, Max Beerbohm was nearly won by this second showing at King's Hall. Miss
Darragh, if a little too modern as Salomé pleased him more than Miss
Murby, but Florence 'was not, alas, the veritable mother of Salomé'
(although Miss Darragh had played 'the veritable daughter of
Herodias.') Her Herodias was 'sympathetic. . . too pleasant. . . out of
key with the tragedy'. [51]

Nothing more seemed to develop for the Literary Theatre.
Florence attempted to interest J.M. Barrie to provide a vehicle but

by the end of 1906 she thought again of an American tour. The years of struggle or the carrying of her 'hard burden', as Yeats would have it, were to receive more than adequate acknowledgement there by various culture hungry Americans.

For the moment it is well to view the relationship of the collaborators in the New Art as it appeared in 1906. Although the poet and Lady Gregory had fashioned many castles in the air with Florence as an occupant, she was a surprisingly inactive part of what was now Yeats's Abbey Theatre. More reason than any was the friction that existed between the theatre's benefactor Annie Horniman and S.S.D.D. Yeats, however, never forgot Florence's part in the pioneer theatre and in 1906 spoke of his regard for his collaborator and for Frank Fay. When celebrating the theatre that year, they had, he said, 'done enough to show that all is possible if the Summer be lucky and the corn ripen'.[52]

That year, too, a more mature Yeats had written to Florence from Dublin:

I want to see you very much now and it will always be a great pleasure to be with you. . . You cannot think what a pleasure it is to be fond of somebody to whom one can talk — as a rule any sort of affection annihilates conversation, strikes one with silence like that of Adam before he had even named the beasts. To be moved, and talkative, unrestrained, one's own self, and to be this not because one has created some absurd delusion that all is wisdom as Adam may have in the beast's head, but not in Eve, but because one has found an equal, that is the best of life. All this means that I am looking forward to seeing you — that my spirits rise at the thought of it.[53]

If Yeats's words imply a fervour after great imtimacy, Florence's remarks to John Quinn the following year should not be dismissed. A 'mutual friendship' with the poet was one thing, she said, but 'mutual scandal' was not to be enjoyed.

For those who believe that Yeats's innovative designs for a Dramatic Art are precursors to the best that is anti-naturalist in theatre, Florence's influence during the years of perfecting the New Art is of vital concern. What the poet imagined from The Music of Speech, imagined, because Florence Emery and her Art were only a shadow of his vision, have not been adequately acknowledged. In the years when Yeats was writing his plays for impassioned speakers, he clearly revealed that his programme for the Noh was an outgrowth of the New Art. When in 1936 he was so passionately stirred by Margot Ruddock's effortless passing from speech into song (and in whom, perhaps, he attempted to create another Florence Farr) surely it was the repetition of that excitement in 1902. At the moment when the priestess in Florence's Egyptian play danced before her god in ecstacy, Yeats knew from then out that the dance was the inarticulate passion of thought, and song, the final ecstacy of speech. That very thought, however, was just another kernel in the seeds of Magic. In 1909 Elkin Mathews published *The Music of Speech,* a slim volume of illustrations and reviews of the Art dedicated by Florence to the poet and to Arnold Dolmetsch. All that Florence believed and all that Yeats used to procreate his genius were immersed in the mysteries of the East.

> Choirs of priests repeat for hours together short formulas, phrases called *mantrams*, while the people sit chatting together — until the spell begins to work. Then their bodies sway to the rhythm and melody of the words, their souls melt under the breath of the inspiring spirit, the sound of the words enters their inmost beings. As in a dream, so they pass away from the life of actuality into the more real ideal, the life as they would have it be! mayhap in this state they first catch a glimpse of the great truth that heaven and hell and God can be with us here and now.[54]

Not so many years after Florence had written the above, she left England to 'catch a glimpse of the great truth'. Yeats was then to mourn that there was no-one left who really understood the supreme unity of words and music. He might also have added, none other who shared with him his vision of a dramatic art, that feast in a monotony of external things, for the sake of an inner variety.

NOTES

1 Alt and Alspach, eds., *The Variorium Edition of the Poems of W.B. Yeats* (New York 1965), 212-13.
2 W.B. Yeats, *The King's Threshold.*
3 Maud Gonne, *A Servant of the Queen, Reminiscences by Maud Gonne MacBride,* (London 1938), 331.
4 Stephen Gwynn, ed., *Scattering Branches,* (London 1940), 39.

5 W.B. Yeats, *Essays and Introductions,* (New York 1961), 19.
6 Mabel Dolmetsch, *Personal Recollections of Arnold Dolmetsch,* (London 1958), 163.
7 Farr, *The Music of Speech,* (London 1909), 16-17.
8 *Ibid.,* 21.
9 Courtesy of Michael B. Yeats.
10 Wade, *Letters,* 312.
11 *Hone,* Letters, 57.
12 Berg Collection, New York Public Library, (April 11 1899).
13 Berg, *op. cit.*
14 Courtesy of Michael B. Yeats.
15 Wade, *op. cit.,* 327.
16 UL, (July 24 1899).
17 Courtesy of John Kelly and Eric Domville.
18 The Pennsylvania State University.
19 UL, (October 6 1901).
20 Foster-Murphy Collection.
21 Farr, 'The Chanting of Poetry', Foster-Murphy Collection.
22 *Study and Stage,* (June 2 1902).
23 Arthur Symons, *Plays, Acting, and Music,* (New York 1929), 180-181.
24 Bax,*op. cit.,* 15.
25 Wade, *op. cit.,* 394.
26 *The Owen College Union Magazine,* (Manchester).
27 *Ibid.*
28 Cornell University Library, (June 23 1903).
29 Foster-Murphy Collection.
30 Academic Centre, (May 24 1904).
31 Wade, *op. cit.,* 435.
32 Farr, 'The London Stage,' No. 3, Foster-Murphy Collection.
33 UL, (October 22 1904).
34 Farr,*op. cit.*
35 *Ibid.*
36 Courtesy of Dan. H. Laurence.
37 'The Albert Hall Theatre,' *Pall Mall Gazette,* (London January 18 1905).
38 Academic Centre.
39 Bax, *op. cit.,* 20.
40 *Ibid.*
41 Farr, 'The London Stage,' No. 3.
42 William Rothenstein, ed. *The Letters of Oscar Wilde,* (London 1962), 16.
43 UL.
44 UL, (May 10 1905).
45 Berg, Permission, Michael B. Yeats.
46 BM.

47 Yeats, *The Autobiographies,* 81.
48 UL, (April 3 1906).
49 Bax, *op. cit.,* 26-27.
50 UL.
51 Max Beerbohm, *Last Theatres,* (New York 1970), 251.
52 W.B. Yeats, *The Poetical Works of W.B. Yeats,* (New York 1912), viii.
53 Wade, *op. cit.,* 468.
54 Farr, *The Music of Speech,* 18.

7

Florence and
John Quinn
1907

Apparently there was no love affair in Florence Farr's life when she met John Quinn, ten years her junior, on his third visit to Europe in 1904. Certainly she was romantically uninvolved with, although not emotionally unattached to Bernard Shaw and Willie Yeats that year, both of whom she considered 'half-baked'.

Yeats brought the successful New York lawyer to 67, The Grove one Sunday in November to hear his collaborator in the New Art speak to the psaltery.[1] Some time during her informal performance that day she hummed a 'weird' tune collected for her by Mrs. Patrick Campbell's mother. In the following week, Florence met Quinn again at Woburn Buildings for an intimate dinner arranged by the poet.[2]

A handsome American of Irish parents, John Quinn became aware of the Yeats family through a notice in a Dublin paper referring to the paintings of W.B.'s brother Jack.[3] Soon after, he was on intimate terms with all the Yeatses to whom he extended innumerable kindnesses, notably to the poet's father. Within the decade he had also become the patron of some of the finest artists in the century. Ezra Pound, for instance, learned that his name did 'NOT spell Tightwad'. Not a rich man in the 'American sense of the word', Quinn 'has what he makes month by month, and most of it goes to the arts.'[4]

Florence corresponded with John Quinn first in 1905; this was the year of her late-blossoming artistic success with *Salomé* for The New Century Theatre. In April she wrote of a new collaborator of sorts in The Music of Speech, an Irish composer called Herbert Hughes whose 'Ninepenny Fiddle' was selling 'all over the place.' At the moment, the young man worked for Yeats at the Abbey Theatre putting a melody to some words by Padraic Colum. Florence questioned the chances of a tour with him in America with a third person going along 'a singer probably a lady.'

There was additional news for Quinn of the Court Theatre 'brimming over with Shaw and Shaw's plays at present. They appear to pay better than anything else. Yeats says he will soon become a public nuisance'.

And there was the 'great lark' Florence enjoyed over a different matter at the Irish Literary Society. At her lecture on 'The Fight Between the Poets and the Musicians' 'there was a strong opposition of musicians present but I got rapturous applause at the end when I did a lot of imitations of the way people speak verse under the existing state of things.'[5]

By October 1906, after the second performance of *Salomé* with Sturge Moore and Ricketts, Florence had prepared a printed announcement to use as advertisement for a lecture tour in America. Dorothy Paget was with Sir Johnston Forbes-Robertson's company touring the States in Shaw's *Ceasar and Cleopatra,* and Sir Johnston's agent, Messrs. Klaw and Erlanger in New York would receive the enquiries. Florence asked for a fee of £10 and expenses with applications between January and March 1907 inclusive. During December Dorothy met John Quinn two or three times to discuss her aunt's impending tour. Once they had lunch and afterwards, Quinn showed the young actress the stock exchange. She thought he was 'extremely nice' and developed a 'great respect' for him.

Aware of her tour, Arnold Dolmetsch, presently living with his wife Mabel in Boston, tentatively arranged five engagements for Florence there. Quinn came up with a lecture for a Barnard Club meeting and on the strength of these Florence planned to cross in January. With Dorothy off to Pittsburg, Cleveland, and Chicago with the Forbes-Robertson company Quinn took it upon himself to make Florence's tour a success. Bring or send photographs for the newspapers, he wrote her, as well as reminding the English woman to travel with a heavy steamer rug, and to take a first class ship. If one could not be found direct to Boston, the fare from New York to there was only six dollars, or twenty-four shillings.

While the lawyer's letter crossed to Florence, she suddenly lost courage to travel for the second time, the association in the Literary Theatre Club providing the first excuse. It was 'too great a risk' without at least ten definite engagements and, as she wrote Quinn, 'You see I am not rich enough to risk losing on the journey and so forth. And I must make £100 to make it possible. . .'

But when she received Quinn's letter, she ordered 2,000 prints from a 'very good man', and decided to go to the States after all. Mrs. Campbell had spent the day discussing the tour with her and whether Florence sailed on the Cunard's *Ivernia* on 22 January depended upon her letting her flat at Warwick Chambers. Writing to Quinn at midnight, Florence thought out a list of names she could use to boost her own, although, she commented, 'it is so difficult for me to call people my "patrons".'

Prince Kapotkin	Mrs. Patrick Campbell
Lady Cromartie	Gilbert Murray
Lady Margaret Sackville	Miss Elizabeth Robins
Lady Lawrence	Professor Herford
Lady Gregory	Gilbert Chesterton
late Frederick York Powell	W.B. Yeats
Henry Nevinson	Miss Jane Harrison
G. Bernard Shaw	late Miss Dorothea Beal
Mrs. Mackail (Miss Burne Jones)	Mrs. Barrington

Almost child-like in her naivity for travel beyond the enclosure of London and its environs, she questioned Quinn: 'I suppose you really think it will be all right & I shan't be left stranded with no means of getting home again. It seems such an undertaking. . .'

Her thoughts wandered as she worked out her plans on paper into the early hours of the morning—

I rather think some French poems I do may be suitable for private houses apart from the chanting & all that sort of thing.

Dolmetsch seems very sure it will be all right in Boston & he thinks Chicago.

I had really made up my mind not to come over until I heard from you because it was all so vague.

There is very little time to get all the necessary things ready; isn't there?

With ever so many thanks for all the trouble you are taking & your kindness to Miss Paget . . . I shall see Mr. Yeats on Sunday . . . Excuse incoherence but I must catch tomorrow's mail.[6]

Four days later, Florence advised Quinn of her booking on the S.S. *Baltic* sailing 30 January. The arrival date of 7 February would permit her enough leisure to rest in New York for a day or two before an engagement with Mrs. Simeon Ford. Was she to 'lecture? or recite? or chant, read?' she asked Quinn; and decided to be ready for any emergency. Then she told the lawyer about Agnes Tobin, a visiting literary figure from San Fransisco, who told her that her friendships with Shaw and G.K. Chesterton would be a 'good thing' for introductions. Moreover, Miss Tobin had got a letter off to Robert Collier, 'son of Collier's Weekly', and had written on her behalf to Mrs. Ernest Thompson Seton, wife of the celebrated Canadian writer of animal books, 'as well known as Roosevelt.' Mrs. Seton was head of the Federation of Women's Clubs, an organization impressing Quinn as

> some sort of political or sociological or economic or constitution body, and I have a vague impression also that they are interested in improving the breed of babies or in shortening the hours of labour for women or some such thing as that, and I don't think any member of the 'Federation of Women's Clubs' would recognise poetry if it was administered to them by electricity.[7]

Because she was still worried about her introductions to the right people, William Archer wrote to John Corwin of the *New York Sun* and to a friend at Harvard. Then Florence was concerned about the press. Yeats told her of the big reception he held in a private room at the Plaza Hotel in the city which indicated to Florence that she would have to stay at a hotel instead of living 'as cheaply as possible.' Dorothy Paget did write that Mrs. Ford could put her up twenty miles outside of New York but Yeats advised her to stay in the centre of things until she saw which set took to her. And Mrs. Ford was 'long-winded'. Quinn told her that 'it takes her about quarter of an hour to begin, about half an hour to tell something that could be told in two minutes, and about quarter of an hour to conclude, and I am seldom in when she calls on the telephone'.[8]

Unsure about her clothes, Florence wrote to Quinn that Mrs. Campbell was instructing her how to dress for the States. She had also commented that she believed in Florence much more *'without the psaltery'*. Anxious too about her fees, Florence did not know why she could not be booked as an artist and not as a lecturer and charge more than £10. When Quinn replied, he was bleak about further engagements at the colleges. It was late in the academic year and 'in any event I don't think the ordinary universities, apart from Women's Colleges, ever have women as lecturers.' This was the sort of policy that provoked an American suffragist to complain 'there is no reason why we should not have what is given to men. We are equal to the other sex in education, I won't say a word about morality'.[9]

As the time approached for Florence to leave London, she was not at all convinced she had made a wise decision. 'It's all very difficult isn't it?' she questioned Quinn; but her trepidations pleased him.

Two Englishmen out of three and nine Irishmen out of ten who come to this country 'know it all' before they get here. Yeats didn't come with any such self assurance, and as the phrase is here he 'made good.' He came with an open mind and that is the way I think to visit any new country.

Now that you have determined to come, let me advise you not to have anxiety about it. We will work to have you make at least the hundred pounds you mentioned in your letter.[10]

Florence spent her last few days in England 'working so hard at clothes and other practical things', and at the last moment, Lady Gregory put her blessings on the venture by sending a book and permission to use her name. In a hurried post card Florence betrayed some feelings of unworthiness as she answered Yeats's friend, 'I am hoping to really get something from this. . . which will make me of more use to all my friends.'[11]

It was 26 degrees in London when the *Baltic* sailed on 30 January. A price war in progress, Florence was booked first class travelling in stateroom number 135 as Mrs. Emery. Quinn met her at the pier in New York during even colder weather and settled her at the Martha Washington Hotel at Fifth Avenue and twenty-ninth street. The generally current impression among New Yorkers was that women, however responsible they looked, had difficulty registering in hotels. The Martha Washington received only women guests and was soon to be run on the principle of a man's establishment. Until these promised changes, the restaurant facilities were still poor. A woman guest put it —

The trouble is that women don't want to spend money for things to eat. They go outside and get their meals at some cheap place around here and then come in, sit around the hall with their toothpicks, and knock the hotel table![12]

Soon after Florence's arrival, she met Pamela Coleman Smith, an American artist friend of Yeats's and a resident at the Martha Washington. The two spent an evening and morning together with Miss Smith telling her friend in Magic a 'lot about the way to get about.' Still in need for Quinn to tell her 'various things I don't understand yet', Florence asked him to call at her hotel, and later, to arrange for her to have a collapsable metal stand, similar to the one she used in England for books and papers. 'It spoils everything if there isn't one'.

When the date occurred for Florence's lecture at Bryn Mawr, arranged by a Miss McKeen in Brooklyn, Quinn sent his office assistant Mr. White to escort her to Pennsylvania Station. After she reached Philadelphia, she took a cab to a smaller station for her train to the University town; there Mr. and Mrs. Mussey of the

College faculty received her. Florence's talk on 'The Music of the Spoken Language' delighted her listeners but later it was agreed both in and out of elocution classes that her theory depended upon her personal charm and was unsuited to the 'world at large'.

Shortly after the Bryn Mawr engagement, Florence lectured at the Barnard entertainment, an 'at home' which had been post-poned because of Ash Wednesday, and then she prepared to leave for Boston. At the last moment Professor Baker at Harvard wrote that her first scheduled lecture was postponed until 21 March. Florence was not put out; she was busy giving private lessons as well as lecturing on Nietzsche. 'The campagne [sic] is a great success everywhere. You must hear it,' she wrote to John Quinn. Attracted to the German philosopher, the lawyer sent his London friend No. X of Nietzsche's *Works, a Genealogy of Morals* and poems translated by John Gray. But the friendship was not running in other ways as Florence wished; her letters to Quinn of 3, 7, 9, 10 and 11 March remained unanswered. What she had done, she could not imagine, 'to be treated to such a long dose of silence'.

Put on her own, she spoke to a New York agent recommended by Quinn in an effort to work up a tour for 1908. She discussed Yeats as well pointing out that if he was invited to lecture, they would not speak together. Quinn had previously warned her 'this is after all, a provincial people . . . for you two to come would be too risky, too easily misunderstood.'

Contrary to her usual regard for women, Florence presently en-joyed herself immensely in their company. Consequently she dined with a Mrs. Drier, and met through an introduction from Mrs. Campbell, Mrs. Clarence Mackay who 'seems to be going in for culture with a vengeance.' There was also Mrs. Thursby whom Florence remembered from an Irish Literary Society meeting in London. She sounded very much like Lady Mary Potter in *The Dancing Faun* asking Lady Geraldine in the same novel whether she had been 'crossed in love.' Speaking to Quinn about Mrs. Thursby —

> she's exactly like an old friend of mine Lady Colvile the wife of the General. But how different she is to the gorgeous lady I remember sitting with Stephen Gwynn at the Irish Literary. Has she been crossed in love or what? It was only two or three years ago when she was what Rossetti and Morris called a 'stunner.' [13]

On Monday 11 March, Florence visited an artist in Columbia Heights to see 'wonderful tapestries and things from Italy.' From there she went to Mrs. Worthington, a friend of Mrs. Ford, who had recently moved to the 'Wyoming' at the corner of fifty-fifth Street and Seventh Avenue. Delighted with her introduction to a Mrs. Merringter at the gathering, the two ladies walked to the Martha Washington, stopping on the way to book a ticket for Florence's journey to Boston.

Quite her most exciting evening before she left the city was spent at the Colliers in Brooklyn. Florence could barely wait to inform John Quinn about her remarkable engagement.

> You were quite right about the Colliers and they were. . . charming. He and I sat at one end of a long table & Mark Twain & she [Mrs. Collier, née Sarah Steward] sat at the other & all the women were beautiful. Mrs. Cushing the artist's wife with red hair & white Gibson girl face. Mrs. J.J. Astor [the former Ava Lowle] & two other wonderful beings in gold and black.
>
> They got me to chant a few different specimens for about 40 minutes and all filed out shaking hands & Hapgood said he'd call here to give me letters to Boston & Collier was most intelligent about it all & they sent me home in an 'electric'. Lo! & behold. . . a cheque arrived for $200 so now I've secured the £100. Isn't it lucky?

Probably for the first time in her life she felt elated, secure, independent of Shaw and Yeats, and outrageously successful. Now that she was 'quite rich' she asked Quinn to make haste in sending his bill for 'all the innumerable things I owe you.'

Yet with all her good fortune, Florence was not uncritical of her new environment. It seemed to her that New Yorkers were a group of feverish devotees at the altar of work to whom doing nothing meant 'hell and damnation'. Even the Manhattan skyscrapers and subways only proved the 'most efficient way of cramming time into space.' And the story she heard of the wanderer who, clasping a lamp-post in desperation, cried 'are you Wall Street or the day after tomorrow', merely expressed the futility of spending one's life in a tunnel 'because the end where he may die may be better than the end where he was born.'

Central Park was little better; 'quite romantic at times', but with 'thin tulip-like magnolias. . .swarming with flowers, and no dreary green leaf, or suggestion of fruit mars the spectacle.' Then there was Fifth Avenue and Tiffany's where the pale amber was paler, the red, redder, and the lapis lazuli bluer than any Florence possessed, and her's was 'collected from all the quarters of the world except Tiffany's.' At the historic restaurants, as in Delmonicos', the meals were too long, but like a Shaw play, they always offered a surprise before the end. Even the antique furniture looked authentic but it was pleasantly adapted to modern convenience. 'America likes a central leg to its chippendale tables and gets it. The venerable and the convenient are united; the sacred with just a little dash of the profane is piquant'.

As for New York women, they were 'delightfully ornamental', working as hard at the art of spending money as their men making it at the offices. Pre-Prufrockian, they

> move in their drawing-rooms with all the grace of a carefully stage-managed scene in a society play. Their voices are soft and carefully trained and they are sure to let you know what they think of the usual person's intonation. 'The poor things have to talk like that because everything is so noisy in the streets, or perhaps it is the climate', they say. The New York smart woman leaves 'the climate' if it is disagreeable, and goes to Florida; so the climate doesn't matter much to her. . .She takes the forces of nature and uses them for her own amusement as ruthlessly as any artist among us; but in America she has the game entirely in her own hands. The suffrage would simply be a nuisance to her; she would as soon think of offering to scrub her own floors as offering to vote; 'that is menial work only fit for men.'[15]

Quinn escorted Florence to the station for her journey to Boston. Outside the city, the train broke down and stood still near the zoo 'or some place of the sort' for half an hour before being towed back to the station. With the unexpected delay, Florence was still only an hour late arriving at her destination. Arnold and Mabel Dolmetsch met her at the corner of Huntingdon Avenue and Gainsborough Street. When Florence reached her room she found it very pleasant, twenty-five by eighteen feet, and filled with roses, violets, and chocolates. The Dolmetsches stayed for a while to have a 'good talk' with the musician warning her she had come at a difficult time; 'as usual', Florence said, Holy Week and Opera Week were coinciding.

The following day the English woman lunched with the Dolmetsches at their 'old-fashioned' dwelling at 16 Arlington Street. Employed by the Chickerings, piano makers, Arnold Dolmetsch was having a 'lovely' time; in fact, they 'simply let him do all he likes.' Of particular fascination to Florence was the harpsichord the musician had made with eight different actions, 'one just like a little warbling bird.'

Mabel Dolmetsch had given birth to her first son in the previous November and Florence's visit coincided with the christening of the child Rudolph. It was their English friend, by chance, representing a godparent who was unable to come out from England, who held the baby for the ritual. Arnold Dolmetsch, incidentally, found Florence a 'fascinating woman', and until W.B. Yeats's death in 1939, he was convinced that the poet was 'certainly in love with her.'[16]

Prudent with her money, Florence was delighted that her expenses were so much less in Boston. All of her washing could be done at the laundry for twenty-five cents, a fact that nearly made her 'faint. . . after the dollars things cost in New York.' But Boston was without Quinn and she missed him 'dreadfully.' When he sent her Yeats's *Deirdre* Florence was especially pleased at his suggestion that she might give it a public reading when she returned to Manhattan. Quinn originally asked Yeats to send the script for Miss Margaret Wycherly, an actress who had performed a few of the poet's plays and presently wanted it for a hospital benefit. If Florence permitted herself any sentiment where the poet was concerned, the play must have held a special meaning. Yeats wrote in October 1906: 'The first musician was written for you — I always saw your face as I wrote, very curiously your face even more than your voice, and built the character out of that'.[17]

By the time Quinn received Florence's letter expressing her wish to perform *Deirdre* he was involved in a financial depression. 'There has been the devil to pay in the market here for the last two or three days and everybody seems to be hard up and anxious and worried'.

His personal entanglement was in what he had imagined to be a 'dead sure thing'. He had put up part of $27,000 for a work contract for the Eirie Railroad Company and now that the work had ceased, he had eight or nine thousand dollars tied up without knowing how to recall them. Florence's strangeness in a new city concerned him, however, and he hoped the Bostonians would be more decent than many of the New Yorkers who invited her to dinner and asked her to perform afterwards, gratis. 'Why wouldn't it be proper when you fear things to accept upon condition that you not be asked to recite?'[18]

The Bostonians paid for Florence and by the end of March she sent Quinn a large cheque to be credited to her account in New York. In spite of her success, the Dolmetsches were little impressed with her performances. Mabel thought that since Florence was not an 'executive musician. . .she could not detach herself from the physical action of plucking the right notes. When carried away by excitement, she had changed the pitch of her voice.[19]

Before Florence left for an engagement in Toronto, Quinn, aware that she might stint on her accomodations, advised her to be sure to engage a berth or sleeper

and always get a lower berth if you can in preference to an upper and always travel in chair cars or in Pullman cars and never in a day coach. Ninety-nine and nine-tenths per cent of all the persons injured or killed on railways in this country are those in day coaches, far ahead near the engine. The people who take Pullman cars are very seldom injured. . .It costs a little more but it is much safer and cleaner and better and pleasanter.

In his letter of 1 April he wrote as well of Yeats whose theatre row seemed 'to have simmered down.' The excitement he referred to in Dublin was created by John Millington Synge's *Playboy of the Western World*. There was a furore over the inclusion of the word 'shift' in the dialogue; but more probably because of the implication that Ireland's hard head was losing its best youth to America, so that a lad who killed his father with a 'loy' was glamorised for want of a better hero. Yeats was deep in the confrontation of religious bigotry and moral hypocrisy — 'It has been for some time inevitable that the intellectual element here in Dublin should fall out with the more brainless patriotic elements'.[20]

Quinn deeply admired Synge, believing him the 'real genius' of the Irish Theatre and he became passionately involved with the *Playboy* issue when the incident stretched to the States. There was in New York a large segment of chauvinistically Irish New Yorkers who were quick to take offence at the slightest hint of derogation of their mother country. An egg throwing riot by a hundred Irishmen at the Orpheum Theatre in Brooklyn, for example, was provoked by a Vaudevillian skit played by the Russel Brothers called the 'Irish Servant Girl'. The enraged opinion was that the Irish lass had been demeaned and no Irish-American was going to stand for a burlesque of the Irish character.

The *Playboy* incident continued for months both in Dublin and in New York. Annie Horniman, who by this time felt she was becoming useless to the Abbey, also feared, as she wrote to Bernard Shaw that

> Mr. Yeats won't understand that Dublin wants to get rid of him too. He has 'had the touch' from that terrible old vampire he calls Kathleen ni Houlihan as he must wear himself & his powers out for nothing. He cannot ever learn to write the ignorant stuff the 'patriots' want; besides he does not know the language in which alone they are encouraged to read. I wish he could be kidnapped & put on board a well-provisioned sailing yacht & not heard of until next Xmas.[21]

Florence finished up her stay in Boston with a seventy-five dollar fee from a Miss Eaton on 4 April and five dollars for a private lesson. The following day she left for Toronto and her lecture at the Chemical Laboratory on 'The Music of the Spoken Word'. Dolmetsch had been there the previous year to speak about the clavichord and harpsichord and now Toronto prepared for Florence to demonstrate there was 'more than one new thing under the sun'.

On the recommendation of Pigott, son of the old play licenser, Mr. and Mrs. Mavor were responsible for Florence's visit and for providing her with a 'jolly' time. It was really a 'great time' with the added enjoyment of Florence mingling with the university professors there. Full of the happiest memories of her stay she left Buffalo on 8 April. En route she decided to take a detour to Niagara. The train was very slow, stopping for an hour and a half first at Hamilton Station. Florence walked in the dreary regions of the platform and then escaped into the coffee shop until another slow train picked up the passengers to take them to the Suspension Bridge. 'The moment we were crossing the gorge,' the conductor collected tickets and fussed 'so only got a glimpse of that.' By then the weather had become chilly and Florence decided not to go around the falls or the whirlpool but to look at them from a distance. Finding out that she had to take a train to Niagara anyway, she finally saw the falls before a 'deluge' began. When the train reached Hamilton Station again, Florence had to wait there with an umbrella until her train arrived for Buffalo. The chilling resulted in a very good imitation of 'what we might have called rheumatic fever years ago.' Quinn's opinion of Niagara was justified, she admitted —

a favourable place for married people to spend their honeymoons, whatever honeymoons may be. I wonder if that is not the reason so many married people express themselves as having been disappointed with the Falls.[22]

Florence agreed, and sounding as if she was hopeful for marriage, told Quinn that she never wanted to go there for her honeymoon. 'It was bad enough to see it alone under the circumstances when one could express one's feelings without hurting anyone's susceptibilities.'

By the time she arrived in Buffalo she had pains in her head and her chest and her temperature was 102 degrees. As soon as her hosts brought her to 80 Jewett Avenue she was 'put to bed and nursed. . . wasn't it all stupid?' she wrote to the Mavors in Toronto.[23] It was with great effort that she pulled herself 'up to scratch' for her lecture in the Sculpture Hall at the Buffalo Fine Art Academy. Dressed in a yellow gown she placed herself between 'pure white Ionic' marble columns and 'shouted' for an hour. It all went very well and her herculean efforts to project in spite of her very sore throat led the audience to believe that their artist had a 'rich, full, resonant voice of remarkable purity.'

Florence enjoyed herself immensely again during her visit to Buffalo. Somehow, both there and in Toronto people were 'warned off' about introducing her to women, so I'm getting along much more amusingly and the women I do meet are quite jolly and not hysterical.' Apart from the good male company, the clocks in Buffalo astounded her with their boomings and musical scales. Rereading the contents of her letter to Quinn, she realised she was full of '!!! all the time.' How wearied she expected him to be of her superlatives. 'One gets hypnotised into egotism under the conditions of a lecture tour.'

Still not well, Florence took her train to Chicago where, John Quinn warned her, she would see the other side of the picture. 'A greater contrast than the serenity and cleanliness of Boston and the rush and dirt of Chicago it would be difficult to imagine.' Francis Hackett, a young Irishman of the editorial staff of the *Chicago Evening Post* and a great 'rooter' of the lawyer met Florence at the depot 'so that she won't have the all-abandoned feeling that is appropriate to a solitary arrival in Chicago.' It appeared to Quinn as if the young man was going to be responsible for connections in that city and he reminded Florence to show proper appreciation for his 'bestirring' himself. But Florence was behaving very well, thanking everyone after a while as 'sweetly' as possible. Especially, it had been no problem with Mr. Hackett; she found him delightful and they found time for a 'lovely' talk as she rested in the apartment of Miss Ella Raymond White before her first recital at Hull House, a social establishment at 800 South Halstead Street.

Florence received a hundred dollars for her lecture on 12 April and in mind of its success asked $200 for an engagement with Mrs. Franklin MacVeagh. Although Florence received her introduction to her from Mrs. Pat Campbell, the American woman 'didn't feel like it!!!'

John Quinn believed that his friend was catching on in Chicago and urged her not to return to Boston. Not heeding his advice, Florence left the city as she had planned and when she arrived in Boston she was 'awfully ill'. After a private entertainment on 15 April and a lecture for the Boston Radcliffe Union to aid a library fund she made up her mind to take a long rest. After all, she had made five hundred and eighty dollars in twelve days.

Resting at the Bartol, this time in suite 33, 'one end boiling hot and the other end chilly', Florence felt her nerves were 'out of order'. She found time, however, to entertain in 'peace and comfort' and when she was alone, to smoke and to recount her earnings. The amount amazed her, but 'I suppose that's nothing over here.'

When John Quinn wrote to Florence in Boston, he attempted to involve her in his concern for Yeats's forthcoming lecture tour. Amazingly off-handed, Florence advised the lawyer that the Pond agency in New York would be able to put the poet in touch with all sorts of audiences and from there, 'he'll have to make himself interesting to the world in general'. By now, Florence was of the opinion that she was totally independent of Yeats in her performance of the New Art, and that she was, perhaps, an even better drawing-card than the poet. Of course, people 'spotted here and there' during her own tour seemed to think quite highly of W.B. In Chicago, in fact, they had even told her 'We have had John the Baptist & now we have you!' It pleased her to think what Yeats might say to that remark. At any rate, Florence did not see why Quinn needed to be bothered with any of Yeats's arrangements.

> I am sure no one will hold *you* responsible whatever happens. But I know Yeats does want to try his luck again. If I do return myself I shall try to arrange for a different time as I don't want to get myself mixed up with him in any way. Mutual friendship is one thing but I don't care about mutual scandal with him. [24]

Mr. Glass from the agency eventually held a long discussion with Quinn and even he expressed fears that a tour by Yeats would now come as an anticlimax, obviously to Florence's own. At any rate, Quinn said, the agent was the sort who could only make good with a man like Lieutenant Peary in his efforts to discover the North Pole. Glass wished to proceed immediately, however, with his advance publicity for Yeats and determined that either January or February of 1908 would be an appropriate time to come. Hearing of this, Florence was 'distressed' that she could not inform the poet of the agency's plans. Annie Horniman was having her wish and Yeats was off to Italy with Lady Gregory and her son Robert until the end of May. For once Florence agreed with Annie that 'Ireland |was| too hot to hold them for the minute. I certainly think the best thing he can do is to go for the public generally.'

After several weeks of illness, Florence still had a sore throat, 'almost like Quinsey', but it did not deter her from mingling. She charmed Mrs. Isabella Stewart Gardner, the widow of John Lowell Gardner, by sitting in a chair more elegantly than any woman she had met before. Even Ellen Terry, then playing in Boston, had been 'most sweet' and told her that everyone was praising her and that she had everything before her in America.

Debating whether to stay on, Florence figured that if she left the States in April she would clear seven hundred dollars. If she went to Chicago again, she might be eleven hundred dollars to the good. San Francisco also intrigued her especially since Agnes Tobin was on her way there to visit her family. Besides, Florence had heard there was a lot of loose money around, and, as she wrote Quinn, she was not aside now from taking advantage of it. Either she would stay in Boston until the twenty-seventh, return to New York or go West. Giddy from over-excitement and the drive of the American tour, that attribute of terrestrial nature she was sure she despised, she loathed the thought of returning to England. Without a doubt she was waiting for Quinn to offer a more permanent stay in the States when she wrote him 'I simply hate the thought of going back to England.' And in one of those moods well-known to Yeats, 'I am sick to death of life altogether & nothing seems to have any attraction for me.'

A few days later, Florence planned to return to New York on Monday 28 April and to sail as soon as possible for England. Typically undecisive, she changed her plans within the day when she heard that Gilbert Murray had arrived in Boston. 'Everybody is chasing after the Earl's daughter.' (Lady Mary Henrietta Howard.) Expedient as she was, Florence supposed it would be diplomatic to stay over to see them. 'They are in such high favour & have always been very nice to me.'

Florence lunched with the Murrays and proposed to meet them for tea on the thirtieth. In the meantime, she notified Quinn she would leave Boston on 1 May. The 'stupid' Cooks people could not book her passage to England without spending dollars on telephone calls so Florence wondered whether Quinn would choose from a list of vessels, selecting a berth for about a hundred dollars. 'What is the use of being in such a hurry away from New York?' he asked. He wanted her to take a few days longer before she returned to 'the city of fog and the land of beef and ale.' But her decision firm, Florence sent a registered letter to confirm her train would leave Boston at 4 p.m. and arrive in New York at 9.30. It suddenly occured to her that she was looking forward very much to seeing the lawyer. 'I hope you won't be too tired; is life worth living when one is always overworked?'

When Florence reached the city, Quinn persuaded her to stay over. They spent an evening with Frederick Gregg of the *Evening Sun* and took dinner another night at the Hotel Belmont. On the evening of the seventh she gave a last recital, a performance 'analagous, perhaps, to the dances of Ruth St. Denis or Isadora Duncan in a poet's pantomime, but transcending these all by power of the spoken word and the low soft voice, that excellent thing in women.'[25] And someone in the audience remarked afterwards, Florence Farr 'makes your blood curdle'.

On 8 May Florence boarded the Norddeutsche's *Grosser Kurfurst*. She 'half-thought' she was in the middle of a labour battle, actually ten thousand long shoremen striking along the waterfront. When she settled that evening in her berth, she realised that she had locked the cabin door and there was no ladder down. She spent much of the night performing 'wonderful acrobatic feats' since she 'just couldn't' discover a way down. 'However I rolled off quite easily when I left off trying to *see* where I was going & resigned myself to fate & feeling with my toe.'

Quinn was unable to get to the ship before it sailed at ten on the morning of the ninth. Disappointed by his absence, Florence spotted instead Mr. White from the lawyer's office. Attempting to attract his attention, she looked hard at him in the crowd but he gazed at the departing faces without ever recognising her's. As the ship left the port, Florence felt strangely exhilarated being on the water. On the voyage out that feeling seemed like pent-up energy 'but it certainly isn't that now.'

Florence left the deck to write a last letter to John Quinn and to bid him good luck. With a tour 'in hand' for the Autumn arranged by Brilt in Boston and Mrs. Babcock from Pond's Agency in Carnegie Hall, she had every belief she would see the lawyer again in six months. As for Quinn, he believed he had done what he could to help, and wrote to W.B.Y. he had 'opened a few doors and smoothed out a few rough places. I think, all things considered, she did very well.'[26]

NOTES

1 Wade, *Letters*, 443.
2 *Ibid.*
3 B.L. Reid, *The Man From New York*, (New York), 8.
4 D.D. Paige, (ed,), *The Letters of Ezra Pound*, (New York), 111.
5 Berg, (April 18 1905).
6 Berg, (January 4 1906). The date is incorrectly written: the year was 1907.
7 Berg, (January 18 1908).
8 *Ibid.*
9 *The New York Times*, (February 7 1907).

10 Berg, (January 18 1907).
11 Berg.
12 *The New York Times.* (February 7 1907).
13 Berg, (March 3 1907).
14 Berg, (Sunday).
15 *The New Age. (London May 23 1907),* 57.
16 The National Library, Dublin.
17 Wade, *op. cit.,* 482
18 Berg, (March 26 1907).
19 The National Library.
20 Reid,*op. cit.,* 48.
21 BM, (June 22 1907).
22 Berg, (April 6 1907).
23 University of Toronto Library, (April 12 1907).
24 Berg.
25 *New York Evening Sun,* (May 19 1907). Reprinted in *The Music of Speech.*
26 Foster-Murphy Collection, (August 23 1907).

8

The New Woman
as Journalist
1907-1908

Strive no more ladies, strive no more
To prove you're wondrous clever;
Remember we have Bernard Shaw —
Sure, that's enough, for ever!
Then sigh not so, but let votes go
(To us they're not all honey);
We want you as your own dear selves,
And like you always sunny.[1]

America had done her 'a lot of good', Shaw remarked to Florence when she returned to England. Indeed, the tour added to her sense of female independence; gave her a new air of self-confidence. Florence said it was as if she had 'lived in a chrysalis' for all her life and was 'unfolding my wings for the first time now.'

Shaw's generous regard for the New Woman influenced his decision to recommend her services as a journalist to *The New Age*. Partly through his largesse, the proceeds from *The Doctor's Dilemma*, he had enabled the purchase of the weekly journal by Holbrook Jackson, and a 'mystery man named Orage', as Shaw referred to him.[2]

As early as 1897, Florence harboured the idea of offering herself as a dramatic critic to the *Saturday Review*. Shaw dissuaded her from doing so then mainly because he was already employed by the paper in that capacity. Then in 1901, the year of the great rumble in the Golden Dawn, Florence enjoyed a brief flirtation with dramatic criticism in a clever article for the 30 November *Free Lance*.

Presently she fulfilled her long-standing ambition by taking her place among a generally unpaid coterie of writers, namely Shaw himself, Anatole France, Arnold Bennett, Edward Carpenter, Edwin Pugh, Hillaire Belloc, and G.K. Chesterton for the new 'Independent Socialist Review of Politics, Literature, and Art.'

Orage, who may have felt an intense regard for his fellow mystic by virtue of their shared interest in the Theosophists, called the New Women's first article for his press 'G.B.S. and New York', a 'good tempered and truthful joke.'[3] In essence, it provided Florence the opportunity for a show of wit to be counted among her other ubiquitous artistic talents; it also indicated that had Yeats not bestowed upon her the 'hard burden' of the psaltery, she might have developed into the first-rate comic actress once groomed for her by Shaw. Certainly the article on Shaw gave Florence the joyous relief of exorcising her resentment at many of the private and not so proprietory rebukes directed at her by G.B.S. during the nearly twenty odd years of their friendship. Shaw, Florence scoffed, was New York city 'incarnate'. Both shared a 'certain delicate brutality', both were brought up 'out of the reach of the influence of a really venerable tradition', both were 'feverish devotées at the altar of work'.

> Play after play, preface after preface, pours from Mr. Shaw. He has been explaining himself for twenty years, but nobody understands. . .Empty Mr. Shaw and New York of work and hurry, the man has a headache and closes his eyes in pain, he feels no reason for existence; and the city is a desolation.

And reflecting, perhaps, on her own roles in Shaw's plays, and those for which he refused to consider her, a further retaliation; for his art

> is not seductive; he does not make hearts glow and expand before he analyses them. Cellini did not fix his model in a chair and copy her form. He chased her round the room giving her a severe drubbing, and no doubt his art got its quality from such behaviour. Mr. Shaw does not pose his model in the ordinary way either, but he seats her in a dentist's chair, puts a gag in her mouth, isolates a tooth as ruthlessly as any dentist and then takes her photograph . . . Mr. Shaw says in the *Doctor's Dilemma* 'I believe in Michael Angelo, Velasquez, and, 'I forget who else, but I don't think it was Leonardo da Vinci. If it was, Mr. Shaw could not really have considered Leonardo and what he means. He means a climber of the air, a dreamer whose dreams come true, a man who incarnates an ageless spirit that will haunt us and inspire us as long as we can look into Mona Lisa's eyes. Mr. Shaw does not believe in giving us a

Mona Lisa, he does not sacrifice to the Artemis who brings such spirits into being.[4]

In 1907, the daily literature was pregnant with the intelligent woman's opinion of where and how she belonged in society; articles on marriages of convenience, breeding, and prostitution were not uncommon phenomena in the Edwardian milieu. Florence, however, managed to distinguish herself by rephrasing relatively current ideas with a special sort of élan. Those, of course, who remembered her startling conversations in the Morris days, would have noticed that the passing years had attached a sharper edge to her present tracts.

Countless wives no doubt endure the horrors of a loveless marriage, and there are other women who bear the disgust with the aid of wine and luxury in order to avoid worse miseries; but no man will ever understand the disgust a woman feels in contact with a man she does not love, because nearly every woman is too polite to tell a husband or a patron in brutal words the real state of the case. The fact is women can be friends with many men and love very few; men can love many women and be friends with very few. Until this fact is clearly acknowledged the sexes will continue their mutual deception. Women will lament because they cannot convince men their love is a great gift, and men will regret that women cannot learn that love is a burning torch to be put out as quickly as possible, in order that they may set about the real work of life. Every man knows that perhaps there is only one woman in the world to whom he can give his intimate friendship; every woman knows that probably there is only one man in the world to whom she can give her passionate love.[5]

It is by now part of a small phase of literary history that Florence Emery was the one woman to whom Willie Yeats could tell 'everything',[6] and the first woman with whom Shaw realised the 'full intellectual and emotional companionship of love',[7] What can only be assumed is that there was none other than Shaw, and perhaps even he could barely qualify to be the one passionate love of which Florence wrote. Certainly many of her articles in the future weeks betrayed she had never quite 'let go' of Shaw. 'Do you want me *for ever* greedy one', as G.B.S. wrote in 1896, appeared in 1907 and afterwards to be an honest assessment. On this subject, one might wonder too, whether in some youthful conversation there was not perhaps a moment when Florence and G.B.S. spoke of family; whether Florence ever regretted her barrenness. That answer may lie in the following:

Great spiritual and mental forces are not necessarily accompanied by physical fecundity; then the purpose of each generation has an end of its own, an end which manifests in mental and spiritual energies having a lineage independent of the mortal bodies of mankind. Those atmospheres, which create strange moods, those enthusiasms which seize whole populations, may possibly be the force of some barren body concentrated on the tremendous progeny of a mind whose influence will be felt generation after generation. Some of our greatest men and women have been childless. They have been the climax of their family, not the foundation of it.

When she was not vying with G.B.S. in her articles, Florence found nothing else quite so bracing as fortifying her known testiness toward Shaw's 'unwomanly' women. The sort who had 'learned to run and shoot and hit hard' were not the answer for sure. But those who debunked the vote because 'every woman knows she has every "right" she can ever want', that is 'the right to govern man completely and draw him everywhere after her like a steel filing drawn by a magnet'.[9] were anathema to Florence. Marie Corelli, the Victorian novelist, advocated the above and the New Woman found her ground rules for ensnaring the opposite sex equally repugnant. 'Refinement, beauty. . .gently reserve. . .chastity' were not, Florence argued the endowments to enrich woman's destiny. Chastity in itself could cover· a multitude of sins, for how could virtue be judged if it existed without the challenge of temptation. Neither could that virtue count for much that arose from an 'innate dislike for the present methods of reproduction'. Chastity was simply an excuse for economic security, its falsehood thriving in a patriarchal society where marriage was a 'profession in which the amateur commands a higher price than a skilled artist.' To be gently reserved meant as little — 'Some women do not care what they say, but are very careful what they do; the rest do not mind what they do; but are very careful what they say.'[10]

One of Florence's more robust articles on prostitution, 'The Rites of Astorath' kindled a sizeable spark within *New Age* readers. Why, the New Woman asked, could Westerners not learn about sexual habits from the East. There religion was the protector of sensuality and Hindus 'tasted the ecstasy of Being' within the female embrace. Because certain women were trained for the gods and their worshippers, prostitution existed as a holy institution. In the West, it was the product of the gutter or the contrast between the temple and Picadilly Circus. Arguing for a more favourable environment for the prostitute at home, so that young men would not become decimated by disease, Florence enquired of her readers 'Is it better that our "Daughters of Joy" should live in the well-regulated house of a "Mrs. Warren", or worse, in insanitary little corners of their own finding', or that

> they should be brought up as dancers in the Temple of Kali
> dedicated to the Goddesses and kept healthy and beautiful in order
> that they may fulfil a purpose that they and their countrymen con-
> sider honourable and not degrading?[11]

When Florence was assailed by a reader in the *New Age* for offering a progressive British society two evils from which to choose, she
reminded the gentleman that his prejudice for the East was merely
an

> ignorance of static power that makes us seem like restless children
> in comparison with the calm sages born of the races we dare to
> despise. Were not Gautama Buddha, Lao-Tzu, and Confucius
> nearer to the ideal than Cecil Rhodes and President Roose-
> velt?[12]

A volley of correspondence concerning 'The Rites of Astorath' continued for some time with Florence's adversary finally suggesting the
only two responsible solutions for prostitution. Socialism, he said,
was the panacea for poverty, and compulsory notification against the
contaminator, with subsequent criminal proceedings, the sole cure
for syphilis. As for the New Women's lame excuse that throughout
her articles she was only addressing herself to those without the
socialist fold, she was advised to turn the 'two remedies into poetry
and to recite them to those without: the fold and the battle will be
half over.'

The issue was not lightly dismissed, and on 9 October a Mr. Alfred
W. Southey of 16 Elm Street, Gray's Inn Road, London came up with
a practical solution, he thought, for a trade union for prostitutes.
Moreover, he would implement his suggestion by becoming its
secretary. Obviously unable to agree and not prepared to withdraw
from the discussion, Florence sought some advice from Shaw. G.B.S.
then proferred his idea of a suitable reply for the gentleman.

Dear Sir,

> There is no doubt that a union among the women would be a
> great advantage to them and to Society, and that it would be the
> first step towards rescuing them from the state of outlawry which
> makes their condition at present so desperate.
>
> But you must allow me to say that the very condition of such an
> organisation must be that it shall be entirely in the hands of
> women. If you can induce one of the 'clever brainy women' of
> whom you write to undertake the work, and if you are a sufficiently
> sensible man, to be able to help her with your advice and guidance,
> then no doubt you can be of service in the matter; but in my opi-
> nion you cannot take any more direct part in it. A male secretary

would be an improper position at the end. When you consider that the mere existence of a Union would be regarded at first a scandal, you will see how undesirable it would be to make the scandal worse by a feature to which even sympathisers might *justly* take wrong exception.[13]

Convinced that such a letter would 'settle' Mr. Southey, Shaw emphasised to Florence that too much caution could not be shown when dealing with 'male champions' of the cause. From a personal point of view, he questioned the feasibility of putting women into a Trade Union at all, especially prostitutes who seldom recognised the permanence of their occupation. 'They all intend to stop it and get married the next month at the latest.' Such a movement any way could only be implemented by a 'very energetic, muscular, and violent woman, with the devotion of a Saint, and the arbitrariness and executive power of a prize-fighter; but such women do not grow on the bushes'.

Two months later, Florence was still defending her position to frightened socialists who were uneasy to share her platform. In a laconic note to *The Spectator,* she claimed to be the 'mouthpiece' of her own opinions.

My articles in *the New Age* are signed, and I have never pretended to express the policy of any association of people. Outcasts can not speak for themselves, it is insidious for men to speak for them, so other women must if public opinion is to be brought to bear on one of the most important dangers to the race. That is all.[14]

One other noteworthy attempt on Florence's part to involve herself in social ethics occured during the famous 'Chesterbelloc' articles. G.K. Chesterton's 'Why I Am Not A Socialist' was subsequently attacked by H.G. Wells, counter-attacked by Belloc, justified by Chesterton in another article and topped by Shaw's *coup d'etat* 'Chesterbelloc'. Then in March 1908 Filson Young came up with 'On Shaw, Wells, Chesterton, and Belloc' and so it continued. Florence's contribution to the game, which the editors made more exciting for the participants by delivering advanced proofs, was in the way of a list of commandments which she interpreted to be the essence of Chesterton's first article. It was very curious to her that G.K. could speak of so many unenlightened non-Socialist working-men with romanticism, and worse, (reminiscent of Florence Nightingale's words to William Farr about nurses) that he could believe 'so many benighted sots were eternally right.' Chesterton's decalogue of humanity appeared to be summed up thus:

1. An Englishman's house is his castle, and he demands ceremonial rites from his guests.

2. That marriage is a real bond, and its natural consequences are jealousy and revenge.

3. That to eat fruit and sympathise with the pain of an animal is a silly fad.

4. That it is worth insuring one's life in the hope that the money will be spent on one's funeral.

5. That it is better to give people what they like than what they don't like.

6. It is reasonable to be furious with other poeple's brutality even if you are in a position of authority.

7. It is allowable to be brutal to your own children, otherwise they are liable to find you out.

8. The working man believes in these things.

9. Other people don't.

10. The working men are absolutely and eternally right.

From her own quasi-Socialist point of view, Florence pitted an alternate credo.

1. My home is where I am at the moment.

2. My wife is whoever I love at the moment.

3. My food is whatever I fancy at the moment.

4. My funeral doesn't matter as long as I don't know the moment when I die.

5. My gifts are what I feel like giving.

6. My temper is what I feel like doing or saying.

7. Other people's habits are often worse than their crimes.

8. These things all men and women would like to believe are right.

9. They all do believe in them without knowing it, and just to round off we will say that

10. We are absolutely and eternally right.[15]

What Florence attempted to accomplish in *The New Age* was probably a little more enlightened than the obvious sport of intellectual catharsis. Never an activist beyong her pen,she did believe, as she wrote in 'Our Evil Stars'[11] that the only people who could awaken the public to the dangers of[16] public health, marriage laws, and the 'well-being' of the race were those who 'lived decently within the law and have no personal object to serve'. Never having publicly permitted her mask of decorum to slip, Florence saw herself well-suited to serve the public interest. But in all those articles which had social issues as theme, a digression into the 'soul's journey' usually precluded any chance for some pragmatic solution. Even her sketches on the women in Ibsen's plays were a melange on socialism and mysticism.

Orage and Jackson in 1907 announced the forthcoming publication of *Ibsen's Women. Studies of the Principal Women in the Plays of Ibsen* in an advertisement in their recent publication of *The Mystery of Time*. The book does not seem to have been published but some portion of its contents was reduced into articles for *The New Age*. *A Doll's House* for one, provided an opportunity for Florence to share a vision she may have experienced in or out of the Golden Dawn;

> Once in a dream I stood with the Principalities and Powers before the Tree of Life. One of the branches was dead, with five, ripe and beautiful fruit still hanging to their exhausted stalks. And the Powers whispered to each other, 'Let us cast off the dead branch and cry aloud that we may become a Tree of Life'. And they said those words as they carried the branch away. Then they ate the fruit and threw away the branch. I said: 'Why did you utter those words?' and they replied:'In order that the other branches may do likewise. The fruit brought forth at the price of the death of the bringer is the fruit we eat with the most relish'. Perhaps this vision is cynical, but such it was, and it is a symbol of man's hope.[17]

Ibsen's Nora, like the fruit of the Tree of Life, entered the world full of hope only to be shattered by her own illusions. Those fantasies of her mind disintegrated in her discovery that man, and in particular a bank-manager, was not (contrary to 'St. Paul's exhortations') a satisfactory representation of the deity.

Unlike Nora, Ellida Wangel in *The Lady From the Sea*[18] was the paradigm of women's complacency. Offered her freedom, she chose to remain in the 'nice humdrum little family' where she could reproduce her species 'and darn her husband's socks. What more need any woman want?' Ellida provided an unfortunate ephitet to the fact that when offered a choice, women would resist the path to freedom. Bribed by the apple dangling from the 'Tree of Knowledge of Good and Evil' she would succumb to the greatest illusion of all: the delusion of knowing 'Good'.

A last article worthy of some respect in the area of dramatic criticism contains Florence's comments on Binyon's *Attila*.[19] Although previously she shared her enthusiasm with Quinn for Binyon's play, her opinion changed after reading the text. It seemed presently as if the four-act tragedy was 'impersonal' and 'without charm'. Also, she wrote in *Goth & Hun*, she could not name a contemporary English playwright who managed to recreate the passions of the Greek poets in blank verse. Scenes in Shelley's *Cenci* and in Swinburne's *Atalanta in Calydon* succeeded, perhaps, but it seemed to Florence as if the very struggle for perfection in verse prevented the playwright's passion and the listener's comprehension. 'Blank verse. . .will never be the equal of vigorous prose until some new means are found of vitalizing it'; a conclusion that was shared later by T.S. Eliot, until, as he remarked, Yeats solved the problem with *Purgatory.*

The New Age proved to be as remarkable an experience for Florence as her American tour. Orage told her she was more quoted than any other contributor and Shaw was requesting off-prints of her articles to send to his friends. Her self-confidence at even greater heights than when she returned to England, Florence reserved a booking on the *Lusitania* to sail to the States on 2 November. Within a few days, she decided not to go; an offer to write dramatic criticism for a new weekly 'at very good pay' induced her to postpone her tour. Three months were all she needed, she wrote Quinn, to tell whether she would succeed.

The new weekly was *The Mint,* a 'new middle-class journal for the home circle.' Its change from a monthly to a weekly publication did not occur until 27 March but in February, while the journal still ran as a monthly, Florence's first article appeared on the 'London Stage' under a page heading of 'Masks and Faces'. The smattering of advertising throughout the paper suggested the hominess to which the paper was pledged: 'Daltoff Tea' for the cure of corpulency, 'Depillos' for superfluous hair and 'Maypole Soap' for home dyeing. To perk up its pages, the journal offered columns like 'Mint Sauce' which included such epigrams of wisdom as 'All men have equal rights, but only a few get them'; and it printed 'Suffragitis: In Chains' which included the verses, 'Remember we have Bernard Shaw/Sure, that's enough, for ever!'

In future months, Florence contributed a series of articles for which she was generally unpaid. 'Alice and the Cheshire Cat' and 'The Cat Preaches the Gospel of Nietzsche' never appeared in print but 'Irving and Toole', and 'Mr. Tree as a Jew became valuable additions to the Victorian Stage. 'Pinero and Shaw' on 23 May 1908 was the title of an article of a different matter. The former's *The Thunderbolt* and Shaw's *Getting Married* at the Haymarket both had their openings the week of Florence's article. Pinero's play came off better than Shaw's, Florence said, because it was 'sharper and clearer cut.' G.B.S.

gives one the impression of writing until he has got down

everything that happens to come to his head. He then appears to go through his books of reference such as Whitaker's Almanac, and finds a list of all sorts of subjects which he had previously overlooked.

The real torture occured for Shaw's audience when after three patient hours of attention, the playwright found he had forgotten to mention the customs of Mahomet and his country, Henry VIII and church confiscation and turnips. But at last, 'Mr. Shaw ingeniously applies Church confiscation and turnips to the subject at hand.' Most people, Florence continued, started with a subject and gradually wandered away from it in various illustrations. Shaw starts 'from the circumference of the contents of Whitaker and only eventually reaches the reality he has at heart.'

Pinero was not without his faults either in never permitting his actors an autonomous piece of stage business or interpretation of their lines. Florence heard that the playwright and Forbes-Robertson quarelled because the actor revolted against putting his hands into his pockets 'at the precise moment' Pinero chose for him.

A chatty column by Florence called 'Plays and Players' usually accompanied her feature article. There were the customary pricks at Shaw whose face 'used to shine pallidly behind the solid cinnamon of his beard, which now glimmers in a dim harmony of drab and gray and silver, giving an almost rosy colour to his face'.[20]

On other happenings in the theatre: John Masefield and J.M. Synge represented to Florence by 'far and away the greatest writers of peasant plays that we have.' Then describing her round of theatregoing in June, she estimated there were certainly thirty first-class theatres in London that were booked by shows. Somerset Maugham's *Lady Frederick* as well as his *Jack Straw* and *Mrs. Dot* were playing. There were some Barries, some Pineros, Shakespeare at His Majesty's with Ellen Terry in *The Merry Wives of Windsor,* and *A White Man* at the Lyric.[21] Florence revealed to her public theatre gossip as well. William Gilette, she had heard, had made the largest fortune ever by an American and Sir Charles Wyndham was supposed to be the richest man in England. Edward Terry was purportedly taking 'good care of his pounds, shillings and pence'; Mr. and Mrs. Kendall were prosperous as well but unlike the Bancrofts, they were not going to abandon the stage. As for Miss Mary Moore, she was no doubt the richest leading actress in England; George Alexander had certainly done well and so had Sir John Hare.[22]

At another time Florence discussed the fact that Lord Howard de

Walden, a friend of George Moore's had been discovered to be the real author of *Lanvalis*. [23] In the same issue of *The Mint* she wrote about a new movement to support a National Theatre as a Shakespeare memorial in London.

13 June was the last instance the weekly printed an article by Florence. Actually the journal had not paid her for seven previous pieces and the editors were advising her to make a claim through a lawyer. More important than the termination of her services was the fact that she was no longer a contributor. Even *The New Age* did not beckon. The paper had become 'very stodgy', but it had a reputation for cleverness, Florence said, with which she liked to associate Shaw told her she was 'one of the victims of the revolutionary paper which is like a woman of bad character always trying to show she is respectable.' [24]

What Florence hoped for by June 1908, was a conservative paper that wanted her services. Much to her disappointment, nothing else was forthcoming, and so she thought once more about an American tour. Journalism had been a spicy divertissement in her life, a rest perhaps between the psaltery and mysticism, but as with most of her pursuits, her aspirations were unsuited to her talents.

NOTES

1 *The Mint,* (London August 15 1908), 643.
2 Wallace Martin, *The New Age Under Orage,* (Manchester 1967), 1, 24,.
3 *The New Age,* (London June 6 1907), 93. Henceforth NA.
4 NA. (May 23 1907), 57.
5 *NA,* (August 19 1907), 214-15.
6 *Bax,* Letters, 33.
7 William Irvine, *The Universe of G.B.S.,* (New York 1949), 151-52.
8 *NA,* (September 5 1907), 294-95.
9 Marie Corelli, *Woman or Suffragette? A Question of National Choice.* (London 1907), 38
10 *NA,* (August 1 1907), 214-15
11 *NA,* (September 5 1907), 294-95.
12 *NA,* (September 19 1907), 334.
13 Academic Centre.
14 *The Spectator,* (London November 9 1907), 706.
15 *NA.* (January 18 1908), 238-39.
16 *NA,* (October 3 1907), 358-59.
17 *NA,*(November 26 1907), 48-49.
18 *NA,* (November 30 1907), 87.

19 *NA,* (September 26 1907), 341.
20 *The Mint,* (May 23 1908) 271.
21 *The Mint,* (June 6 1908),334.
22 *The Mint, (June 13 1908), 366.*
23 *The Mint* (May 23 1908), 271.
24 Berg, (June 18 1908).

9

'Second always . . . yet this is you.'
1907-1912

An autobiographical statement by Florence Emery of her life in the following few years describes her as a 'hermit' with mitigating friends and enemies and a life full of 'unusually . . . varied interests'. Without reservation she could claim that her failures were part of her rewards, and her moments of bitterness, the cause of her greatest contentment. Reflecting on all she had written, no doubt in *The New Age* and elsewhere, she also confessed that her own 'tranquil' nature never permitted her to practice what she preached.

Unlike many other 'transitional' women, which is the way Florence referred to the *fin de siècle* genre of New Women, she was perfectly aware of her driving requirements for intellectual companionship with men. She had always refused to serve the male ego in 'unwomanly' ways, yet, because she needed an emotional relationship with a male of her choice, she made certain allowances for John Quinn. That is, she made herself available to him when, ostensibly, there was not an equitable return of her regard. Fortunately, Florence never experienced the defeat of May Morris who received baskets of apples in lieu of affections from the lawyer. But then, neither did Florence fall in love with Quinn.

Still buoyant from the New Yorker's attentions to her during the American tour, Florence was disconcerted when he did not communicate when she returned to England. On 6 'June, while she wrote for Orage's paper, she decided to remind him that he had not sent word since she sailed. In an attempt to keep him abreast of the London news, she wrote that Mrs. Campbell had invited her to tour: 'Clytemnestra is the bait.' Also, Yeats had said that he did not wish to return to America until Bullen published the Collected Edition of his

Works. By July, Quinn still did not write, and Florence sent news of Yeats who was at Coole for the summer and autumn, and lastly, her expression of annoyance with Brilt, the Boston agent, for making a 'hideous' job of her circulars.

Florence went to Wales for a _'lovely' summer holiday as the houseguest of Mrs. Bligh Cilmery in Builth Wells. The country was beautiful, and the weather, not atypically 'horrid cold' with rain nearly every day. In spite of this, Florence was having 'great fun' learning how to ride 'equally well as a man or a woman'. Her holiday ended 5 August and when she returned to London there was still no news from Quinn. It was not until September that he wrote that the markets had 'all gone to the devil' with 'failures after failures'. Banking and brokerage clients consequently insisted that he remain in the States which left only a small hope for a visit to England later in the month. Referring to Florence's past news that Synge's *Playboy* was a success at Oxford he replied, 'I am so glad':

> This will bring about another classic instance of Irish critics' fairness, namely, abuse of a play or a work in Ireland as anti-national, next its presentation in England with   success and favourable notices in Ireland or a comment on them as proof conclusive that the play was writing down the Irish in English eyes.[1]

Florence answered Quinn at once: 'You see one doesn't even know that you have not been swallowed up by an earthquake.' She quickly reviewed the London scene: Yeats in town for a week; Robert Gregory's forthcoming marriage; Laurence Binyon's play *Attila* which she attended with Lady Gregory and Yeats. The scenery was by Ricketts, and the dresses 'very delightful . . . made by people I know, who have helped in our Literary Theatre productions.' Her tour with Mrs. Campbell was on again but Florence fancied Mrs. Pat would probably perform her old repertoire and not *Electra,* 'so my Clytemnestra is off.' They planned to sail in November although they would not stay at the same hotel, Mrs. Campbell's is 'frightfully expensive.' Referring again to Synge's *Playboy,* Florence told Quinn she had seen it for the first time in London; it was a 'fine play, a new genre, a farcical tragedy'. While she wrote the longest letter 'since I was grown up', the hall porter at Warwick Chambers came to her rooms to report a burglary in the next block of flats. Florence was insured by Lloyds but since she was on the first floor, she hoped she would not 'be burgled too.' Looking around her she stopped to admire the garden she had made on one of the window sills. 'It is really such a lark after always seeing flowers one bought dying to really see them flourish and look as well as they do at the florists.' For the moment she liked her flat and told Quinn she would keep it on when she came to America in November, letting it furnished, or putting her things away.[2]

The contents of Florence's letters to Quinn suggest that she was on easy terms with him, probably for several reasons. He offered her no artiistic competition or complaint, and it seemed as well, as if she enjoyed a relationship with a man who was financially and philosophically independent. There were also few holds barred when it came to the frank discussion of the sexes. In no other correspondence did Florence write with such personal abandonment or with so little thought of literary style. Careless penmanship, ink blots, and words continually cancelled give her letters the tone and appearance of an enthusiastic schoolgirl.

Yeats at this time, wrote freely, as always, to Florence, A long letter written during the period of her journalistic activity presents his own battles, which were, of course, far removed from the social conflicts in *The New Age*. His letter is important in many ways. Firstly, it betrays his anger with the embittered people he professed to cherish. Secondly, he admits a condescension to an individual who never fitted into his concept of a dramatic art; lastly, he makes it perfectly clear that the Fays were in many ways destroying much that he was attempting to create. Despite the fact that the poet wrote in 1906 that Frank Fay was 'the most beautiful verse speaker I know — at least you and Mrs. Emery compete together in my mind for that', the Fays represented the type of theatre which Ireland, or more specifically Dublin preferred: a theatre of realism. After Yeats's inevitable complaint that Florence had neglected her correspondence to him, the letter went as follows.

I have no doubt that Mrs. Campbell has told you the news and so I feel that you are the less entitled to hear it from me, but why don't you write. I have nobody to tell me your news, and God knows how much longer I shall have to stop here. Another month possibly, certainly three weeks, I see nothing for it in spite of all good resolutions but keeping hard at work here in Dublin, except when I can hand the Theatre over to Lady Gregory. If Fay is not constantly watched he is away idling with his paint box, or what is still worse down at the Theatre painting out our decorative scenery and putting his own damnable landscapes in its stead. Mrs. Campbell came in for one of these. Mrs. Campbell has won my heart for ever. I am fifty times more grateful to her than I would have been if she had put the Play on in a London theatre. It is really a beautiful romantic thing. You do not often see me in this mood but I am really touched. I have been thinking of her as giving up too much to

Society and of the people who are not Artists, but now I see her once more as the great Artist. You who love London will not understand me, but it is this narrow, imbittered in many ways stupid town that touches my imagination. Elsewhere we become like other people, here perhaps because other people are rather disagreeable we remain ourselves. I believe this promise of hers, the mere promise, will help me more than anything I have said or written these five years back, and that the performance will win the battle. She made a beautiful speech from the stage of the Gaiety promising to return in November next year to play at the Abbey 'in Deirdre by my dear friend and your great Poet.' The day before I caught an old journalist who probably hates the Abbey, because he thinks it is the centre of advanced ideas trying to stir up, though' naturally in vain, Miss Allgood's feelings, trying to rouse her jealousy. On Saturday he began questioning me, with a queeer bitter tone in his voice looking I could see for some fact that might help him prove that this was a mere act of friendship on Mrs. Campbell's part and not a compliment to the Abbey. In reporting Mrs. Campbell's speech which he, for I have little doubt it was he, did for every Dublin paper he left out the word 'great.' On the other hand those who do care for my work are delighted. This is a litany not a letter, a list of beatitudes what you will . . .

Accompanying Yeats's letter were some songs, 'if I can call them songs' for the 'golden helmot' [sic]. With typical casualness when it came to the composition of music for words, (although he was sure that nothing concerned him more) he asked Florence to recall the script when she set the words to notes. 'You will remember the play is noisy and violent.'[3]

The poet had asked Florence for all of her music prior to September when he corresponded with Miss Lister at Bullen's discussing its inclusion in his *Collected Works*. Anticipating that Bullen's reader would not be in sympathy with Florence's settings, he wrote that they get their meaning 'from the method of speaking and [are]a necessary record of that method. It is important to me that people whom I cannot possibly teach and who may produce my work shall know my intentions.'[4]

Later in September, the publisher decided the music would fit best at the end of the Prose plays and Yeats withheld the settings until 1908.

After Florence decided to cancel her November tour of the States to write for *The Mint*, John Quinn replied[5] to her October correspondence. The Bank of Commerce which he represented refused to clear $60,000,000 or £12,000,000 for the Knickerbocker Trust Company and the failure was like a 'thunder clap'. A dozen other Trusts

conducting investments on a similar basis followed suit and the
public, which thought the institution as strong as the United States
Treasury, panicked. Fortunes were being wiped out and prices had
dropped from ten to sixty per cent. People were feeling poor
everywhere; some curtailed living expenses by selling their
automobiles or moving to Europe to live more cheaply; others rented
homes in the city in order to move to the country. Factories were
shut down and thousands of people were out of work. In spite of all
this, Quinn told Florence at her asking, that he would be delighted to
see her again, although he could not withold his judgement that the
following year looked more prosperous for a tour. He had had to dis-
suade John Butler Yeats as well who wrote to announce his plans of
bringing Lily to America. Mrs. Ford, 'you remember her — the
woman who aspires', promised Yeats some sketching when she
visited his studio in Ireland. Conditions were since changed, and
Quinn was aware that two or three sketches would in no way pay for
the Yeatses' expenses. With remorse he replied to Yeats that he had
chosen the worst possible time for his journey.

There was additional news concerning Shaw who had written a
'disgusting attack' on America in *Everybody's Magazine.*

It was not clever; it was only ignorant and stupid and conceited
and it will do him no good. There wasn't a bit of wit in it and he is
still talking about old Comstock. He forgets that there are stupid
policemen everywhere in the world, and it was only a Police Com-
missioner that stopped temporarily the performance of 'Mrs.
Warren's Profession.' When it got into Court the Judges threw the
prosecution out.

Quinn suspected that Shaw was rankled by the fact that the play was
not a success in New York even though Mary Shaw, a popular and experienced actress performed the leading role. G. B. S. should
recognise, he added, that his plays were appreciated in the States
long before he was acknowledged in England. 'Besides, no man has a
right to criticise a country he has not visited.'

What angered Quinn, in turn, was Shaw's opening statement in 'A
Nation of Villagers'. The playwright had attacked the Trust Companies ('integrated Capitalism as distinguished from disintegrated
competitive capitalists') which revealed the 'political imbecility' of
the country. Shaw also singled out the 'personal braininess and hustle
of the American Man of Business' which Quinn took personally.
Consequently, the lawyer was not upset that Mrs. Campbell, on tour
in America, was 'hitting a kick' at G. B. S. in her conferences with the
press. Conversely, he was especially pleased that she was saying

some very nice things about Yeats. They were well-timed with two unsuccessful productions of the poet's plays at the Berkeley Theatre; Margaret Wycherly had performed *The Hour Glass* and *Kathleen ni Houlihan* very poorly.

Personal news followed; Quinn had acquired a new 'Jap' houseboy. His mother was a Christian, and his father, a Buddhist; the boy, a chemist, was an atheist, since 'he finds an inability to mix up, chemically or otherwise, chemistry with Buddhism.' Several jokes came next, the type that imply the ease and informality of his relationship with Florence. 'Have you heard the story' Quinn asked, 'of the man whose wife sent him to buy a pair of corsets?' 'The girl behind the counter reached down to get the box and then lifted her head and said: "What bust?" The man said: "I didn't hear anything".'

The best story Quinn had recently heard was one he expected Florence to appreciate since she knew the fast American trains. 'The Twentieth Century Limited' which made the distance from New York to Chicago in eighteen hours provided the setting.

> There was a man on one of the Pullman sleepers and he met a charming lady, and being in an amorous mood he asked her if she had the time, and she replied she had if he had the money. Then they hit upon a novel scale of compensation. He agreed to pay her at the rate of a dollar a mile (The train goes, not counting the different stops, at the rate of sixty to seventy miles an hour.) They took a reckoning from the next mile post and retired to a state room. When they emerged they again took a reckoning and discovered that he owed her $49. She said she hoped he didn't consider the rate extravagant, and he said no, that he was satisfied and then he said; 'But some day I'll get you on the Erie and at that rate I'll work you to death for $2.'

To assure himself that Florence got the point, Quinn reminded her that the Erie was the slowest rail in America, the popular estimation being that it made six miles an hour.

The lawyer closed his long letter with a request for Florence's opinion of the Augustus John drawing to be included in Yeats's *Collected Works*. He had indicated his desire to purchase the etching if he was not charged a 'millionaire's price'. In September, Yeats wrote to Florence that Augustus John had done numberless portraits in preparation for the etching, 'All powerful, ugly gypsy things'[6], and later, that he 'shrunk from the John Thing.'[7]

In December, Florence decided she would go to America after all. Quinn began a letter at once expressing his delight but the next morning, with his letter uncompleted, he received word that his English friend had cancelled her plans yet again. Poor economic conditions in America were her present excuse. Quinn repeated his disappointment several times throughout his news of J. B. Yeats and Lily. Contrary to his advice, they had arrived in New York and were staying at the Grand Union Hotel as the guests of the Simeon Fords. The 'old gentleman' was 'having the time of his life . . . It is too bad Mr. Yeats is not a few years younger . . . He is a man with a young heart in an ageing body.' On one occasion, Quinn entertained the artist and Lily at a dinner for twelve at the Belmont before bringing the evening to a close with highballs at the New Plaza Hotel. At another time, J. B. Y. wanted to sketch Evelyn Nesbit Thaw during the New York trial of her husband. Harry Thaw was accused of the murder of an architect, Stanford White, who allegedly took advantage of Evelyn Thaw when she was a chorus girl of fifteen. Quinn had asked Justice Dowling for two good seats for J. B. Y. but when he came into the courtroom, there was Yeats seated fifty feet away from the witness, at which distance, Quinn said, Evelyn Thaw resembled any other woman.

There was another story for Florence which was told to Quinn by the poet's father.

A man was engaged to a girl and was pressing her for the enjoyment of the fruits of marriage . . . and she was resisting. He was pressing her for reasons of her refusal. First, she said, it would be immoral: secondly, if she did it would forfeit his respect; and thirdly, she said, it always hurt her back.

Quinn was fond of J. B. Y. especially since neither he nor Lily complained about the city or made 'odious comparisons' between countries. They did not comment upon the heat in the rooms or the ice water; delighted with everything, they took the strangest events as new experiences to enjoy. 'That isn't the way though, that the English and Irish generally take America'. It was a general psychological problem, Quinn believed, with the inhabitants of the British Isles being able to accept the freshness of mind in a younger race. 'For that is really what is in the making here, a new race, a compound of many races.' The country might not become admirable, but it was efficient, and when standards were more settled and there was greater wealth, cultivation would follow. 'Some day it will produce fine art and good writers.'

Quinn did not complete his letter until 10 February. By then, disappointed that she could not find a paper to write for, Florence sent a letter card to announce her journey to the 'sunny south', the French Riviera.[8]

The American tour had contributed to the New Woman's feeling of restlessness and for the next four years, the penultimate period in her life, she often toyed with the idea of leaving England permanently. Her associations with G.B.S. and Willie Yeats were still strong but they were also too long-standing to offer her any special gratification, and certainly, any excitement.

Believing that Florence still planned an American tour, Yeats wrote to enquire whether she had let her rooms at Warwick Chambers. He believed he could not stay on at Woburn Buildings and thought he might rent her flat. In the following day's post he sent along *Deirdre* 'at last'. After much revision the play looked well to him, and betraying his impatience with actors, he remarked that he had finished reading it with 'some content. I can judge it now for the first time for the actors' voices have begun to fade.' His gift also included the American edition of his plays which Quinn had previously sent to Florence with his name written in Volume I. The poet expected that his mention of her in his preface and appendix 'may be of use to you in America.' He spoke of his preparation of a volume of prose plays for Bullen: the *Hour Glass, Pot of Broth, Kathleen ni Houlihan,* and *The Unicorn From The Stars;* the last was nearly finished, in 'three acts and thrown back in time a little over a hundred years.' It was 'tamed' enough to be possible to play in Dublin. Yeats's letter was written from Coole where he delighted in a 'double "war of sex".' Until the parental hearts 'softened, a young man and his bride who had eloped the month before were the house guests of Lady Gregory. The young husband was extremely depressed and as his depression grew, his wife became 'more and more cheerful'.

> She grows pinker and whiter & her hair seems yellower every day & she eats enormously. He watches with a look that seems to say 'I never thought you would be like this — I wonder how much longer I shall last — O my God.'

(Yeats's image of the young girl's hair seems to commingle with Anne Gregory's golden locks in his poem 'For Anne Gregory'.

> 'Never shall a young man,
> Thrown into despair
> By those great honey-coloured
> Ramparts at your ear,
> Love you for yourself alone
> And not your yellow hair.'

Nothing , Yeats told Florence, was said or done between the young couple that was unkind. On the other hand, Robert Gregory and his wife, Margaret, were 'fighting for mastery'. One day the depressed husband brought a 'dangerous little yacht' to the lake at Coole which upset twice in three days. Robert had already forbidden Margaret to sail unless the weather was calm, but on a certain day she walked into the library holding the 'cheerful bride' by the hand. The depressed husband refused to take them sailing because of the storm and so the ladies set out for themselves. Once at the lake, the 'cheerful' bride became afraid and returned to the house. When Robert eventually went after Margaret he found her in the water up to her 'middle.' That evening, to his 'great joy' his sweetheart came down with a cold which she was presently calling 'hay fever'.

Florence left London at the end of January 1908, staying for two nights in Paris on her way to Mentone. As she approached the south by rail, she was enchanted by a 'series of visions', which, by the time she reached her destination, turned into 'loveliness of all sorts'. By 2 February she was comfortably settled at the Regina Palace Hotel on the sea-front (now a block of flats) situated between the Promenade Col. Le Clerk and the Avenue Fauré. In the midst of 'oranges, lemons, mimosa, almond blossoms, siroccos', was this the region, she asked Quinn 'where you said you wanted to spend your old age? It is perfectly heavenly and I only wish you were here now. There are hundreds of lovely places to see.'[10]

Before long, Florence arranged two concerts in Mentone and one in Bordigherri in Italy, early in March. In addition, she was negotiating with 'some wiseacres at Monte Carlo'. Restless, all too soon, she shortly lost her enthusiasm for her hotel which was 'intolerably dull . . . full of old Germans and bores.' By the end of March she moved to the Hotel-Pension Annonciata, a 'lovely establishment on top of a hill, close to an old, dismantled monastery. For the moment, Florence found it incredible that within a half an hour she could pass 'from a kind of monastic reverie into the wild excitement of Monte Carlo. The contrast amuses and delights me.' Hopeful that Quinn might join her there she suggested a meeting at a town farther west like Nice before going to Marseilles around Easter time. She had actually sold her return ticket to London, and was of good mind to sell up her flat and return to France to end her days. Some little hermitage for a dwelling and occasional visits to Monte to break the monotony were her *idée fixe*. Inclined to be rash in spirit when away from London, Florence hoped that when her new novel *All Sorts and Conditions of Love* was finished, she would be free to live wherever she chose. Hughes Massey, an American agent who was working at the Curtis Brown office, was attempting to place the book for her. She was sure it would be a sensation and that she would not be in need of an American tour. Besides, she told Quinn, the country would probably be no more anxious to welcome her in the following or any other year, and, if the novel really did create a sensation, it was not the sort of book to 'appeal to the heads of colleges'.

For the first time in her life Florence was living without any particular friends, except for a Miss Hearne and a Miss Tucker, guests at the hotel. Apart from the three becoming 'very sage' occasionally, Florence wandered about as a 'ghost', thoroughly unattached. There were certainly no male conquests, or she 'wasn't conquered anyhow.' Everyone bored her, even the embellished prose in the reviews of her concerts at Mentone merely amused her. H.V. Barnett, an old confrère of W. E. Henley the poet, wrote several articles about Florence for the local *Green Paper*. After a particular concert which was attended by the singer, Christine Nillsen, Barnett wrote of a 'new troubador' who had come 'chanting through Provence',

> I am persuaded that she is more splendid, more skilled, more subtle, more various, and far more expressive than were any of her predecessors of the Middle Ages . . . [The music] is beautiful, the outcome of a great intelligence . . . you have only to taste such an experience . . . as was vouchsafed at Mentone on Monday to understand why so many of the acutest intellects of our time have welcomed it with wonder and praise.[11]

Yeats kept in touch with Florence during her stay in the south writing to ask whether she had 'lost all yet'. Presumably he spoke of her gambling at the Casino if not of her heart. He was amused to tell her of the tale Robert Farquharson, her 'marionette', was spreading that Granville Barker was Bernard Shaw's son. 'I shall begin searching everywhere for the mother I suppose — I shall discover here his nose and there his earnest gaze.'[12] On 21 April he wrote again wondering if there was a chance that he might meet her in Paris. London was 'unendurable' in her absence; 'I have no real friends — I have been away too long'.[13]

Mrs. Campbell, the poet said, had announced she would perform *Phèdre* in London and he wanted to be sure Florence played the second heroine. It 'is a very fine part and would suit you in some ways well.' Another letter in April requested all of Florence's settings for the *Collected Works*. Mrs. Lister presently considered her music quite beautiful and Yeats was anxious to make the book a complete record of their work together . Most of all, he hoped that the volume, in time to come, would represent their influence. Bullen had shown him a finished copy at his new establishment at Stratford-on-Avon:

> It will be a most beautiful edition . . . I think nobody of our time has had so fine an edition — I believe it will greatly strengthen my position — for my work is far stronger when put all together. I have been myself surprised by the unity of it all & by its general elevation of style I think.[14]

Volume III of the edition Yeats spoke of did indeed include his description of Florence's work in 'Music for Lyrics' which was followed by her own note. Printed as well were her settings for 'The Wind Blows Out of the Gates of the Day', 'The Happy Townland'. I have drunk from the ale from the Country of the Young', and then the songs from *the King's Threshold, On Baile's Strand*, and *Deirdre*.

Florence spent a fair portion of her time in Mentone travelling the short distance to Monte Carlo to gamble. For a while she enjoyed being ahead with £80 but toward the end of the season she was disappointed by a 'bad' day. All at once she 'lost courage' and stopped her bet always a turn too soon. Annoyed with herself for trying to cut her losses, she came away from the Casino with only £6.10 to the good. Soon afterwards, she left the south accompanied by Miss Hearne and with two hundred francs between them. It was a 'most heavenly' journey to Milan where they spent two nights before travelling to Lugano. The rail between Corno and Lugano cut across the 'most beautiful' country Florence had surely seen; 'everyone agrees about that', Florence told Quinn, 'and we saw it with Spring blossoms, all the pink peaches, just at sunset on a perfect day.'

On the way to Rheims to visit the 'magnificent' cathedral, Miss Hearne discovered that the contents of her handbag had been pilfered. With only some small change left between them, the two ladies had a 'narrow squeak' on the last lap of the journey back to England. But, it was all 'great fun'.[15]

Quinn did not correspond with Florence during her visit abroad but when she returned to Warwick Chambers he sent an apologetic letter informing her about the winter panic. The banking situation was just then improving, 'but we poor devils of lawyers inherit many troubles'. J. B. Yeats and Lily were still in New York and Quinn was doing a 'great deal to make their stay pleasant'. Indeed, though Lily was returning to Ireland 6 June, Yeats had decided to stay over. Quinn commissioned him to paint a portrait of the poet and one of George Moore. The work on Moore never progressed beyond a sketch but Quinn kindly paid J.B.Y. for both and then added an additional £30 to the sum for an oil portrait of himself. The artist thereafter came to Quinn's apartment every Sunday to paint from 11 to 1 retiring for a short lunch before resuming his work again from 2 to 5. Quinn sat for nine or ten sittings and then he 'struck'. Mr. Yeats insisted upon painting him from a distance and consequently the portrait did not progress beyond the third sitting.

Quinn was better pleased concerning another matter. He had been offered the refusal of a chalk drawing of W.B. Yeats by Sargent. Shannon had painted an oil of the poet for him as well which Quinn expected Florence would see in exhibition in London before him. In addition, he was gratified that he had received recognition in his own field. The National Democratic Convention took place in Denver in July and Quinn had been elected a delegate. On a different topic, Quinn was distressed to learn of Synge's grave illness:

> I am afraid the poor fellow is done for. I wonder what the 'pathriots' think of their attack now. A man with a latent disease in his system never ought to have taken the worry and vexation of managing a theatre. At times I feel like saying 'Damn the theatre, anyway!' It has kept Yeats from doing his real work of writing poetry in the last five years; it has killed Synge, and it gave the Fays to the United States for one winter, which is quite enough of them. They got fine notices in New York, but their acting was awful. In Chicago they got good notices but did no business, and I understand they sailed for the other side a couple of weeks ago.

Florence was of course pleased Quinn had written. Back at her 'old diggings' she was preparing for a change in address in a week or two (which she did not make) and advised the lawyer to send letters to the Union of London and Smith's Bank in the High Street, Kensington. The thought of J.B. Yeats having such a splendid time in America convinced her that it would be fitting if the poet's father would live in Jane Addam's Hull House in Chicago; there he could lead the talk. Not only had Florence acquired a photograph of the Sargent portrait, she had in her possession the Mancini photograph too. Also, Shannon's portrait, she wrote Quinn, was showing at the Franco-British Exhibition, 'the site of the Greatest show on Earth! The Entente Cordiale! and all that useful humbug.' But Willie was very pleased about the portrait, arriving at Shannon's studio at 'cockrow' for the sittings. 'That was quite necessary as it took him all the time to arrange his tie and his hair.'[17]

Florence mentioned to Quinn the music which she had written for Volume III of Yeats's *Works*. In turn he replied that the poet certainly had loyal friends. He was 'lucky' in this, 'even if he is not so lucky in his love affairs.'

By June, Florence was disappointed that her new novel was un-published so that she was not able to 'wander about the world'. Her only item of income since her return from Mentone was for a charity recital. When she talked over her possibilities with Mrs. Campbell, the younger actress advised her that London simply wasn't worth troubling about when it came to recitals. So, Florence told Quinn, she wasn't exactly 'on the make'. The only bright spot in her future was a recital she planned of Nietzsche's 'Dance Song' to be held after a dinner at the United Arts Club. The group met at Rumplemayers in St. James Street; a rather nice club and only four guineas a year. 'Beautiful teas as you can guess there.' Then too, she looked forward to attending a 'great Woman's Suffrage Demonstration in Hyde Park' with Mrs. Todhunter and her daughter. Everyone was beginning to take to the idea, Florence said, and the militants would soon realise their demands

> I think it is doing a good deal for the sex they don't hate each other so much as they did & its making them think of something besides keeping up the fiction 'that home is the foundation of the Empire,' a cry which pays so many of them so particularly well.18

As a matter of fact, Florence could not see what was to become of the aged and the ugly unless they interested themselves in politics and economic independence. England was undergoing a very dif-ficult stage of transition, 'the middle class young and pretty all seem to be taking to free love on the sly.' She had been reading Nevinson's book on South Africa in which he remarked that in Africa the laws were ahead of their customs. 'It strikes me our customs are getting ahead of our laws.'

John Quinn wrote to Florence again in July. He was preparing to leave for Denver and with his cusomary preciseness accounted for his itinerary. His tailor had made him some light suits for the trip, a short gray silk coat, and a 'long passionate-looking, yellow pongee duster and motor car coat.'

> I don't need to wear anything under these but my pyjamas if I want to. I am going to have some white shoes and I think I will add white stockings, and then I will have a suit of light pyjamas, and then the long yellow duster, and with a light cap I think I can give a fairly good imitation of a Buddhist priest or a Capuchin monk, on my way to a political convention.

J.B. Yeats, meanwhile, was sorely annoying Quinn and the lawyer was about to throw out the whole matter of his portrait until he decided that after sitting for sixty hours he would make Yeats finish up at any cost. Certain rules were enforced: Quinn would allow the artist one half hour more for the eyes and the same for the hair. At the moment, one of his eyes looked as if he had a squint, and the other, a cataract. Worse, Yeats had painted his hair in a fashion that made him resemble an English butler. Not that Quinn objected to looking like a butler. 'That is to say, the side whiskers down on my face — side-boards we call them.' Yeats began to paint again after Quinn extracted an additional promise that he would not 'pink and white' his whole face, but after sitting for fifteen minutes, he caught the artist doing just that. Then he exploded; there was a 'devil of a scene' with Quinn telling Yeats he 'would put a knife through the canvas and never frame or keep it.' When the dreadful confrontation ended, Quinn thought he was most generous for permitting J.B.Y. to finish; he even sent him a letter of congratulations. To his amazement, Yeats, with his typical attitude of independence, replied that the portrait would have been completed sooner 'if he hadn't interference from without.' With peace made between them, Quinn gave the 'old man' an additional £20 for an impressionistic paintng of his houseboy, Sadajiro Kumantani, and a sum of money for another four drawings: two of Professor Dowden of Trinity and one each of John Hughes the Irish sculptor, and the Irish writer Standish O'Grady.[19]

Florence 'shrieked' with laughter over Quinn's encounter with 'Father Yeats' as the wife of the painter Edwin Ellis referred to him. In London it was cold and raining and she lit a fire in her sitting-room before replying to her New York friend. Referring to his story of the Twentieth Century Express, she hoped that the 'passionate looking yellow pongee duster' had not been fatal with the ladies. As for his comparison to the Buddhist monk, 'our monk', one with whom she studied, wore bright orange dress which was called the 'yellow robe'.

Yeats had gone to Paris, Florence informed Quinn; in fact he had disappeared for a whole month. Supposedly he was visiting Maud Gonne; and then a remark that might establish the nature of her own relationship with the poet, 'I suppose his long years of fidelity have been rewarded at last!!!' For all Florence knew, she might be imagining the whole thing but she thought Quinn would enjoy her idea. There was additional talk of personalities with a discussion of Mrs. Campbell's 'brain breakdown' which consisted of 'awful pains in her head'. On occasion, Florence was called in to soothe her with Mrs. Pat saying she had a 'healing touch.'[20]

By the second week in September, Florence was in Edinburgh touring with Mrs. Campbell in Pinero's *The Thunderbolt*. From the Lyceum Theatre there, the company went to the Theatre Royal at Glasgow, and then to Southport in October to play the Opera House; following which, they travelled to Newcastle-on-Tyne to appear at the Tyne Theatre and Opera House. By 24 October the company was at Liverpool adding *Electra* and *The Second Mrs. Tanqueray* to the bill before going to the King's Theatre, Hammersmith. The large audiences, attracted by the predominantly West End cast, appreciated Florence's 'clever' Ann Mortimore in *The Thunderbolt,* and when she played at the Theatre Royal in Dublin the following month they thought her 'capital'. Florence saw a great deal of Lady Gregory while she was in Ireland. Lily wrote all about her visit to her father.

Back in London after Mrs. Campbell's promised performance of *Deirdre* at the Abbey, Florence performed in a series of matinées with Mrs. Pat at the New Theatre in St. Martin's Lane. On 27 November, and 1, 8, 9, and 11 December the company repeated Hugo von Hoffmansthal's *Phédre* translated by Arthur Symons, and Yeats's *Deirdre.* W. Dixon Scott, young man about town, wrote of his impressions of *Phédre* to his friend Mary McCrossan. He was enchanted by the beauty of the ensembles: 'venemous, nightmare colours, the blotted swollen rather morbid lovliness of the whole thing — like a great black and scarlet snake lifting up its head and then dreadfully extending the dark fang'.

Plot there was none, neither real action, and the construction was 'puerile' but there was glamour everywhere. After an added evening performance the young critic saw Florence home — 'Twas a gory and colossal time.' An onlooker walking along Princess Raod at 10.30 p.m. would have remarked at an 'amazing spectacle',

> A wonderful Egyptian-looking person, habited in purple and umbers and scarlets and great hats and veils . . . The Scarlet Woman was Florence Farr . . . and we talked and talked; and she is very glamorous and vivid.[21]

Yeats came over from Dublin to see his play and seemed in 'high feathers' although he wrote his father that Mrs. Campbell did only 'fairly well'. *Dierdre* was not generally appreciated; it was, perhaps, that London had not yet learned to suit the theatre to the play and Yeats's one-act simply did not carry in a large theatre. As for the poet as playwright:

> He is one of the archconspirators in the cleverest literary fake of modern times . . . The Celts have given modern English literature almost everything of value it possesses; their last insult was to give us their traditional tales . . .Mr. Yeats should find the one-act play

a good form for his art, for his characters are static, they do not develop, they 'are' . . . To say that Yeats's plays are inhuman is not to expose their defect but to define their quality.[22]

Florence, too, was in 'high feathers' after her autumn tour. Travelling with Mrs. Pat had done her no harm 'in the way of prestige' and she was free of the inertia that settled in after her return from France. A lecture tour was coming up in December and she expected to go to Glasgow, Liverpool, Leeds, and Chesterfield, and to have a 'lively' time staying at the houses of her benefactors. So sure was she of her future in England that with typical misjudgement, she did not accept Mrs. Campbell's new invitation to accompany her to the States. Florence did not feel like playing 'seconds' to her, besides, her cousins (the Whittalls) had come into a lot of money after their parents' deaths, and there was talk of one, a singer, teaming with her for an extended tour around the world.

Quinn wrote to Florence in December, neither married nor 'done for' as she assumed, but attempting to recuperate from a nervous breakdown and neuritis. His friends's past news of the poet and Maud Gonne amused him indeed and he hoped Yeats had not fallen in love again with 'M.G.' or, if he had, that his years of fidelity would be rewarded. 'It would be an amazing thing if he married her'.[23]

Sometime in 1909, Florence met the young American poet Ezra Pound. In February, Elkin Mathews who published *The Music of Speech* for her that year, introduced Pound to the Poet's Club.[24] The group met at the United Arts Club for which Florence had performed the 'Dance Song'. In general, the American found those gathered there a bore in spite of such presentable company as Bernard Shaw and Hilaire Belloc. Florence may have met young Pound at this time but certainly by April when he joined a new group of poets organized by T. E., Hulme.[25] The latter was a member of the Poet's Club until an attack on him in *The New Age* by the poet F. S. Flint. After the article appeared, Hulme formed a new group called the 'Secession Club' to which Flint, Edward Storer, Joseph Campbell, Francis Tancred, Padraic Colum, Ernest Rhys, and Florence belonged.[26] Alternate dates have been suggested for Pound's introduction to this group and Florence may or may not have shared their impression of the American as 'a rebel against all conventions except sanity'.[27]

Ezra Pound was especially interested in the Troubadors and so it is not difficult to imagine that from this mutuality he proceeded to engage in what must have been a very piercing friendship with Florence. Rather unexpectedly, it was not the spokeswoman for the revolutionary spirit in England who brought the American to Woburn Buildngs but Yeats's intimate friend Olivia Shakespear and her daughter Dorothy. By the end of 1909, Pound convinced the elder poet of the brilliance of his sort of music for poetry. Yeats wrote to Lady Gregory 'It is more definitely music with strongly marked time and yet is effective speech. However he can't sing as he has no voice. It is like something on a very bad phonograph.'[28]

I doubt whether Pound pleased Yeats for any great length of time with his own brand of 'lilting'. But his robustness of attack must have provided a cathartic effect on the elder poet who was tiring of his own life style. He had, after all, outgrown the *fin de siècle* period of his life and with it, the psaltery which had become a symbol of the years of his indefinite twilight, lacking in vigour and concreteness.

There were probably many occasions when Florence visited Pound when he moved to 10 Church Walk in Kensington. Asked for his recollections of those who came to his room in the next few years, he replied:'Actually IN the front room, Florence Farr reading Tagore, D.H. Lawrence missing train from Croydon.'[29] By the following year, Pound knew Florence well enough to write her biography in a poem that is unequalled in the accurate observation of its subject. Noel Stock in *The Life of Ezra Pound* refers to 'Portrait D'Une Femme' only as a 'modern' subject in 'modern terms.' During his confinement in St. Elizabeth's Hospital in Washington, D.C., however, Pound told Jayanta Padmanabha, a visiting professor from New College, Ghana, Africa, he wrote the poem for Florence and he believed it influenced T.S. Eliot to write his 'Portrait of a Lady' (although not on the same subject).

Rejected by the *North American Review* in 1912,[30] 'Portrait D'Une Femme' bears the date of 1913 in *Rispostes* but Florence uses or repeats the words 'dull man' in quotes in her book *Modern Woman* published in 1910. Her portrait, painted no doubt in the small rooms at Warwick Chambers evokes an earlier vision by Yeats wherein he describes the reflections of her mind in the wall hangings of Brook Green. Pound wrote:

> Your mind and you are our Sargasso Sea,
> London has swept about you this score years,
> And left you this or that in fee:
> Ideas, old gossip, oddments of all things,
> Strange spars of knowledge and dimmed wares of price.
> Great minds have sought you — lacking someone else.
> You have been second always. Tragical?

No. You preferred it to the usual thing:
One dull man, dulling and uxorious,
One average mind — with one thought less each year.
Oh, you are patient. I have seen you sit
Hours, where something might have floated up.
And now you pay one. Yes, you richly pay.
You are a person of some interest, one comes to you
And takes strange gain away:
Trophies fished up: some curious suggestion;
Fact that leads nowhere: and a tale or two,
Pregnant with mandrakes, or with something else
That might prove useful and yet never proves,
That never fits a corner or shows use,
Or finds its hour upon the loom of days:
The tarnished, gaudy, wonderful old work:
Idols and ambergris and rare inlays,
These are your riches, your great store; and yet
For all this sea-hoard of decidious things,
Strange woods, half-sodden, and new brighter stuff:
In the slow light of the differing light and deep,
No! There is nothing! In the whole and all,
Nothing that's quite your own.
Yet this is you.

Florence was anxious to return to the theatre in March 1909, and asked Yeats whether she might have his permission to produce Synge's *In The Shadow of the Glen*. Synge's being in hospital 'he is perhaps dying', Yeats wrote — would prohibit a decision for some time.[31] The playwright died on 24 March and for some reason Florence did not mention his death when she wrote to Quinn in early April. Neither was news sent to him from Dublin; the information came to him by chance from a man in his office who showed him a clipping from a Dublin paper.

Florence was especially effusive in her letter as she presented Quinn with an old question of whether 'you are really and truly coming over this summer. I do hope you are.' She was 'frightfully active' again giving recitals 'all over the place', and a new membership in the Eugenic Education Society interested her. Her real passion was to 'stir up' people and 'revalue their values' for them a little but the association with the group was proving more beneficial than she had hoped. 'I think hitherto I've been dwelling too exclusively on the sunbeam in my own eye and not attending enough to the motes in my brother's It's a much more cheeful occupation.'

She was full of ebullience and thought again of Quinn's proposed visit.

It's such a lovely day & we could take a motor cab and drive to some nice place in the sunshine & see the almond blossoms all coming out.

Mind you don't back out of it again or I shall have to come over to New York to fetch you.[32]

Yeats wrote to Florence in April of being unwell.[33] Headache stupidity, & the rest.' From 3 May he expected to be perfectly free until about Christmas. 'I think another year of the theatre would have broken me down utterly.' His work at the Abbey was presently lightened by a new manager, an Irish novelist and playwright named Conal O'Riordan, but the theatre was in the middle of 'great trouble'. Only a fortnight after his death, Molly Allgood was told she was the sole benefactor of Synge's money which entitled her to the large sum of £80 a year. But the ownership of copyright was not decided and endless delays were being caused by Synge's brother-in-law Stephens. As a result, the Abbey players could not perform *Deirdre of the Sorrows* until the winter. Yeats wished he might play it in June after completing the script with the help of Lady Gregory. 'But we will only have to write a few lines. It must remain a magnificent sketch of what would have been his greatest work.'

Temporarily freed from the Abbey, Yeats planned to come to London the following week and 'do nothing but *The Player Queen* for months.' The Abbey was a burden in so many ways and the emotional atmosphere was stifling him. Annie Horniman's association with the theatre was coming to a head and she, Yeats, and Lady Gregory were all attempting to find a solution which would terminate Annie's legal ties. Largely through Shaw's ability to act as mediator in Abbey politics, her relationship was eventually severed. One of the determinants in the break was the Abbey's financial coup with Shaw's *Showing Up of Blanco Posnet* which gave Yeats some new courage for independence. The Lord Chamberlain refused Shaw a license in England but since Ireland did not come under his authority, G.B.S. gave the play to the Abbey players. A letter from Annie written to him 30 August 1909 after the successful performance at the Abbey shows her influence in the production there and the rapport which she shared with Shaw so many years after the Avenue affair. The playwright obviously asked her to produce the play at her Manchester Theatre and a triumphant entrepreneur wrote that her dander was up and she was willing to 'go for' the Lord Chamberlain 'or any man in a position to bully me.' But fighting against the patriots and everybody else in Shaw's country prevented her from saving enough to help further.[34]

Before he left for his European holiday, John Quinn wrote to Florence to congratulate her for the new interest in the Eugenic Society. He believed it had similar virtues to Socialist Societies —

They fail of their direct objects but shake people out of their thoughtless laziness and bring about reforms; extremists usually fail; but they are idealists, — pioneers — and they bear the flag of progress . . . But don't get so deep in the business of correcting other poeple's lives that you begin to worry. I don't worry any more. We can't make the world over. All we can do is our part to prevent useless suffering and to help, within our means, those who suffer.[35]

Florence was overjoyed to read that Quinn would really be over. Social life was not dull with Americans 'swarming over' and everyone busy with dinner parties and theatre but she was anxious to arrange expeditions with the New Yorker. Meanwhile, she sent him news of his friends; Yeats and Lady Gregory were in England for the Irish play week but the poet would probably be in Paris when Quinn arrived. He was considering a holiday with Maud Gonne in Italy with a cousin, Miss Clay, going along as chaperone. Since Quinn was especially disturbed about Arthur Symons who had suffered an emotional breakdown, Florence assured him that the writer was on the mend with Mrs Symons being 'packed off "to rest" ' by Miss Tobin. Although he was still under medical supervision, the American woman was bringing him to concerts and galleries, and Florence heard 'he talks quite interestingly I believe'.[36]

It was Quinn's habit to dictate his letters; therefore the news that he would go to Paris for a week before London 'to take some motor trips with a friend' acquires added significance after reading Florence's reply. 'I think we'd better arrange Paris as we made up our minds before, don't you?' Future correspondence does not refer to this arrangement but Florence did of course spend time with Quinn in London. In September, when she reflected upon their many conversations during his visit, it was apparent that Quinn's feelings for her were other than amorous. When she wrote to him after he returned to the States, she wondered 'how many men had died to prove that the women they loved had no passions — It is a funny state of things brought about by immoderate modesty, isn't it?' For an instant it appears as if the passionless woman might be Florence until later in her letter when she asks the lawyer to take care of himself and not to let logic be overcome by 'apparently pathetic situations. They can all work up so easily & you only hear one side.'[37]

Much to her disappointment, life for Florence continued as usual while Quinn was over. She still looked for work in the theatre and, being out of luck with her novels as well, decided to turn to Shaw for an agent. 'Why depend on agents?' he answered. They were useless except in the case of very incapable or busy people. Confronted with another gloomy complaint concerning her eyesight, which had actually begun to deteriorate in 1906, G.B.S. reminded her that everyone's reading sight diminished after forty.[38] Compared to Quinn, Shaw played the role of a sort of dull black knight while the lawyer, ephemeral though he was, suited her conception of an attractive consort.

After a journey to the west of Ireland, the playwright returned to London in October with his own headache and 'millions' of letters attacking him. Replying to Florence's information that in his absence her eye problem had been diagnosed as astigmatism, he wrote that it struck him as an ordinary infliction which was 'the common lot of mankind'. Meyrowitz at the Picadilly end of Bond Street, he added, carried invisible glasses but since the kind he referred to were rimless and fragile, he recommended a sturdier pair for ordinary use. 'Meyrowitz is abominably expensive, so you had better let me pay the bill.[39] The gesture gives the lie to his repeated denial that he ever helped Florence out with money.

Florence spent a late summer with friends in Brittany having a 'gorgeous time' going without stockings as she walked the sand, and sleeping in the midst of heather and granite. Inclined to be overweight, she had lost pounds in the 'most satisfactory manner' Back in London by 8 September she went to an exhibition of Beardsley drawings in Burton Street. A print from a second edition of her blue and green Avenue Theatre poster was selling for ten guineas. She offered the gallery one of her first edition copies for six pounds to which they would add a 25 per cent commission. The original drawing was with Francis Byrne at Chickerings in Boston. Charles Ricketts had told her it was worth forty guineas and so she advised Byrne to release it for sale. He was unsuccessful and eventually Dolmetsch shipped it back to England where it immediately went into the *Fair Lady* exhibition at Grafton Street.

Florence went on a motoring trip in Chesterfield at the end of September and by 8 October she was bothering Shaw again for an agent. This time he advised her to publish at her own expense, or his, or on commission. Fifield the publisher was available for that kind of arrangement or Everleigh Nash. Sorry perhaps at his impatience with her, he nearly apologised that he was so occupied by work of all sorts that I have become a two-headed monster of the most callous selfishness and the most devoted self sacrifice; and I am growing elderly and crazy and unscrupulous and so forth; but still, if I can be of any use, let me know.[40]

Florence continued to worry G.B.S. about a publisher until, in answer to what must have been a request for money, he wrote 'horror . . . I haven't a rap.' He had undergone an 'eclipse' in America and in England for eighteen months, and two plays had been censored, 'and deuce knows what else, I have sailed round this years' end closer in the wind that I have been since my days of destitution. Of course this only means loose cash: I have plenty of money locked up'.

Until the end of the year, he would be counting 'not exactly my shillings, but my sovereigns'. He attempted to steer Florence toward Fifield still with the most indelicate argument. The publisher could not afford to be independent of common work and therefore he did 'common work well'. It may be of Frank Palmer who ended up publishing *Modern Woman* for Florence the following year for whom Shaw invented the maxim:

If a man has friends, one can forgive him for having no policy; if he has policy one can forgive him for having no friends; but when he has neither friends nor policy where are the compensating advantages?[41]

By the time Florence's book was out she was allegedly lagging in her awareness of the changing morality in Britain. In her own ingenue days, chorus girls drank champagne and 'went to the bad'. In 1910 they drank milk and married peers. Moreover, girls with brains were cautious enough to exert prudence in order to make a better bargain, and were deliberately not marrying. The intelligent woman refused to enter into a game of love unless she was animated by ardour; 'passion served up with cold sauce as in the Shaw-Barker school of sex revolts them'. As much as Florence attempted to be thoroughly innovative in her ideas in a text she had sat upon for over a decade, the results were merely like 'flies buzzing around a stinkpot', or so H.M. Paget told Geoffrey when he asked permission to read it.

Yeats's verses from the second version of *The Shadowy Waters*
> Another fire has come into the harp,
> Fire from beyond the world, and wakens it:

were odd guests across from the table of contents; yet, no less confounding than the incongruity of a woman who searched for the ineffable while cautiously playing the roles of quasi-socialist and suf-fragette. In a book which was three thousand words longer than Palmer wanted, Florence took the position that one set of readers would think her outrageously advanced while the other would call her absurdly conventional. In reality, Florence really did enjoy the comfortable role in life and in literature of setting foot in neither strata while applying herself to the enviable freedom of uncensored discussion.

Pleased with the book's reception, and the publication of her *Calendar of Philosophy* that year, Florence wrote to John Quinn that she had not wasted her life 'this twelvemonth'. She had dis-covered a way of getting thin too: 'It's the stretching system instead of trying to develop one's muscles one stretches one's sinews. It's most successful'.[42]

Florence would not have broken Quinn's silence this time except for Mrs. Worthington who disclosed his illness durng a visit to Lon-don. Sarah Purser had been over from Ireland and she too spoke of the lawyer which prompted Florence to 'break the ice'. Although 'I am not at all sure you don't want to be quit of the whole boiling [lot?] of us.' She wrote about the costume party at a debating society at 'The Mitre Tavern'. G.K. Chesterton escorted her as Dr. Johnson while she was disguised as Mrs. Trail. They had 'great fun' and a 'very good talk' with Hilaire Belloc joining them for desert.

Quinn did not reply to Florence's letter of June until 2 November,[43] (1910) ill health and overwork consuming him. Near to a total breakdown in the spring, he had come as close to the breaking point as could be possible without going to pieces completely. Insomnia ac-companied exhaustion and he finally put himself into the hands of a 'great' physician who tinkered enough to keep him going. J. B. Yeats was still in New York 'flourishing' although age was beginning to tell with his hair looking whiter. The painter had a small coterie of artists and writers about him and he enjoyed life very much.

Florence answered immediately for 'if I don't answer at once I never answer at all.' She was sitting by the fire in her sitting-room, attempting to wipe off the smears of the cinders on her writing paper. A new project interested her, she wrote, 100,000 words which she was writing in a big library book on 'great women characters in the Drama.' She had a new diet too, 'muscatels' with only one big meal a day and 'snacks'. Pleased that Quinn was fond of 'old' Mr. Yeats, she remembered him herself as a 'lovely talker . . . "Sweet-voiced" telling stories'. Quinn must have been told, she expected, that George Pollexfen, Willie's uncle had died leaving the Yeats family £5,000. Willie and his brother were to receive £1,000 between them and Lily and Lolly $2,000 each. 'It will be a great boon to them'.[44]

The first half of 1911 brought no new artistic opportunities for Florence and by June, she moved her things into a smaller flat at 20 Glebe Place, off the King's Road and a turning away from her sister Mary Catherine. The packing and unpacking of old possessions, and the 'most beautiful' procession of George V's Coronation which she saw from the Carlton Club, filled her with sentiment and nostalgia. All of a sudden, she thought of Edward Emery and scribbled John Quinn a line asking him whether he had ever seen Edward act. 'I hear he's one of Schubert's leading lights!!!' As a matter of fact, the lawyer had seen Mr. Emery a year or two before in Clyde Fitch's *The City*. He did very well with the role playing a 'sort of drinking fellow.' Quinn thought he looked the part, seemed a clever man, and 'I should say was a good actor.'

Bernard Shaw bought the Beardsley drawing from Florence that month paying £63 for it although he remembered the sum as £60, and his wife had it for a birthday present. In 1941, Shaw insisted to Clifford Bax that it was the only sum of money that ever crossed between them and he thought it might have been for a book with which he was not familiar. 'But as she always lived within her means, this must have been the purpose for which she sold the drawing.'[45]

It was true that G.B.S. gave Florence a sum of money to publish *The Solemnization of Jacklin* but Florence used the money from the Beardsley for a different purpose. The transaction may have taken place at her flat because Shaw was certainly a visitor there. A promise which was not kept to see her on one occasion was the reason for a letter from him written 'en voyage' at Annency 12 July.

It was no use — I mean my attempt to get to Glebe Place before I left. I had to get away at once, having worked myself to a standstill & realised that I should have gone a month earlier; and the preparations for a motor tour are appalling; for instance, I had to pay more than £200 to secure the privilege of dancing backwards and forwards across the Alps and Vosges in & out of France, Germany, Switzerland, Austria & Italy. Of course I shall get it back. I only mention it as an impressive sample of the sort of thing that leaves me, when I start on a holiday, as exhausted as if I had produced another play. Foreign money, maps, routes, hotels, customs duties, insurance of car, spare parts, clothes, provision for inevitable business during absence, &c.: it ends in your sitting down and crying because you can't bring your mind to grasp the question of how many socks to put in your trunk. Beardsley, black

and spotty, loomed through it all as something forgotten that would nevertheless not get out of my head & leave me alone. My sordid intention of selling it was promptly checkmated by Charlotte, who not having paid for it, loved it greedily. You had much better have pawned it to me, and kept it on your walls.[46]

Florence went to Mentone again for four months during the winter of 1911–1912 on the proceeds of the Beardsley and with a 'system', (presumably for the casino) Lily Yeats told her father. She sketched much of the time capturing the 'spirit of the olives' and finished her novel *The Solemnization of Jacklin.* In Florence's words, the story was about a 'woman who found matrimony rather tiresome & took a lot of settling down.' The characters were created out of the prejudices of a lifetime. John Woods, the husband who snored, possessed a characteristic implying a 'certain subconscious tactlessness, an ineptitude in the conduct of life.' The heroine, Jacklin, divorces 'dull' John Wood and marries a philandering artist Tim Callands with whom she engages in a dialogue taken from one of the *New Age* articles.

> 'Tim,' Jacklin cried, 'don't you know that a woman can be the friend of many men — she can only love one with all her passion.'
> . . . and a man can love many women. He can only be the friend of one,' said Dorus,

a sort of male counterpart to Florence's characterization of herself.

Within a collage of semi-autobiographical experiences, Jacklin gives birth to a Yeatsian fairy child who is led by a mysterious person with black, wet hair (the young Yeats) singing on 'a five-note Celtic scale'. The mystical child, more properly at home in *Land of Heart's Desire,* does not save Jacklin's marriage to the unfaithful artist and she leaves with their child to return to John Woods. Never does she deceive herself that she is not returning to the hideousness of 'mutual charity', the ugly epitome of tolerance, dullness, and forgiving. Florence's idea, no doubt, of how her life might have gone had she returned to Edward Emery.

Before the ghastly novel ends, Florence hints at her desire to leave England for all time. A character says:

> Quite lately I have met some women who live in India. They tell me of quiet places there, on the shores of the Ganges, which make one willing to give up all the power money gives and all the excitement of Western life; if one could hope to live in one of them.

Fifteen years after Bernard Shaw prophesised that after this period of time she would fit herself in somewhere, Florence was about to make a drastic decision in her life as she prepared to leave the south.

NOTES

1 Berg, (August 24 1907).
2 Berg, (September 6 1907).
3 Academic Centre,
4 Wade, *Letters*, 492.
5 Berg, (December 9 1907).
6 Wade, *op. cit.*, 493.
7 Academic Centre.
8 Berg, (January 21 1908).
9 Foster-Murphy Collection.
10 Berg, (February 29 1908).
11 Reprinted in *The Music of Speech.*
12 Academic Centre.
13 Wade,*op. cit.*, 508.
14 Academic Centre.
15 Berg, (June 18 1908).
16 Berg, (June 5 1908).
17 Berg, (June 15 1908).
18 *Ibid.*
19 Berg, (July 1 1908).
20 Berg, (July 13 1908).
21 Mary McCrossen, ed., *The Letters of W. Dixon-Scott,* (London 1932), partially quoted in Ian Fletcher,*Romantic Mythologies.*
22 *NA,* (December 10 1908), 142.
23 Berg, (December 20 1908).
24 Noel Stock, *The Life of Ezra Pound,* (London 1970), 61.
25 Patricia Hutchins, *Ezra Pound's Kensington,* (London 1965), 128.
26 Stock, *op. cit.*, 63-64.
27 Martin, *The New Age,* 151.
28 Wade, *op. cit.*, 543.
29 Hutchins, *op. cit.*, 69.
30 Stock, *op. cit.*, 111
31 Wade, *op. cit.*, 525–26.
32 Berg, (April 5 1909).
33 Academic Centre.
34 BM.
35 Berg, (June 1 1909).
36 Berg, (September 8 1909).
37 *Ibid.*
38 Bax, *op. cit.*, 29-30.
39 BM.
40 BM.
41 BM.
42 Berg, (June 20 1910).

43 Berg.
44 Berg, (November 13 1910).
45 Academic Centre, (May 22 1941).
46 UL.

10

Ceylon
1912-1917

And they wanted more from their women,
Wanted 'em jacked up a little
And sent over for teachers (Ceylon)
So Loica went out and died there
After her time in the post-Ibsen movement.[1]

Why 'Loica', as Ezra Pound mistakingly wrote for Shaw's 'Louka' in
Arms and The Man[2] so suddenly took off for Ceylon in 1912, actually appeared to defect from the comfortable environment of London, was part of the mystery that surrounded Florence Farr. Her
friends could only guess at her motives. Arnold Dolmetsch, for one,
was sure she left England because of disappointment that W.B. Yeats
would not marry her.[3] Then there were the rumours reaching
Dorothy, presently married to Sir Percy Rhodes, that her aunt knew
she was 'doomed to die'. Florence herself was vague about it all.
When asked by her family whether she would return from Ceylon,
she never provided an answer they could rely upon. Once she said
that it all depended upon 'how she grew old'; which could have been
so, Dorothy thought, for she knew Florence wished to be
remembered 'moving among interesting people — keen witted and
alert. . .The withering of the leaf before an audience was not for her.'

Florence was still 'lively — nice — quite girlish — hair a greying
brown-pretty-still there-bubbly-talked twenty to the dozen —VITAL'
was the comment of another contempory.[4] But she had missed her
chance again to become an important actress, in her maturity, by
refusing to play 'seconds' to Mrs. Campbell. Her recitals were
dwindling in number, a recital in the Arts Theatre at Liverpool 5

January 1911 alone is on the record.[5] Even her writing achieved, as
she surely knew, no lasting recognition. Neither was there a
relationship pertinent enough to keep her at home; the price she
eventually paid for her insistence on independence and her demanding standards of other human beings. In truth, she was 'second
always'.

It was a matter of chance in 1912 that Sir Ponnambalam
Ramanathan had nearly completed his College for Girls in Ceylon.
That year Florence was ready to abandon the thought that she would
be 'lost' if she did not 'stamp' herself upon her age. She decided,
therefore, to test her promise made to the Guru in London in 1902.
Certainly there was correspondence between Sir Ponnambalam and
his disciple in Theosophy as letters from Edward Carpenter
(Florence Farr's colleague in *The New Age*) testify.[6] And Florence
may have discussed a future in Ceylon with Ramanathan's nephew
who prepared for his law examinations in London in 1906.[7] This was
the year that W.B. Yeats wondered if it was not the Eastern
meditations that had changed Florence, and 'fired' her; although he
considered her immersion in 'the Eastern supersensualizing state'
one that was 'upwards out of life'.[8]

In June Florence had almost decided to leave England. Her words
to John Quinn were 'I may be off to Ceylon the end of the year to end
my days in the "society of the wise" as the Vendantist books say one
should.' A septet of which she had been 'delivered' captured her
mood after seeing Albert Einstein's 'great' monument to Oscar
Wilde. The marvel of it inspired her to write[8]

> Neither in Anuradharpoura,·
> Nor Nineveh, nor Babylon;
> Nor cut in porphyry at Itzalan,··
> Nor carved for Khefren's tomb ··· tomb in diolite
> Has a wrought stone
> Set prouder seal of silence on the dead,
> Then that enchanted, winged hermaphrodite.[9]
> Ceylon ··Mexico ··· Egypt 4000 B.C.

After many months of silence, Quinn, though pleased to hear from
Florence, was not impressed with her plans. The idea that she might
end her days in Ceylon sounded 'romantic' enough and would undoubtedly 'read well in a book', but he was deeply concerned that she
had perhaps not considered the adventure carefully enough. Had the
decision been his, he would have enquired about the flora and fauna,
the types of insects, the neighbours, the cooking, and especially
(since Quinn was a hypochondriac) the availability of good doctors.
Then he would have questioned the condition of the roads, the prox-

imity of the post-office, and whether the English who had settled there had remained 'sane and comfortable'. As for himself, illness, worry, and the disgust which arose from having taken on a new legal partner deterred him from travelling to England. The new man was 'conceited, superficial, impossible to work with', and more sensitive than any neurotic woman Quinn had ever come across. A conference was like 'Sherman's March to the Sea — a frontal attack, a flanking movement, a detour, another frontal attack, another diversion, another flanking movement, and so on'.[10]

Four days after revealing the news to Quinn, Florence wrote to Bernard Shaw whom she must have seen more than a little during the early summer. A 10" pastel of the playwright, probably painted by her at Glebe Place during those months, was presented to Geoffrey Paget when she packed for Ceylon.[11] Recommending that Shaw 'soothe' his 'weary brain' listening to a woman she did not name who played 'deliciously' Florence broke the news that she was off to Ceylon in August for 'five years certain'. Fifield the publisher wold pay him the royalties from *The Solemnization of Jacklin* in her absence.[12]

By July William Butler Yeats knew of Florence Emery's plans. Topped by what appeared to be an 'old fish basket on her head', but 'absolutely no swan bills on her body', Florence, obviously garishly dressed, came late one evening to Woburn Buildings. W.B.Y., Lady Gregory, Sturge Moore, Will Rothenstein, and 'a Rajah who is also a poet', (Tagore presumably) heard that Florence was 'going to Ceylon for five years to meditate in an Indian School for mystics.'[13]

Not unmindful of the enormity of the looming responsibility she faced at Ramanathan College, Florence went up to Cheltenham Ladies' College sometime in July to enquire about the latest ideas in Western education. She was delighted to learn of an 'elaborate thing called the "Montessori System" ' which she looked forward to practicing in Ceylon. In August she left Glebe Place and moved in with the Pagets at 76 Parkhill Road, Haverstock Hill. What became of those 'idols, ambergris, rich inlays', Ezra Pound catalogues, during the dismantling of his aunt's possessions, Geoffrey Paget does not know. They may have been as carelessly dispersed as her vast collection of books which she sold to a casual book-seller for a paltry £15. Geoffrey, who asked for her library, was horrified to witness her recklessness when among the collection were cherished editions of William Morris, Yeats, Shaw, Blake, and the Cuala Press books. The 'particularly fine' psaltery was given to William Butler Yeats, as the poet reminded Arnold Dolmetsch in a letter in 1935.[14] But what has become of it now Senator Michael Yeats does not know, nor thought to enquire of his mother while she was alive. Fortunately, Florence decided to save certain of her correspondence for posterity. When Harriet Paget asked what would be done with the letters her sister replied that Clifford Bax would know how to manage them. And so she gave several of these locked in a black box to the London writer requesting they should not be examined until after her death. The eventual destiny of her legacy is worthy of a small digression.

One 'dark evening of May 1940' when 'France was about to fall', Clifford Bax sought some divertissement during a bombardment on London.[15] Having put aside Florence's locked black box for several years he removed Shaw's letters to read to two Shavians, one of whom was Leon M. Lion. Both friends were delighted with the contents and soon thereafter Bax decided to seek Shaw's permission to publish. The name Florence Farr, long dead, would not have created a special stir that year, but its association with W.B. Yeats's who died in 1939 and Shaw's who was very much alive, made a fetching trilogy. Bax wrote to or saw the playwright's cousin Sarah who acted in the capacity of secretary, and after establishing a preliminary communication received word from a flabbergasted Shaw. Incredulous he had ever written to his one-time mistress, and more than curious to learn there were letters from Yeats he wrote to Bax 9 August: 'Supersarah tells me that you have some letters I wrote to the late Florence Farr. I am surprised to learn that I wrote any; for I saw so much of her that any intercourse was viva-voce and not literary'.[16] If such letters existed, Shaw was dumbfounded that Clifford Bax possessed them. 'How the dickens did you get hold of them?' he asked. Sarah had given him the 'inevitable black box story' but he could not fathom why Bax was designated their keeper. 'Florence claimed 14 lovers. Were you the fifteenth?'

Shaw's first suggestion to Bax was to sell the G.B.S. part of the cache to Gabriel Wells who 'has tons of my letters', and failing this, to give them to Lily Yeats who had 'begged' for them for the Cuala Press. 'Yeats's letters. . .as well as mine. . .would be a godsend to Lily, as Cuala is always on its last legs.'

By 15 August Bax decided to publish. He had been invited by the Shaws to lunch at Whitehall Court, and had turned over the letters to G.B.S. who thought they were not 'up to much, but enough, perhaps, for Cuala.' Charlotte was about to look them over and following this, George Yeats the poet's wife would communicate, with Lily Yeats being the 'next step'. But before the end of August there was a sharp 'hold on to the letters'. The playwright was tangling with Lily about titles. Cuala wanted to announce a book by Shaw and he wanted it entitled *'Florence Farr, Bernard Shaw & William Butler Yeats, edited by Clifford Bax.'* Included in Shaw's grumpy remarks to Bax was his opinion that the latter spent far too much time in the shelters. 'Why get out of bed before you are blown out?' G.B.S. slept through six hours of a raid 'like a baby'; and Charlotte, her husband wrote, dreaded shelters more than bombs preferring death 'to getting up and dressing'. In the following year with '750' words on the way to Cuala for an introduction to his letters Shaw, with waning brio, acknowledged his approval that Bax was in the country and 'not sleeping in doomed London. Was anything ever so utterly foolish?'[17]

Not included in the slim volume of the published letters of Shaw and Yeats was a poem Clifford Bax noted was composed by G.B.S. Dan Laurence is unsure the verses are Shaw's, but in case there is the remotest chance G.B.S. is the rightful owner, they are included here with a question mark.

> 'Hollo, pilgrim!
> Whence came thy nettle crown?
> Loosen thy tongue.
> Why art thou so cast down?'
>
> 'My tongue clacks dry within my teeth:
> My thoughts are all defiled:
> I flee the witch who plucked this wreath,
> And slew my youngest child.'
>
> 'Ha ha, pilgrim!
> What sort of child was that?
> Wasn't hers as well?
> Why did she slay the brat?'
>
> 'Enough, pilgrim:
> This we may not believe:
> Void of all sense,
> The riddles thou dost weave.'
>
> 'Rest innocent — far happier so:
> This that the witch decrees
> The heart in deepest pain may know:
> The brain can never seize.'[18]

Much in the poem, especially the words 'youngest child' in the second quatrain, bears the tone and jest of the letter from Shaw in

1891 in which he addresses Florence as 'my darling youngest child'. And of the 'witch,' this well could be Florence herself who could not oblige Shaw by becoming the child-actress par excellence he attempted to gestate. The child G.B.S. wished to create in his own image and whom he eventually rejected should have been, as he wrote in 1891, the 'happiest of all my great happinesses, the deepest and restfullest of all my tranquilities, the very inmost of all my loves'.[19]

(Of course, there is also the vague possibility that Florence *might* have 'slain' an unborn child.)

After Florence moved in with the Pagets in August 1912 she forwarded her new address to John Quinn. In this last letter from England she attempted to ease his trepidations about her new adventure. Ceylon, she wrote, was an 'earthly paradise' with fourth century B.C. ruins and 'the most beautiful fruit . . . in the world' were cultivated near Jaffna where she would eventually live. As for insects, mosquito nets would protect her and zinc lined boxes would keep out the white ants.[20]

Quinn received Florence's letter before she sailed and hastened to reply he was sending a subscription of *Scribner's Magazine* to Jaffna which would begin in September to print George Meredith's letters. He was still unable to share her enthusiasm for the Ceylon educational experiment so convinced was he

> after having had experience with forty or fifty men during the last fifteen or twenty years, some public school graduates, most of them college and law graduates, that the modern system of education results in the enfeeblement of the mind. Not one in fifty thinks for himself, or is able to pick himself up and carry himself along. Nearly all seem to seize upon any excuse for stopping and want to be pushed along. Yet that does not seem to stop them from marrying or begetting. They do not seem to need much urging or pushing in that line.[21]

When September came it was time for one more new experiment in Florence's search for 'reality'. In *Modern Woman* she wrote that the 'object of life is to make experiments' and since she believed herelf to be a 'real experimenter — quite ready for solitude', she saw no reason to 'stop at home by the fireside'. Therefore, she was 'so happy . . . saying goodbye to the lot of us', Mrs. Campbell wrote to Shaw.[22] That day, 5 September, Florence boarded the S.S. *Leicestershire* and dutifully wrote postcards to the friends who were not aware she had sailed. But when the ship docked at Marseilles, the postcards seemed to have disappeared except for one that got off to Charlotte Shaw.[23] Leaving the coast of France, Florence settled down to an active crossing of 'balls, concerts, skittles, bridge,' and, as she approached Naples, the bluest of blue seas. The colours excited her about the possibilities of painting in the East as she thought about her 'post-impressionist' style at Mentone the year before.

At Naples, some new women passengers boarded bound either for Cairo or Ceylon; 'rather charming gossipy creatures', from whom Florence chose to keep her distance. No less hostile to their male companions, she saw them as 'funny little civil servants sombre-eyed officers comic song singers — hard drinkers — miserable little pimply objects'.[24]

In an attempt to categorize the lot she decided they fit well into a Marie Corelli level of people and in shades of Charles Dodgson's 'Walrus and The Carpenter' burst out in her letter to Quinn, 'Oh God! What quantities of sand.' Florence wondered if he too had not tired of his 'fellow creatures'. No and yes, he later replied:

> I am tired of many of them! All men are not born equal and when Mr. T. Jefferson in the American declaration of Independence said they were he uttered an . . . Like the rumour of Mark Twain's death, he slightly exaggerated.[25]

In quiet desperation of 'this race of fools', Florence resorted to the ship library and on her second reading of H.G. Wells's *The New Machiavelli* decided that the 'Cambridge parts' struck her as very exact. This led her to think of Geoffrey Paget who had recently earned his B.A. at the University and was presently seekng a Museum post in Biology. The brightness of her nephew's future reminded her of the limitations of her own sex. 'I expect he will be a clever writer some day & I hope will do all the things I would have done if I'd been a man. Yet I don't know after all if men have more courage to express themselves than women.'[26]

On further reflection of her 'old' life, Florence thought she had perhaps said more than she might have had she known all that men knew, or, for that matter, all she knew at fifty-two. To this Quinn replied that few people had the courage to express themselves 'as you say fully and wholly. Who has done it? Strindberg, perhaps, among men of our day and Cellini and Casanova and Cardinal Newman'.

Bernard Shaw must have crossed his mind when he added that Florence had somehow managed to join this list by writing courageously without maiming others in her criticisms. Aware of his own peripheral existence in the world of commentators he apologised 'With me it's hard work and the more one works and makes the more one spends and buys and the less time one has to live and the more hours work like a machine one has to put in'. [27]

As the voyage progressed there were constant introspections between lemon squashes which prevented a quite lonely Florence Farr from turning into a 'little heap of dust'. Sharing her ponderings with Quinn, it amused, perhaps even startled her that she was beginning 'the world all over again'. Imagining her new life among the twenty Europeans in Jaffna she thought she would probably be suspect of 'upsetting the empire' as she worked among the 'clever, industrious' Tamils.

In spite of her wish for privacy Florence finally made friends and occasionally joined in for bridge before the ship docked at Cairo. One evening she was even gay enough to recite Verlaine in an imitation of Sarah Bernhardt; the nearest she could come to satisfying the passengers' taste for the 'Music Hall spirit'.

The S.S. *Leicestershire* docked at Port Said in the middle of the month and Florence spent two weeks in Cairo, perspiring constantly, and intrigued by the 'rich golden' light. When she continued on the Bibby Line to Ceylon she felt eccentric as she removed herself from her fellow passengers and wandered about in her Chinese robe and spectacles. No longer even amiable she was overcome by nostalgia and in her loneliness wrote to Shaw to ask him when he would be out to India. Somehow that hot afternoon at Hampstead Heath G.B.S. recorded in his diary in 1893 comes to mind when from somewhere in the middle of the Indian Ocean Florence reached out —

> We have passed through the fairy land of Egypt and Arabia. Seen the sun setting in pyramids of glory over pink hills and blue seas and now we've left Socrata behind and have 5 days of plain green with purple patches — plain apricot sunsets and no more glamour of Africa . . .

And is not the foreboding mood of *Heartbreak House* lingering in

> The ship is dripping tonight but there is no mist to see — just wet salt woodwork & deck.
> A gale last night drove the sleepers in. I had fever & was below. Tonight I shall be the only one aloft I think. It is delicious to sleep on the sea under the stars with the spices of Arabia wafting their odours through your toes.

Optimistic after a momentary 'I don't know if I shall like this so well', she felt as if 'something real' was going to happen at the College in Jaffna: 'Everything seems to be falling right for it.' [28]

Florence landed in Colombo in October. That capital had been described by Aleister Crowley with a blending of loathing and ecstacy.

> Its climate is chronic . . . architecture is an unhappy accident, its
> natives are nasty, the men with long black hair cooped up in a comb,
> smelling of fish, the women with waists bulging black between
> coat and skirt . . . its English are exhausted and enervated. The
> Eurasians are anaemic abortions: the Burghers-Dutch half-castes
> — stolid squareheads . . . In the matter of religion, the Hindus
> [Tamils] are . . . servile, shallow, cowardly, hypocritical . . . But
> then how rich, how soft, how peaceful is Colombo! One feels that
> one need never do anything more. It invites one to dream delicious-
> ly of decidious joys.[29]

Near to Colombo is the district of Sukhastan and it is here that
Florence first lived as the guest of the Ramanathans. The elegant
vicinity of the Cinnamon Gardens was the happy playground for
Europeans in executive positions who could afford the exotic man-
sions as well as the unexpected retreat of the Guru who occupied a
large 'bungalow' there. His establishment was divided into several
wings accommodating his eldest son by his deceased first wife, and
his young daughter, an unmarried son from Ramanathan's first
marriage, his first wife's father and two more of his children. In an
upper storey that resembled a guest house, Florence occupied one of
the two bedrooms. The long verandhas which surrounded her accom-
modations gave her the privacy for walks, or reading and meditation.
Of special pleasure to her were the lavish grounds, tall palms and a
series of lawns and tropical flowers which reminded her of the
hothouse at Kew Gardens. When the torrential rains stopped she
walked here in the 'grey' light marvelling at the servants who were
stationed at every corner to serve her needs.Treated as a sort of
'royal personage', she sometimes journeyed beyond the grounds in
the victoria or motor car and became dazzled by the tropical richness
everywhere. 'Beautiful creatures' walked the streets like 'exquisite
mahogany statues come to life'; even the 'crooked and the old'
resembled 'extraordinary' works of art.

Daily amenities were observed with quiet discipline within the
Ramanathan household. Florence was served coffee at 7.30 a.m., a
curry meal at one, tea at three, and a second curry meal at eight.
Ramanathan came to the curry meals and had 'great talks' with her
'about the nature of the soul'.[30] Florence's report to Yeats of these
discussions left an indelible impression with the poet for eight years
later he wrote in 'All Souls' Night' that Florence Emery had 'ravelled
out'

From a discourse in figurative speech

By some learned Indian
On the Soul's journey
How it is whirled about,
Wherever the orbit of the moon can reach,
Until it plunges into the sun;
And there, free and yet fast,
Being both Chance and Choice,
Forgets its broken toys
And sinks into its own delight at last.

There is the opinion that Yeats wove himself into the character of Florence and that the learned Indian included the personalities of Mohini Mohan Chatterjee and Rabindranath Tagore.[31] All is possible in the mind of a poet but the above stanza is written from the suggestion of Tamil verse Florence sent to Yeats during her years on the island and even, perhaps, from a suggestion by York Powell who in 1902 remarked that Florence played with her life as if it were a toy.

Florence first wrote to Yeats after coming across a metaphor only the day before she thought might interest him. It was contained in the transaltion of *The Yoga Vashishta Maharamayyana of Valmiki* (Vol IV p. 314) which she hoped Yeats could find in the British Museum. The passage suggested to her

> that the seeds of our dreams are the seeds unknown to each other and the seeds of waking life are those in which a number of seeds grown in the same pod as it were are united by the unripeness of their state & produce the delusion in common which one feels is so difficult to account for.

Ramanathan had explained 'delusions only consist in our reversal of the truth. We consider the solid things to be changeless and the unseen to be changeable instead of the reverse'.[32]

Florence was fast familiarising herself with Tamil spending an hour every day at two studying with Sir Ponnambalam's secretary. In preparation for her work on the island she soon accompanied her learned host on a visit to the Minister of Education and in true New Woman style, it was soon 'she' who did the interviewing. Education in Ceylon was just commencing to be compulsory for Tamils and Sinhalese alike. Before this, the missionaries, so bitterly despised by Florence, had brought to Ceylon the only education available to the poor. Her prejudices not withstanding, the Church's attempt to bring Western Christian ethics into the lives of Buddhists and Hindus had, in many ways, enabled the island to produce a group of representative educated individuals who were able to supply a balance in Colonial rule. Ramanathan, fast becoming known as the 'foremost

parliamentarian of the day', and still remembered as 'a leader of out-
standing talent and foresight' [33] was the first member of a new party
known as the 'educated Ceylonese' to be elected to a new seat in
Parliament in 1910. Florence's association with the man who acted as
a buffer between the Empire representatives who sat in the
Legislative Council and the small number of educated Ceylonese af-
forded her an instant position of esteem. Soon she was drawn into
political discussions and for some reason gathered from her observations that Bernard Shaw's old friend, Sidney Olivier, was to
become the future Governor. Sir Henry Edward McCallum was in
residence when Florence came out to Ceylon but it was Sir Robert
Chalmers, later Lord Chalmers, who took office in 1913.

Apart from her enthusiasm for island politics, Florence looked
forward to becoming active again on a nationalist newspaper that
Ramanathan planned to print on his own press in March. The paper
was to appeal to the most affluent of Ceylon, an improvement to *The
New Age,* Florence wrote to Yeats. The problem with Orage's
paper was that it could never find advertising money and so was
always in the red.

When Ramanathan College scheduled its opening in January 1912,
Florence left Colombo for Jaffna, a dry peninsula of scrubland at the
Northernmost tip of the island. A temperature of 90 degrees caused
her to continue to perspire and she suspected that her diet of
vegetables and curries 'drenched' her clothes with 'a spice laden
cloud over & over again'.

Ramathan College was situated on twenty-five acres in the region
of Induvil in the centre of the Jaffna peninsula. The imposing but
austere buildings of the School were arranged around a courtyard ap-
proximately 150′ square with a verandah running along the entire
perimeter of the building. The Indian system of *Guru Kula Vasa*
would be practiced in which students in their constant association
with their teachers would develop the highest spiritual, moral, and
intellectual qualities of character. Instruction would be in Tamil as
well as in English following the standards prescribed by the Director
of Public Instruction in the Code and by the Universities of Madras,
Cambridge, and London.[34] Opening day was scheduled for 17 January
until the local inhabitants discovered that the date coincided when
the moon would be in conjunction with Pleiades, the seven stars of
Taurus. 20 January was then agreed upon but shifted once more
before the College finally opened with parts of the building still incomplete. Construction materials took as long as a week to arrive
from Colombo although the journey from Colombo to Chunakam

Railway Station, a mile away from Induvil, took twelve hours. Florence was frankly amazed that the institution stood at all in a country of such primitive conditions and while she restlessly waited for its opening, wrote to Yeats for a copy of Tagore's poems for the library, if he felt 'benevolent'.

February saw the beginning of a well-ordered life for Mrs. Emery, the Lady Principal, as she was known at the College. An Assembly room upstairs provided space for the several religious and musical functions, and the dining room, an architectural jut at the rear of the building, space for eighty noisy students who ate their curries from banana leaves. Observing their indigenous loudness and untidiness, Florence immediately forgot the Montessori system and instructed the *Brahman* to teach the girls to eat so that each mouthful was dedicated to the service of God. Her magic provided a 'most lovely calm' to pervade the dining hall but she was displeased with the general permissiveness that surrounded her. Not in a manner un-mindful of her autocratic behaviour in the Golden Dawn, she made it her business to secure 'public' support for a disciplined environment of 'quiet games' and 'decent behaviour' to which the children soon responded; especially because of Mrs. Emery's 'light and countenance'. But whenever Florence needed to extricate herself from an awkward situation she resorted to more of her magic. Once a child with fever did not want to sleep alone and laying a finger on her eyes, the Lady Principal spoke in English 'go to sleep'. Mesmerized by Florence's voice and without understanding her language, the child went to sleep without a word. 'They must be a very susceptible race', was all Mrs. Emery could make of it.

One of the brighter moments occurred during the early days of the establishment of the College when some musicians came to tell stories with songs to the students. Florence was especially fascinated by the principal musician who held his violin between his chest and his knee. He with the other two sat on the ground as they played 'like figures out of [a] Beardsley drawing'. But it was the drummer who impressed Florence most. Playing his drum with his fingers and wrists he gazed into the eyes of the violinist as both worked up 'their final runs and thumps as if they were lovers producing their progeny in immediate ecstasy.' The music was planned out like a 'Dutch gar-den', Florence wrote to Yeats, and the verse was so exciting that she knew how affirmatively the poet would respond if he could hear it spoken with its correct pronunciation. She sent an example of Tamil verse and a translation.

Nomy menge, nomy nenge
Poon pulatta meranda sheretei neringil
Kadkinya malar pultu mudpayandango
Iniya seyta kadelei inna cheygil nomy nenge

Hurts my heart hurts my heart
Where grass grows and fades the sweet smelling neringil
To the eye sweet blossoming flower — thorny fruit brings forth
Sweet doings once beloved—sweet doings not now Hurts my heart.

Whether the next comment was for Yeats or for 'great ' poets universally, Florence was convinced that 'the thing one wants to know about a great poet is the sort of sounds his verse made. One doesn't particularly want to know anything else about him that cannot be put into prose'.[35]

Soon disciplined by Tamil (sweet) customs Florence felt she was acceding to the rules without too much fuss by becoming a vegetarian, a teetotaller, and a non-smoker with 'the best tobacco from Cairo' in her cupboard. All her vices were forgotten except 'laughter'; it was all that stood between herself and the 'proper' concept of life preached at the College as 'a means of bringing self-willed spirits into communion with God.' So 'there', she joked to Quinn.

The daily rituals at Ramanathan were not really dissimilar to the Victorianism she rebelled against at Cheltenham and at Queen's but something more was added, the consistent magnificence of Sir Beerbohm Tree's pageants. Customs were one part medieval and the other like the life of a royal family with its etiquette, seclusion, and marital arrangements. Florence was even assigned her own cook who doubled for her personal servant. It so filled her with wonder that she questioned whether she was not 'born again'. Of course, she told Quinn, she had been born many times in her previous life as Florence Farr but this time, she hoped it would be final.[36]

With March, Ramanathan placed Florence in a position of total authority and with a power of attorney while he and his wife left for India. Although the architect of the college knew all the 'ins and outs' he defected in his assistance to the Lady Principal after receiving a wound from a man's tooth. Apart from the *Brahman* whom she occasionally relied upon to threaten the pupils with magical retributions, Florence assumed the total supervision of 'gardens — stores — servants — teachers — sick children — money.' When she wrote to Yeats of this she told him she was really governing a little kingdom, of laying out a garden, of supervising the construction of walls, the feeding of cows, the tiling of the building, the children who have fever — the children who steal — the children who are so naughty no one else can manage them are brought to me, I hear evidence & give decisions. It is exactly like being Queen Elizabeth. [37]

There was news as well of an astrologer who told Florence of her fortunate horoscope during the past year, and calculated she would be prosperous for fifteen years then die at the age of sixty-eight. In three years time he predicted a pilgrimage during which she would suffer great unexpected privation. Somehow that prophesy brought to mind Mabel Beardsley who had been so surprised to learn that Florence Emery was actually in a girl's school. Mabel had a supply of her own naughty stories but Florence's store made even Beardsley's sister blush. [38] Florence asked Yeats several times how her friend, ill since June, was faring. After reading the poet's discouraging news she answered that she was 'glad to hear of someone making a brave end. I came here to make mine brave & I seem to have started another incarnation.' The remark was to suggest to George Yeats when preparing an introduction to her husband's letters for Cuala Press that Florence suspected she had not long to live when she left for Ceylon. This was not so. Instead, Florence enjoyed the drama of her statement to Yeats and impressing him with her noble work. The poet understood it all —

> On Florence Emery I call the next,
> Who finding the first wrinkles on a face
> Admired and beautiful,
> And knowing that the future would be vexed
> With 'minished beauty, multiplied commonplace,
> Preferred to teach a school
> Away from neighbour or friend,
> Among dark skins, and there
> Permit foul years to wear
> Hidden from eyesight to the unnoticed end.

Florence's letters to Yeats were full of the customs of the Tamils; their inhibitions and uncensored lives, and nothing to 'blush about.' Men talked to her freely of the state of their child's puberty and servants made new toilet arrangements which she approved or disapproved in open council for all to hear in front of the College. Male servants discussed the condition of female servants who were temporarily 'unclean' and Florence had to decide whether they should put oil on their heads and continue to work or be confined to their rooms so as to be separated from the older girls. Leaving the land of one's birth indeed had unusual rewards and she compared herself to John Butler Yeats who still flourished in New York. His hair was whiter than ever, Quinn wrote, and certainly he was the best talker ever. Yeats's father had set an excellent example without a doubt, Florence told the poet.

Leave all your old associations and go to another country when your work as householder is over.

It gives one new youth the whole place is full of curiosity & interests you. Your oldest jokes are new. The platitudes of one country are the discoveries of another.[39]

Nothing, she wrote, could quite match the colour of her new experiences except, perhaps, 'Miss Davidson's adventure on Derby Day' with George V's stallion.

During the College break Florence experimented with the Vina she had acquired. Ramanathan called the stringed instrument 'an image of man's subtle body.' After finding a book of instructions which helped her to tune it, Florence discovered as many varieties of sounds as there were in Dolmetsch's harpsichords. Seldom performing her old New Art in Jaffna, she did in the future make an attempt to sing a Tamil devotional song with the College choir leaving such a 'strange and funny' impression on one young civil servant. [40] And once she gave a reading at Amanda College in Jaffna. 'Many. . .were duly impressed,' but there was one who was neither 'thrilled or even amused.' Florence looked 'solid, substantial, masculine'. . . . 'Would have done credit to a drum-major. Face could not have launched even a dozen ships. Handsome perhaps, but nothing more'. [41]

Another young man scolded Bernard Shaw in 1948 for not visiting the town where Florence worked during a future visit by G.B.S. to Ceylon. Having heard his one-time mistress, he was not enthralled 'by her charms, or was it that she had already lost them.' [42]

Ramanathan returned from his cataract operation in India soon after the College break and complimented Florence on serving her stewardship with great tact in the cases for which diplomacy had arisen. An exclamation mark in her report of this to Yeats indicated they were both aware of the enormous control she had exercised on her outspokenness. In May, with some time to spare, she investigated the farms in the surrounding countryside. Impressed with the bounty of extraordinary possessions that could be bought, she decided to establish a sort of courier service between herself and London. An old Tamil agreed to disassemble, mark and pack pieces for shipping and Florence wrote to the only 'honest' antique dealer she knew in London for the purpose of creating an English market.

The rainy season was approaching in Jaffna after nine months of continual sun. Florence was used to the 90 degree heat and sundown always brought cooler air. Much in the same mood when she wrote to Shaw on her journey out, she spoke to Yeats this time of the evening's beauty.

It casts up great pink pathways between itself and the moon like a great fan of pink and blue with the gold and purple flowers varying the effects. In Egypt & here the full moon rises like a strange green disc in a pale mauve sky. I have seen that colouring over & over again. [43]

The meddlesome Christians, the only available assistants at the College, cast the only penumbras on the landscape. These were the Church missionaries Yeats referred to in a letter in 1906, those of the

holy church — now alas steering its malignant way. . .through the Indian Ocean — a sort of diabolical Aengus carrying not a glass house for Etain — as did the Irish one — but a whole convent, altar lights, vegetarian kitchen and all. [44]

What they really needed at the College was a good pagan like Jane Harrison at Durham, Florence wrote Yeats. Ramanathan was prepared to pay a hundred pounds a year, free board, and travel paid in both directions to a BA who was expert in English. With nothing to spend the money on, Florence thought Yeats should be able to come up with a candidate.

A year after leaving England, Florence was immensely happy in Jaffna, the 'land of the lute players'. The Tamils were of special fascination and she described them to Quinn as the 'Irish of India. He, not knowing if this meant good Irish or bad, wrote that in a recent article Shaw spoke of the bad Irishman as being the worst person in the world, and the good, a saint. But Florence meant that the Tamils enjoyed an oral tradition of poetry and learned their grammar by singing poetry. Truly, she wrote to Quinn, she was living in the 'midst of all times'. Ceylon was an ancient country suspended in the middle of the twentieth century. Goatherds dressed 'as in the time of Theocritus' kept the goats from entering the gardens with violent protestations from the animals. And Sidney, Spencer, Milton, Gray and all the poets school spoiled for her were challenging her to create splendid memories for the girls she instructed for the Cambridge Examination. [45] Each day brought a new experience as well. A father of one of her students died and as a matter of etiquette Florence visited the family home. Twelve women were wailing in the first room and 'he daughters against the pillars of the inner court in order to be hidden from the sight of men. Most tragic of all was the mother of the student who walked up and down 'wailing like Hecuba'. They all did it 'beautifully' and Florence found herself happier when she left the scene to think they did not suffer in 'our tight civilised way'.

In her response to a letter from Quinn where she spoke of his acquisition of several post-impressionist paintings, Florence expressed her elation that 'art is really becoming a religion at last'. Furniture scavaging was her own particular way of collecting artifacts and she purchased a fourteenth century Jacobean chair for eight shillings and a satin wood table red with age for £1 1s. 4d. In what appears to be a private joke with the New York lawyer, Florence mentioned in quotes there were 'no legs in the way'. Somehow she did not manage to save very much from her stipend and when she found an old ebony box inlaid with ivory and in perfect repair she asked Quinn to advance her fifty dollars and postage if he wished her to make the purchase for him. He did not reply until June 1914. By then W.B. Yeats had made his March tour and the two men made up the quarrel that began in Ireland over Quinn's mistress. The poet spent the last two weeks staying in the lawyer's apartment and he was guest of honour at a 'swell' dinner hosted by Quinn the night before he sailed. Yeats made a 'good' speech to the forty guests and Quinn thought he looked younger and stronger than when he had seen him last.

Florence was pleased about the reconciliation for she now believed life was so mixed that it was impossible to find any relationship where all went smoothly.

> The feelings we have that other people ought to behave according to our ideals leads to nearly all our unhappinesses & desires for a false kind of progress. We fix our attention on tomorrow when we have the greatest treasure of all with us today if we only knew it. Bergson speaks of it as 'the rare moment of philosophical clarity,' when we understand something we might call 'existence in itself.' How can we see what is in our house if we are always looking out of the window?[46]

This sort of attitude and Florence's work in Jaffna impressed Quinn very much. Thinking her rather unnecessarily as a missionary who brought succour to the underprivileged, he was reminded of an antithesis occuring in America with private and federal funding for the needy.

> Not withstanding the Rockefeller Institutes and the Carnegie Institutes and the Cancer Research Institutes and the discovery of cerebral spinal meningitis anti-toxin and the diptheria anti-toxin and the cure for tuberculosis, and radium, and the marvels of sur-

gery, and so on, the poor people in the South don't consult a doctor until they are in pain, and then they consult someone almost as ignorant as themselves, and when they die of typhoid, small-pox, diphtheria, meningitis, hookworm, and so on, they call it 'a visitation of God'.[47]

The responsibility of running the College lessened by 1914 and Florence began to experiment with verse based on Tamil poetry. A poem, she explained to Yeats after his return from the States, was capable of at least six different interpretations. Burlesquing the Tamil tradition she sent a quatrain of her own making.

> Mutable mindings of amazing men
> Mutable windings of a mazy fen
> Disputable mindings of apraising men
> Disputable bindings of a crazy pen.

Surely Yeats played with 'wandering' and 'pondering' in similar fashion in 'All Souls' Night'. Another attempt, 'rather Elizabethan', which Florence worked around five lines, five stanzas and five words in the first verse of each stanza represented the four elements, earth, water, fire, and air, and *Akasha*.

> I see the narrow gate —
> Away! fortune and hate
> With me no more to mate!
> All hearts annoy
> Out of the world!

> A silver bell may sing
> A dewy drop may bring
> Lightening that will fling
> Trembling and joy
> Out of my world.

> What is that narrow gate
> Rids me of joy and hate
> Never again to mate
> In hearts annoy
> With this maz'd world?

> A sound upon the wing,
> A sight I may not sing,
> A going — ne'er to bring
> Returning joy
> To fright my world.

> Above me is a stone
> Below me is a bone,
> I pass the gate alone —
> I was a toy;
> I am — the world.[48]

'I am a toy' becomes in 'All Souls' Night' forget its broken toys,' and 'I am — the world' is transformed into 'Sink into its own delight at last.'

In April, after recess, the college opened with some long-awaited efficient teaching staff. For the first time Florence found some real quiet in her routine brought about by her abilities to keep the pupils subdued. She spoilt herself by the purchase of a rickshaw for £12 and every evening she was 'dragged about' by a coolie. One evening they approached a great fire alight in the field and passing some drummers along the way Florence learned that a cremation was taking place. Each musician carried a special drum made either of stone, skin, or a wooden head. Sent for when a 'good' *Sivite* died, the drummers' function was to warn the world away from the dead. The rules of procedure were imparted to Yeats. All the women connected with the deceased began their wailing in their respective places in the house, as she had previously informed him, and continued their sorrow until twelve hours after death. For the ceremony, the exquisitely robed body rested on a board with a huge block of wood placed on its chest. Florence was convinced that the people were frequently buried alive so that the big block of wood prevented the victim from rising to tell his friends! Additional wood was piled upon the first block and then the barber and washerman circled the body while the barber struck an earthen pot with a knife after each circumambulation. On the last gyre the pot was struck until it broke into pieces. Immediately upon this, the eldest son or other relative walked around the body with a lighted torch and then with his back to the pyre lit it and walked away without ever turning back. In consequence of their duties, drummers, barbers, and washermen were looked upon as being under a special curse and so received excellent wages. Florence told Yeats that she thought they resembled William Morris's 'Golden Dustman'.[49]

As she told her story it occured to her that so many people died in Ceylon that it was not at all like England 'where only other people's friends seem to die as a rule'. The exception was Mabel Beardsley: Yeats had implied she was 'serious', a word the servants used in Jaffna to explain that someone was dying.

From her preoccupation with death she turned to livelier matters in her discourse with Yeats. Ezra Pound had enclosed some lines in the elder poet's last letter and Florence asked for his address. Then her conversation was of Mrs. Campbell. Shaw filled her with little except scorn perhaps when he wrote that he 'had fallen in love' with Mrs. Pat. Now that the lady had married George Cornwallis-West Florence wondered how the marriage would go. Mrs. P.C. always told her G.C.W. was 'so delightfully merry'. She also wondered by chance whether Yeats had seen *Pygmalion* which must have reminded her of 1891 when Shaw played elocution master to her Eliza. Thinking still of Mrs. Campbell who appeared to have supplanted her with fascinating both playwrights she asked if the poet ever finished his *Player Queen* for her.

In spite of her questions Florence was estranged from her former existence. She spoke of 'rounding off' her life and attempting to prove her adeptship in a different way from the Golden Dawn by becoming 'true of voice'. The meaning of 'Will' in Eastern philosophy required the understanding that once it asserted itself an individual must carry out its desires even at the expense of one's life or the lives of everyone valued most. In essence, it truly resembled the 'superhuman morality'.

A letter to Shaw bore more humour than the serious exposition of the death scene to Yeats or the chatty correspondence to John Quinn. Whether Florence was aware that her 'most faithful friend' had prepared a Will on 3 August 1913 in which Clause 31 he bequeathed to her £104 per annum upon his death is not sure. It read

> I declare that if Florence Farr (who in One thousand eight hundred and ninety four produced my play 'Arms and the Man' at the Avenue Theatre in Northumberland Avenue London) formerly the wife of Edward Emery. . .[50]

Beatrice ('Mes') Webb obviously asked Shaw to find out from Florence the exact procedures for death, sex arrangements, and women's periodic indispositions which Florence accounted for in great detail. Just as interesting to her at the moment of her writing was a moth, the size of of a mouse, which had flown into her lamp shade and had to be taken outside the building. No insect or animal was allowed to be killed and the only reptile which even *Sivites* were permitted to kill were the small poisonous snakes. Presently able to brag to Shaw about her own habits of vegetarianism, 'we are people', she told him, who live on *Satvic* food, a diet of milk and its products, many vegetables excluding coarse beans, and 'drumsticks' with a taste of fowl, prepared from the fruit of the acacia tree.[51]

Vegetarianism impressed Florence very much for the moment, and she attempted to convince Quinn as well of her abstinence from the sins of Western society, or the fact that she never touched 'eggs or wine or tobacco'. Not the least touched by her abandonment of a prior life, Quinn reminded her she seldom drank wine and he had never seen her smoke. Neither could he agree with her total acceptance of Ceylon. 'Don't you ever take a vacation? Have you no plans for returning to England? Where do you go when you want a change?'[52]

By the time Quinn wrote to Florence in August 1914 the first World War had begun and would be a more lengthy affair, he was convinced, than was commonly thought. He guessed at the strong possibilities of the Germans overwhelming the French and the English providing a negligible alliance. England, he speculated, would be well out of the war sustaining, perhaps, a few thousand losses out of her 80,000 soldiers and losing a ship or two. British sea supremacy, he was sure, would scare the Germans to the point of withdrawal. As if to confirm this thought he wrote of the eighteen ships belonging to the Hamburg-American line which were tied up in New York harbour afraid to leave port for fear of capture by the British. Quinn was not in particular sympathy with big countries who in times of stress held smaller countries in submission with promises 'galore'. England, in his opinion, had been the first of the 'promisers'. . . . 'Ulster was split up and now Ireland is to get everything at once — bigger than ever — for her loyalty during the war'.

Florence took the world's events quite casually 'devouring' the daily papers but unable to find room on her writing paper to discuss them with Yeats. The unrest that was to occur in Ceylon in 1915 had not yet begun its rumbles. In that year Sir Ponnambalam was in the middle of a clash between Buddhists and Muslims in the ancient city of Kandy. The Governor, convinced of subversive activities instigated by German propaganda, subsequently imposed martial law. It was Ramanathan who came to the defence of the Sinhalese and supported their position in the Legislative Council. Attempting to convince the British that an act of treason was an unmitigated accusation the learned mystic couched his words after his censure of the Empire in what resembled a Brooke sonnet.

England, Sir — my heart melts at the sound of England. I feel that my whole life has been protected by England. I have from my infancy upward been bred by England, benefitted by England, and I am deeply grateful for it not merely for the benefits which I have personally received, but for the reputation it has for justice, humanity, mercy and honour. . .however painful my duty may have been, I have discharged it because of the great and good who are standing up for the glory of the British Empire, because they want us to do our duty, in order that England may continue from genera- tion to generation as the greatest, the best and the noblest country on the face of the earth.[53]

The nearest Ceylon came to actual physical involvement during the war was during the incident of the German cruiser *Emden* . After its destruction by the Australian warship *Sydney* in the Bay of Bengal in 1914 Florence wrote to Yeats 11 November to admit that Ceylon's incapacity in the matter was a trial. She was glad to hear that morning it was all over. 'What a time she had! Dodging the Navies of the "world domain" & always winning with honour & rob- bing as gallantly as any Eighteenth Century highwayman'.[54]

It was the native music and the story of the soul's journey that real- ly interested Florence and of the first she wrote to Yeats about the weekly performances of the Priest in the College of the Holy Siva. The chanting of the stories of the Gods were sung 'full of shakes and quivers and quaverings and modulations', accompanied by silver cymbals, violins, and a stringed instrument called the 'thambam'. It was a very special experience to listen to the Tamil girls who joined in with their 'song-speech' whenever they knew the songs and hymns by heart. And of the other, she discussed with Yeats how the *Jiva* or the Western conception of soul was surrounded by a film of etherial matter which bore the impressions of the individual's desire for par- ticular magnetic influences caused by meditation of some great soul like *Brahma*. In its dream-like state *Jiva* developed and matured from its encounter with experiences. When upon death the con- sciousness 'sinks' to the tip of the spine, the *Jiva* in its dream body travels straight away to Death. Once judged it is sent to heaven, to hell, remains on earth, or is liberated; liberation meaning a clear conception of the 'real'. To remain on earth after death meant a liberty of sorts but *Jiva* was in constant peril from the actions of 'careless persons' who could subject the dream body to injury. Sen- sitive to this limited liberation *Jiva* sought refuge in 'weak-minded' persons and entered their bodies to forever cause embarrassment. Bedevilled by its uninvited guest, the host could not be set free until a priest willed the *Jiva* into a cocoanut shell and sank it to the bot- tom of the sea. It all reminded Florence of the 'button molder basin'[55] (presumably in Ibsen's *Peer Gynt*). There was surely another association for Yeats in Florence's explanation it 'sinks' to the tip of the spine when he wrote in the same 'All Souls Night', 'and sinks into its own delight at last.' And is there not something of Florence's influence in his knowledge of the soul's bedevillment in Hindu lore in what seems to be the Christian mystery in *Purgatory?*

Of the personal news between them, a fetching remark by Florence implies that Yeats deeply missed his companion of the spirit, that her absence perhaps motivated him to find a life-long companion apart from his perennial rejection by Maud Gonne. In answer to a statement by him, Florence wrote 'I suppose you stop your memories on the day you first met me?' There was word as well that Geoffrey Paget was about to marry Nora Dryhurst and Florence wondered what Mrs. Campbell was doing now she had married George. Ezra Pound, meanwhile, had married Dorothy Shakespear and not without cynicism Florence asked Yeats whether Dorothy's family name had driven her to marry a poet. War news seemed remote, she added, although the astrologers were prophesying a big battle in December. Certainly there was no thought of war panic in her life and she suggested that 'any starving vegetarians from England can find work and shelter here'.

Quinn wrote about the war in February 1915.[56] A man of great compassion, he thought often of the 'poor devils' in Europe who were condemned to death every night in the trenches from bullets or pneumonia. Loathing the leaders of the nations who were responsible for their slaughter, his sympathies, nevertheless, were with the Allies. Among those of his friends who shared his allegiance were some who believed that all that was needed to win the war was a spell of good weather. Personal acquaintances in Petrogard had expressed their disbelief of Russia's ability to whip Germany in the East but somehow Quinn thought that if Italy joined the allies, the mess would be over. Had he his wish, even food would be with-held to starve the Germans into submission. This reminded him of Lincoln's dramatic decision during the American Civil War to issue his proclamation to liberate the slaves. 'That was a dangerous doctrine, but there are times when such a decision is the only right one.'

Quinn wrote again in March.[57] Mr. Edward Emery had played the lead in Sutro's play *The Clever Ones* 'and his acting was good'. Of other news, the English and Irish still came over in spite of the war. Granville Barker and his wife and company performed Shaw's *Androcles* which went well but *Midsummer Night's Dream* was 'simply rotten'. Lady Gregory had been over and 'lectured' fairly well, but his sentiments were presently vituperative when it came to several of the Irish.

> As usual the rag-tag bobtail Irish who have always been wrong on every subject are with the Germans here. It comes from having lived in an atmosphere of falsity and lies. They come over here to this country and are grabbed up by this, that, and the other association and are coerced into subscribing to this, that and the other Irish paper and suddenly find they are heroes, patriots, and bards. I use the word 'bards.' I love it. They find out that the Irish race have a mission to perform. From the patriots they get the blab that they have the mission of civilizing the rest of the world. Both of them in one great stream of slush is poured down their throats on the 17th of March so that they think they are hells of fellows. An atmosphere of lies and falsity. Out of this grows the idea that England is going to be licked and this is Ireland's chance to become a big country. I would like to see the Prince of Wurtemberg or the Prince of Saxony in Dublin Castle. There would be a whole lot more for them to really holler about then and Shaw's prediction in his *Man and Superman* that the way to treat the Kaiser was to give him Ireland to play with would be realized with a vengeance. They would have a damn lot to holler about then and besides they would have to go to work. That wouldn't please them a bit.

It was a rare moment when Quinn found something in Shaw's writing to commend. Once he wrote Florence that like H.G. Wells, G.B.S. had no style and therefore would not last as a writer.[58]

A highlight occurred on the College calendar in March 1915, when, after losing his two sons on the Western front that year, Sir Robert Chalmers attended the Prize-giving ceremonies. Florence was required to read the school report on this occasion and afterwards the Governor expressed his amazement that a Principal read so well. Being a 'wide-awake-individual', according to Florence, he became curious about her background. Since she was extraordinarily secretive in guarding her identity on the island, the headmistress informed him only that she had sometimes lectured in poetry. Impressed with her abilities Sir Robert named her the 'Elocutionist'. Various celebrations in honour of the Governor's presence lasted for three days and his departure was celebrated by a display of fireworks. Sir Robert, Lady Ramanathan, and Florence motored outside the College grounds for the entertainment at which Florence sat on the Governor's right and next to Mrs. Ramanathan. Opposite, the Tamils stood in a congregation dressed in long white robes, the line-up reminding Florence rather 'ridiculously' of her six year old visions of being asked to sit on the right hand of God. It was difficult for her, or so she imagined, to adjust to the distance observed between the races in the presence of a white official.

Florence took her first holiday in two and a half years in April, a self-imposed rest-cure at a British hotel in Kandy. Nestled at the foot of the central hills of Ceylon, the city offered a feast of artifacts acquired in its ancient Sinhalese history from the occupation by the Portugese and the Dutch. After the first surprise of tasting English cooking vegetarianism was forgotten and Florence was 'stuffing' herself with English food cooked in 'English ways'. Hill-climbing and her participation in the many activities that were not available to her at the College in Jaffna awakened her to the limitations of her life on the Island. Very shortly she seriously thought of not 'ending her days' in Ceylon even though she had considered the possibility of becoming a *Sanyasin,* one who abandoned the world. She realised after all that a white person in Ceylon had great difficulty behaving 'eccentrically'. Whites were expected to 'play the game and demand more than less'.

Releasing herself from her sense of loyalty to Ramanathan, Florence entertained the idea of going to San Fransisco and asked Quinn in her letter to him whether Agnes Tobin was back in America. Of course, she wrote from Kandy, China and India were both on her mind and she decided to visit these countries on a trip around the world. Nevertheless, San Fransisco was where she would 'end my days'. In a British atmosphere war became a reality and Florence told Quinn 'We are having the experience of centuries packed into our life times, aren't we?'

After Florence returned to the College John Quinn answered with a report of Agnes Tobin. Arthur Symons ended the relationship treating her like a sister, and unhappy, she left for America in 1913. Although Quinn did not choose to be quoted, Miss Tobin was having 'obsessions' due to 'stomach trouble'. He had heard her complain of 'growths on her insides' and rave about operations that never took place and of parents whom she was sure were trying to declare her 'incompetent'. It struck Quinn that Florence would not want to bother with her if she returned to England via San Francisco. Not taking her wish to end her days there too seriously, that particular route, he estimated, would be a safer way to travel if she returned to England during the war, a turmoil that should last for another two or three years.

There was news of friends. Lady Gregory had arrived back in Ireland after laughing at Quinn but finally accepting his warning against returning on a Cunard Liner. Shaw and his wife stayed with her at Coole for three weeks on her return and Augustus John was over to do 'three heads'. One of them reminded Lady Gregory of the prophet Ezekiel, or 'Zeke' as Quinn referred to him. Then the American revealed the news that Lady Gregory's nephew had drowned on the *Lusitania*. Quinn had become fond of him during his two weeks in New York. They discussed the possibility of the ship being torpedoed by the Germans but Lane refused to accept the idea of such an atrocity.

> It is the most horrible thing that has ever happened, worse than the St. Bartholomew massacre. I have no patience with those who defend the Germans because they are patriotic or honest or sincere. And the leaders of the Inquisition were certainly sincere and honest men. It is their lack of humanity that condemns and shoud damn them.[60]

Florence was restive after her return from Kandy and unenthusiastic in her role of Lady Principal. Not until March, the following year, could Ramanathan relieve her of her responsibilities. When the time approached for her stepping down, plans were made to celebrate her departure with due signs of 'sorrow and cheer'. On 11 March two hundred and fifty pupils with their parents and the 'elite' of Jaffna gathered on the College grounds to feast on lavish servings of fruit and delicacies. During that afternoon, the tolling of the bell signalled the guests to file to the Assembly Hall for the ritual which would acknowledge Florence's resignation. Three Tamil girls garlanded their retiring Principal before all sat for a musical interlude of songs of 'gladness and distress'. A Miss Murgascoe then expressed to Florence the grave sentiments of the College before the retiring Principal was presented a 'beautiful silk gold lace *chelai* and a purse of money'. After more songs of praise Ramanathan came forward to give eloquent praise to Mrs. Emery and to explain that her resignation took place because of the heavy strain of work over the last three years. Florence answered the Guru's address with an expression of gratitude for the innumerable kindnesses extended to her after which the assembly closed with a procession to the Temple for worship and 'heart-stirring music and song'.[61]

At this juncture, and Florence being mercurial by nature, she could not decide how to approach her future. Nowhere else could she live in such tranquility and independent comfort. Yet there was still no surcease to her restiveness. The war presented a deterrent to travel but her wish to visit China and India did not re-occur now that she had her choice. Even a visit to America was no longer in her mind although Quinn would surely have welcomed her there briefly. For the moment there were two immediate choices: to accept the

Ramanathan's invitation to remain at the College in the capacity of Bursar, or to settle in a cool bungalow in Jaffna for the remainder of her life with 60 rupees a month to manage on. Perhaps sensitive to the sentiments of the pupils and to the music master's wooing with 'magic' songs, Florence decided to postpone a long-range decision and to remain at the College. As a compromise she decided to change her living quarters to a remote wing where she would not be subject to the worst noises of the daily routine. Twenty-five violins at practice on different *ragas* at the same time presently struck her as a dreadful experience in a building that seemed to be constructed so that every sound uttered became audible throughout the entire structure. She had forgotten that this very principle had inspired her reveries with The Music of Speech.

Now that she was keeper of the 'cashbox', Florence wrote to Shaw, her only responsibility was to dulcify the relations between the new Principal, Miss Mabel Needham, and the girls who were rather too fond of their former headmistress. So high was their regard for her that she permitted them to call her 'mother', an endearment brought about because she made no objection to their placing ashes on her head. Generously, she always indicated 'their religion is just as good as my own.'[62] What Florence considered her 'own' at this point, she did not clarify to Shaw.

In contrast to her previous hard work her days were now halcyon-like and Florence decided she never wanted to leave Ceylon. She missed certain of her friends, especially Bernard Shaw who had not written since the start of the war (although he did send her his 'Christ' book). Florence was sure he must have some time to spare unless he was making 'guns or socks'. She was tired, she wrote in April 1916 of hearing the Germans referred to as 'Huns', and she could not fathom why the English should not be called 'Saxons'. Was it he or someone else, she asked, who said that since the Allies could not wipe out seventy million people and because they all had to live on the same planet they might as well recognise it and attempt to harmonize.

Too many people arrive in one place and they have to be cleared off — I am very glad I cleared off to a nice part of the world that no-one else is likely to want. . .Do you remember how you always tried to prevent me from associating with *Moonshees*? I must say my experience with *Moonshees* is that they become very practical when it comes to getting things done. I think Mr. Ramanathan has worked the inner history of his country to much more purpose than the people do who. . .have no. . .knowledge of the 10 Yogic trances & the final liberation.[63]

Twenty years after Shaw warned mankind to 'beware of a woman with large eyes, and crescent eyebrows, and a smile, and a love of miracles and moonshees', the Hindu interpreters had relieved her of many fears.

> I have spent all my years getting rid of many barriers between me and liberation — all my little disagreeablenesses & the things I never noticed about myself as bonds have loosened. Also my secret horror of death. I mean the deathbed scene — I have been through with it once or twice & it's nothing after all.[64]

What she did not add was that she had spent her life preparing for the liberation of her soul in death; an unusual occupation for one endowed with so many earthly talents for living.

The days passed quietly during the summer months of 1916 and the war looking 'as if it might come to an end within our lifetimes'. She wrote that she had 'settled down to it & shall quite miss it'. Often that summer she sat on a favoured stone bench beneath a jasmine bower 'lost in thought or meditation',[65] and when Sir Ponnambalam came up from Colombo she talked to him in his office for hours on time. Occasionally she 'read' to the Ramanathans in their bungalow nearby; for the rest, she was reading from 'cover to cover' the *Aeneid*, the *Odyssey*, the *Endymiou*, and 'grappling' with Montaigne's *Essays*. Bundles of newspapers that did not sink to the bottom of the ocean came out from England sent to her by Charles Oliver, 'the little man in the Golden Dawn' from Knightsbridge, as well as her cousin who once loved her, Willy Whittall. Florence thought they were both rather noble but she hoped her contamination with the 'society of the unwise' would not delay her attainment 'of real saintliness for some years'. On the other hand, Ramanathan assured her she was 'all right' and her mind had 'lost its hold on most of the *Malams* or evils which cause a soul to subject itself to birth or death'

Thinking back to the Golden Dawn, Florence told Yeats she had heard that A.É. Waite had a flourishing Order of his own which met in expensive hotels.

> It is extraordinary to think of all the changes that old original 1888 order has gone through. It is like the last incarnation of a soul which rushes here and there to 'eat up' all its karmas* before liberation. .
> *Karma our old friend which can only be escaped from by an elaborate process of detecting the various gods who inspire us at their work & attributing our apparent deed to the real doers.

There was another question for Yeats about the Third Order of St. Francis (not identified) which Florence supposed was 'on the outskirts & not like our Third order.'

The poet had previously written that he was writing his memoirs and wondered whether Florence preferred to appear as herself or under an assumed name. 'Certainly', she answered, 'I think it would be safer to be known as myself. My experience of being the 'green lady' in Moore's book was not exhilerating.'

She talked of Woburn Buildings as well, especially since the poet wrote it was to be pulled down, and asked if he still had his Monday evenings. Then there was a comment concerning Maud Gonne whose reception of 'the news' (Major McBride's death in the Easter Rising) was 'very characteristic of her'. There was also an exchange of gossip about Herbert Hughes, with whom she hoped to travel to the States in 1905. He had married a South African girl who wrote to Florence that Hughes was an officer in the British Army training recruits at Sandown. Mrs. Hughes supplied the additional spice that 'Orage had set up with a lady of social distinction.' [66]

It was the third week of November 1916 when Florence felt a 'twinge' in her left breast. Thinking it was only her imagination she hesitated to act until the first week in December. At that time she decided to consult a woman physician at the Dispensary at Inuvil. Arriving in her customary conveyance of a travelling cart drawn by two white bulls, Florence discussed a sick pupil she brought with her and then asked for an examination for herself. The Doctor's probing of her breast revealed a small lump which the physician rapidly diagnosed as cancer. Dr. Curr, a second practicing physician at the Dispensary came in for another diagnosis and both doctors agreed that it was an early case and advised Florence to go to Colombo for surgery. [67] Sir Ponnambalam accompanied his friend on her immediate journey there and to the General Hospital where Florence was admitted as 'Mrs. Winifred Emery' After the 'eminent' surgeon Dr. S.C. Paul examined Florence he told her there was little doubt that she had cancer.

Resting in a private room on the eve of her surgery, her left breast 'swathed in iodine and cotton wool', Shaw was the one person Florence needed at that moment. Although she had not heard from him for years she was still unavoidably bound to him. 'Talk of galloping Consumption' she wrote to G.B.S., 'this is galloping cancer with a vengeance.' Never ill enough in her life to have required even a nurse, for the first time since her infancy she was 'guarded & taken care of as if I were a baby again.' As she reflected on the 'tragic moment' only a fortnight past when she became aware of a 'dead place' in her breast, she admitted to Shaw that she told herself 'cancer'.

> & felt the force of doom but I didn't let anyone see & went & lunch- ed & laughed & talked with the British Principal & teachers. — Then when one after the other had confirmed the doom I felt less & less doomful & now I feel full of interest in the experience. . .Goodbye remember me to your people. [68]

On the following day 8 December Dr. Paul performed a mastec- tomy and removed a major pectoral muscle leaving Florence's side 'a beautiful slab of flesh adorned with a handsome fern pattern made by a cut and 30 stitches.' [69] For a week after surgery she was not per- mitted to move but later, during her convalescence, she wrote to Henrietta very 'merrily' about it all. Florence's decision before her surgery was to withhold the truth from the Whittalls and the Pagets 'because it might make them more nervous for themselves'. Now her sister presently assumed Florence was quite well.

Back at Chunnakam Florence Emery was feeling *'piano'* but well enough to explain the events to Yeats. A 'sort of piece of rubber' which turned out to be a tumour had spread 'long roots' under her arm. The doctor said that it was not malignant 'so I don't know whether it would be called cancer in England, but that's the name they give it here.' Everyone told her she was making a speedy recovery and so, she told the poet, she finally wrote to Etta and to her other relatives that it was a tumour without mentioning the *'taboo* word cancer' Forgetting that such a short time before she asked Yeats why Mabel Beardsley could not have had 'consumption a much pleasanter feeling for the end than cancer', she did not now conceive

> why it is considered so awful to have *cancer*. I know when I found a report was being spread that I had a *boil* I felt most indignant be- ing supposed to have such a nasty disease. The other seems decent & dry. So much for that. [70]

She spoke of enlarging her soul and her success with a new way of translating poetry. The trick, she discovered only the evening before, was not to worry about the subject matter but to think of the mood and then to translate each series of vowel sounds, (and consonants if possible), into English words that had the same kind of vowel sounds. A verse of High Tamil poetry she had learned and translated con- vinced her of that method.

> Omen of ancients — Omen of ancients

The moon in pearl attire palely shimmers through Syringa
Scudding over the blue dome, muddy patches hang and go
In the sky. Clouds in the sky. Ill-omen of ancients; omen of ancients,

Her letter to Yeats concluded with a poem she had composed around Fechtner's idea of 'our being senses and thoughts'. The signature of 'Florence Farr' at its ending was in lieu of her usual autograph, Mrs. Emery of F. Farr Emery.

The Earth and We

We are the eyes, the sense, the vision of Earth
And she is just a Kerub face that floats
Dancing and laughing round the sun. In mirth
She hides in cloaking masks of night and gloats
In shadows ov'r her aureol of beams
Like coloured feathers in St. Michael's wings.
When we are dead she makes thoughts of our dreams;
And if we are remembered when she sings
Her song to the sun; 'tis because our wild ghosts
Clamour within her, till she suddenly screams
Tragic notes — wakening tremendous strings
Reverberating, calling Fame's starry hosts.

Surely this last verse prompted Yeats to Write 'On Florence Emery I call the next.

In March 1917 Florence returned to the Dispensary at Inuvil complaining of a slight cough and shortness of breath. Her physician noticed she was pale and thinner and proceeded to examine her. She did not tell Florence of her discovery of secondary deposits of cancer in the lung but called in Dr. Curr. Again, they told Mrs. Emery to go at once to see Dr. Paul in Colombo.

For the second time Florence entered the General Hospital accompanied by Ramanathan. Dr. Paul examined the patient while the Guru waited outside the Passenger Ward. Not long afterwards, the surgeon appeared and disclosed that Florence's condition was too far advanced for further surgery. Mrs. 'Winifred Emery' was subsequently transferred to a private room and placed under the care of the acting Senior Physician Dr. Lucien de Zilwa. Little could be done for his patient 'beyond alleviating her sufferings on the *via deloroso* which lay before her'.[71]

After attending the dying woman for several days, Dr. de Zilwa was confused by the name of Winifred Emery. He was so sure that the woman reminded him of the actress Florence Farr whom as a younger man he had seen at the Court Theatre in 1906. He even treasured a souvenir programme of *The Hippolytus of*

Euripides. 'You remind me of Florence Farr', he told her, and she, confessing the truth of the matter, asked him to reveal her identity to no-one else.

In the weeks that followed Sir Ponnambalam waited every morning outside of Florence Emery's room to hear the day's bulletin. Beyond Dr. Thornton the Medical Superintendent, the Ward Sisters and the Tamil women who daily filled her room with flowers, the Guru was her only visitor. The English woman might well have laughed had she known that during her dying days her physician saw her as a reformed wanton who, like a somnambulist, finally awakes to perceive that she stands on the edge of a precipice, realizing the folly of her old, promiscuous way of life in England. His last words about what must have been an exquisitely painful death were 'She had no nostalgic longings for her homeland, never expressed a wish to have her kith and kin about her. She was at home with devoted friends . . . and appeared to be perfectly happy.'[72]

Florence Farr Emery died on 29 April 1917, not yet fifty-seven.Her body was removed to the Ramanathan bungalow in the Cinnamon Gardens and on 30 April she was cremated according to the traditions she had once observed belonging to the Hindu rites. In absence of a close relative Mr. K. Viswalingham, the headmaster of the Ramanathan Tamil Training School, lighted the funeral pyre. Florence's ashes, so the legend ends, were then scattered in a 'sacred river

Henrietta Paget first read of her sister's death in the Ceylon newspapers which she thought Florence had sent on as a joke to show how papers exaggerated. But by 27 June Etta received official word of her sister's passing. 'The immediate cause of her death was heart-failure'. Henrietta notified Shaw; "Forgive me for troubling you about this, but you worked for a long time together & she was fond of you."[73]

NOTES

1 Canto XXVIII
2 Revealed to Jayanta Padmanabha by Ezra Pound.
3 National Library, Holloway Collection.
4 Revealed to Dan H. Laurence.
5 Researched by Ceridwen Oliver.
6 UL, (May 1906).
7 UL, (December 1906).
8 Bax, *op. cit.,* 56.

9 Berg, (June 18 1912).
10 Berg, (July 26 1912).
11 Sold at Sotheby's to an unknown buyer.
12 BM, (June 22 1912).
13 Foster-Murphy Collection, (July 2 1912).
14 Courtesy of John Kelly and Eric Domville.
15 Bax, *Some I Knew Well,* (London 1951), 97.
16 Academic Centre.
17 Academic Centre.
18 Academic Centre.
19 Bax, *Letters,* 4.
20 Berg, (August 9 1912).
21 Berg, (August 26 1912).
22 *Bernard Shaw and Mrs. Patrick Campbell. Their Correspondence,* (London 1952), 44.
23 BM, (September 1912).
24 Berg, (September 14 1912).
25 Berg, (September 20 1913).
26 Berg, (September 14 1912).
27 Berg, (January 20 1913).
28 BM, (September 1912).
29 Crowley, *Equinox,* Vol. 2, 53.
30 Letters from Ceylon, permission of Senator Michael B. and Miss Anne Yeats. (October 26 1912).
31 Amiya Chatiravarty, *The Modern Review,* (Calcutta March 1939).
32 (October 26 1912).
33 Zeylanicus, *Ceylon,* (London 1970), 118, 150.
34 M. B. Yeats.
35 (January 1913).
36 Berg, (September 18 1913).
37 (March 18 1913).
38 Wade, *op. cit.,* 574.
39 (1913).
40 Padmanabha, 'In Memorium,' *The Ceylon Daily News.* (April 30 1947).
41 *Ibid.*
42 BM, (August 14 1948), S.H. Parinbanyagam.
43 M.B. Yeats.
44 Bax,*op. cit.,* 55-56.
45 Berg, (September 3 1913).
46 Berg, (July 17 1914)?
47 Berg, (June 4 1914).
48 (November 29 1913).
49 (May 17 1914).
50 Chapelow, *Shaw,* 481.

51 BM, (February 12 1914).
52 Berg, (August 24 1914).
53 Zeylanicus, *op. cit.,* 159.
54 (October 3 1914).
55 *Ibid.*
56 Berg.
57 Berg, (March 22 1915).
58 Berg, (January 20 1913).
59 Berg, (April 5 1915).
60 Berg, (June 8 1915).
61 BM.
62 BM, (April 7 1916).
63 *Ibid.*
64 *Ibid.*
65 Lucien de Zilwa, *Times of Ceylon,* (February 27 1966).
66 (September 23 1916).
67 Padmanabha, *The Ceylon Daily News,* (April 30 1947).
68 BM, (December 7 1916).
69 M.B. Yeats, (January 18 1917).
70 *Ibid.*
71 Lucien de Zilwa, letter to the author.
72 *Ibid.*
73 BM.

Index